Sex, Youth, and Sex Education

•◦ A Reference Handbook

Sex, Youth, and Sex Education

•◆ A Reference Handbook

David Campos

A B C 🌊 C L I O

Santa Barbara, California • Denver, Colorado • Oxford, England

Library of Congress Cataloging-in-Publication Data

Campos, David
  Sex, youth, and sex education: a reference handbook / David Campos.
    p. cm. — (Contemporary education issues)
Includes bibliographical references and index
  ISBN 1-57607-776-4 (hardcover: alkaline paper)
  1. Sex instruction for teenagers—United States. I. Title II. Series
HQ57.5.A3 C36 2002
613.9'071'2—dc21
                    2002002830

This book is also available on the World Wide Web as an e-book.
Visit www.abc-clio.com for details.

07 06 05 04 03 02   10 9 8 7 6 5 4 3 2 1

ABC-CLIO, Inc.
130 Cremona Drive, P.O. Box 1911
Santa Barbara, California 93116-1911

This book is printed on acid-free paper ∞.
Manufactured in the United States of America

For my father, Agapito D. Campos,
who dreamed his sons
would work far from the crop fields
in which he once labored

⚭ Contents

☞ Series Editor's Preface

The Contemporary Education Issues series is dedicated to providing readers with an up-to-date exploration of the central issues in education today. Books in the series will examine such controversial topics as home schooling, charter schools, privatization of public schools, Native American education, African American education, literacy, curriculum development, and many others. The series is national in scope and is intended to encourage research by anyone interested in the field.

Because education is undergoing radical if not revolutionary change, the series is particularly concerned with how contemporary controversies in education affect both the organization of schools and the content and delivery of curriculum. Authors will endeavor to provide a balanced understanding of the issues and their effects on teachers, students, parents, administrators, and policymakers. The aim of the Contemporary Education Issues series is to publish excellent research on today's educational concerns by some of the finest scholar/practitioners in the field while pointing to new directions. The series promises to offer important analyses of some of the most controversial issues facing society today.

Danny Weil
Series Editor

✦ Preface and Acknowledgments

Make no mistake about it, youth are exposed to sex on a daily basis. Images of sex are quite pervasive in our society. Sex can be found on television, in magazines, in newspapers, at the mall, and in school. A recent magazine advertisement for the prime-time sitcom *Friends* featured a full-page photo of the six cast members lying in bed with a caption that read, "Who's Pregnant?" *Friends* is a popular, humorous, clean show with very little violence, but there are often subtle instances of sex intended for the mature audience. The 2001–2002 season, for instance, featured Rachel getting pregnant and her friends trying to find out who the father was. Many adults understand the humor of the situation, but what impact does watching shows like this one have on youth? *Friends* is only one example of the many shows that are lighthearted, and yet sex is still occasionally embedded in the situation. Imagine the sexual content of shows found on the premium cable channels. What impact do they have on youth who watch them?

It is not the purpose of this book to provide large-scale empirical data to support the contention that watching sexual images on TV increases the sexual appetite of youth, nor is it to render judgment on youth and expect them to conform to a social standard of yesteryear. Instead, the book considers sex as a healthy aspect of life, one for which youth need sex education to acquire certain information, skills, and concepts in order to have a fulfilled life. Youth need sex education to learn to put sex into perspective. They need to know that sex is good. However, they also need to know that having sex is often accompanied with untoward consequences—including pregnancy, disease, and even death—for which they may not be prepared. Moreover, youth need to learn that sex should be reserved for when they are emotionally and cognitively capable of handling the consequences that will follow.

This book examines the dynamics of sex, youth, and sex education. Current statistics are provided on youth who have sex, and an overview of the sex education debate is discussed in Chapter One. Another chapter is devoted to the history of sex education, and the information therein seems to suggest that society has unfailingly been concerned with sex education and supported its implementation in schools.

Subsequent chapters are devoted to sexual violence among youth, sexual orientation issues and youth, and the sex education of youth with disabilities. Two resource chapters are available for further information on sex education, and a concluding chapter discusses recommendations for sex education.

ACKNOWLEDGMENTS

I extend my deepest appreciation to my colleague Dr. Valerie J. Janesick for her full support throughout the writing of this text. I am especially grateful to you for the many hours we spent discussing the issues that impact higher education. A special thank you to my editor, Danny Weil. You were unfailingly supportive, positive, and helpful. My colleague and friend, Dr. Kenneth A. Perez, was a great source of encouragement throughout the writing. I always knew I could count on you for professional guidance and support. Finally, my deepest love, appreciation, and respect to my parents, Guadalupe and Agapito. Thank you for your moral support. I couldn't have completed this book without you.

David Campos
Chicago, Illinois

Chapter One

◆ Introduction

SEX AMONG YOUTH

A dire concern exists regarding the sexual education of youth. Our society reacts strongly when confronted with the sexual activity of youth today and recognizes that many youth have not acquired the cognitive and emotional skills they need in an array of sexual encounters. Findings in recent studies, government reports, and stories reported in the media lead many parents, educators, and politicians to believe that our youth are experiencing their own sexual revolution. Indeed, youth engage in sex at earlier ages than ever before (American Academy of Child and Adolescent Psychiatry 1999), have more sexual partners than older adolescents (Burack 2000), and the number of youth that have sex is steadily increasing (Donovan 2000). Despite the fact that the teenage pregnancy and birthrate is in decline, the U.S. rate continues to be the highest among developing countries.

Youth who choose a sexually active lifestyle risk their physical and emotional health. One of the most serious consequences of engaging in sex is AIDS. Nearly 20 percent of adults living with AIDS are in their twenties. Because of the relatively slow incubation period between the time the AIDS virus (HIV) is acquired and AIDS develops, researchers believe that many of these young adults acquired HIV in their adolescence. Although there is a general decline in the number of reported AIDS cases in the United States, the rate of infection among youth remains steady (Forsyth 2000a). New drug therapies have slowed the progression of HIV for thousands of reported cases, yet the fact remains that AIDS is incurable and fatal.

Sexually transmitted diseases (STDs) such as chlamydia, genital herpes, gonorrhea, and trichomonas have invariably concerned society. Today, however, with twenty-five STDs, one-quarter of all reported STDs occurred among adolescents, and sexually active adolescents have the highest rate of STDs in comparison with other sexually active age groups (Braverman 2000). Although STDs are treatable, the long-term consequences of contracting an STD can be life-altering for female youth. Medical research has found that some STDs can cause infertility, cervical cancer, and chronic pelvic pain.

Youth who engage in sex also risk becoming pregnant. The pregnancy rate for youth has captured national attention since the early seventies when the birthrate for adolescents increased. Although the birthrate for this age group has decreased in the last decade, one million adolescents become pregnant each year with nearly 480,000 giving birth. Nearly 35 percent of the adolescents who give birth get pregnant again within a year, and about half get pregnant within two years (Coard, Nitz, and Felice 2000). Research suggests that long-term costs exist to these young mothers, their infants, and society.

Youth who engage in sex face emotional consequences as well. Some youth may become worried about getting pregnant or acquiring AIDS, regretful in having sex, and depressed. Little quantitative research is available to substantiate the effects of these concerns. However, one study noted that youth frequently expressed worry over their sexual activity, and a national survey found that adolescents are concerned about acquiring HIV and STDs. In the latter survey, the adolescents ranked teenage pregnancy as their third most troubling concern, and casual sex ranked twelfth.

The sex lives of youth are undisputedly well documented with well-defined repercussions. Our society recognizes that many youth do not fully understand the risks associated with sexual relationships as many of them maintain an unrealistic perception of their vulnerability. A consensus exists in our society that our youth do not have to suffer needlessly, that they can change their behavior to refrain from having sex or acquire the skills to protect themselves from the long-term consequences of having sex. The ultimate challenge, however, is how to teach children about sex.

Sexuality education elicits much controversy. On the conservative end of the sex education spectrum, a faction of parents and professionals believe that youth should refrain totally from sex until they are married. The premise is simple, if youth abstain from sex and "just say no" to sexual experimentation, they will not have to contend with an unwanted pregnancy or STD. This abstinence-only curriculum is a form of sex education that has generous support from the federal government. Provisions were made in the 1996 welfare reform measures to allocate $50 million yearly to states that offered sex education through an abstinence-only curriculum. These youth learn: to resist peer pressure; that becoming sexually active is deleterious; that contraceptives are ineffective.

On the liberal end of the spectrum, a faction acknowledges that youth will have sex irrespective of the probable harmful consequences. This faction maintains that youth should be encouraged to abstain from having sex but also learn the skills to protect themselves when they do have sex. This form of sex education, known as comprehensive sexuality education, teaches that sexuality is a positive and healthy aspect of humanity. In a comprehensive sex education program, youth learn about "sexual development, reproductive health, interpersonal relationships, affection, intimacy, body image, and gender roles" (SIECUS 2000).

In addition to the statistics on the sexual behavior of youth, STDs and AIDS, unwanted pregnancy, and the sex education debate, the role of schools with regard to the sexual harassment and sexual abuse of youth must be acknowledged. Schools have the legal duty to eliminate sexually hostile environments and protect youth who are harassed on their campuses. Title IX of the Education Amendments of 1972 (P.L. 92–318) prohibits discrimination on the basis of gender, protects youth from the sexual advances and harassment of other students and school employees, and is the basis for lawsuits of sexual orientation discrimination and harassment. The number of sexual harassment lawsuits has increased since the Supreme Court ruled in 1992 that students could file suit and collect damages (Crisci 1999). This ruling has forced many school districts to initiate critical discourse about gay and lesbian youth in relation to school policy, curriculum, and lives of other youth (Jones 1999).

Forced sexual contact committed against youth is perhaps the most destructive form of manipulation. Approximately one in four girls and one in ten boys are sexually abused each year (Lanning, Ballard, and Robinson 1999). The repercussions of such abuse can be devastating, leaving victims withdrawn, depressed, fearful, angry, sick, or causing them to become sexually active. One study revealed that 61 percent of adolescent mothers had been sexually abused prior to their pregnancy. Although most of the reported cases of sexual abuse occur outside of school, schools share the responsibility of educating youth to prevent or respond to such abuse. Sex education programs exist to teach youth the skills to protect themselves from perpetrators who abuse them sexually, and numerous programs are available to reduce the number of youth who become pregnant or infected with an STD.

SEX EDUCATION

With no standard national curriculum on sexuality, sex education remains politically contentious. Most factions agree that youth deserve to learn: how to maintain emotional and physical well-being; the skills to apply in sexual situations that are potentially risky; to postpone sex. Exactly how long to postpone sex, whether until marriage or until they can act maturely and responsibly in their relationships that involve intercourse, is one of many debates. Other points of contention are centered on the delivery of sex education. Many parents and experienced professionals argue over who should teach sex education, how to teach it, when to teach it. Knowing the source of these contentions is relatively critical in that sex education programs have a tailored agenda to consider. Before discussing the issues of contention, however, a definition of sex education is necessary.

Definition

Sex education is difficult to define. Twenty years ago, Bruess and Greenberg (1981) mentioned the difficulty of locating an adequate definition of sex education, so they described the underpinnings of sex education. Very few dictionary-style definitions surface in an extensive literature search, and definitions that do arise merely describe sex education in terms of goals or objectives. In the broadest and modest sense, sex education can be defined as finding out about sex from parents, family, friends, teachers, adults in general, or mass media. The work conducted by Patricia Schiller (1973) enhances this definition. Finding out about sex means

- learning factual information on all aspects of sex
- learning about sexual self
- learning about the opposite sex
- learning about the sexual behavior of others
- learning that sex is a part of life.

For the purpose of this text, sex education will mean curriculum that is used to teach youth about any of these aspects.

Goals

Numerous programs that teach youth about sex are available commercially, and many local schools and communities have developed their own programs to meet the needs of particular youth. The programs are extremely diverse with their own political and local goals to satisfy. To better understand how these goals can be classified, a cross-section of sex education programs is provided in Figure 1.1. The illustration can be

Figure 1.1. Types of Sex Education Programs

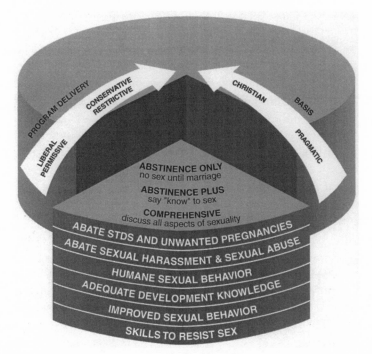

viewed as a continuum of sex education programs. Issues in contemporary education can be thought of as figurative cake slices with the layers of cake as common elements in consensus. The outer end of the slice represents a liberal spirit, and the center represents a conservative one. The layers of the slice illustrate how there is an agreement that sex education programs should: benefit youth and society; inform youth of human development, STDs, and reproduction; prepare youth to resist sex; teach youth to exhibit humane sexual behavior; improve youth's attitudes toward sex and the opposite sex; and abate sexual abuse and sexual harassment. The top of the cake, however, represents the goals of sex education as they vary among proponents. As diverse as sex education programs are, any one can potentially be identified somewhere along the continuum.

Abstinence-only

The conservative end represents the goals of the abstinence-only curriculum. On this end, most programs have a Christian basis and are more restrictive in their view of youth having sex. Program goals are founded on the biblical principle that sex outside of marriage is morally wrong, and the only effective method for youth to avoid STDs, AIDS, or an unwanted pregnancy is to abstain totally from sex until marriage. In many programs, youth cannot engage in any sexual behaviors, including experimentation that could lead to intercourse. Abstinence, these programs promote, also prevents youth from the emotional damage created by having sex. Any discussion of contraceptives is short and falls in the context of their failure. Proponents of abstinence-only maintain that discussions about contraceptives or making them available to youth encourage them to have sex.

Abstinence-only supporters strongly contend that this type of curriculum has emerged as a direct result of society's frustration with the ineffective "Safe Sex" curriculum of the eighties. They assert that in the span of thirty years, over 3 billion federal dollars were wasted on family planning/sex education programs because teenage pregnancies and abortions continued to increase (Andersen 1998). Rosemond (2001) cites two federal studies that find no progress in the reduction of risky behavior, teen pregnancy, or the transmission of STDs in comprehensive sex education programs. Moreover, supporters applaud the work of Barbara Dafoe Whitehead (1994) of the Institute for American Values for her article, "The Failure of Sex Education." Her report emphatically underscored that the then current sex education programs were unsuccessful. Although Doug Kirby's research in the 1980s found that students who had sex education knew more about the aspects of sex, supporters of the conservative viewpoint argue that knowledge about sex does not correlate with youth's decision to postpone sex.

In their argument for abstinence, the Family Research Council has found studies that reveal that condoms fail to protect youth from STDs, HIV, and unwanted pregnancies. Farish (2000) underscores that condoms have a 31 percent failure rate, and the Medical Institute for Sexual Health (MISH) espouses that condoms offer little protection against chlamydia and human papilloma virus. Moreover, Hartigan (1999) indicates that distributing condoms increases the sexual activity of some youth. One study found that after some San Francisco high school youth were provided coupons to be exchanged for condoms, the population of females engaging in sex increased 25 percent. Two other studies conducted in St. Paul and Dallas found 30 percent and 47 percent increases, respectively, in the pregnancy rate after condoms became available for students. Proponents contend that the distribution of condoms promotes sexual activity among youth because of the false impression that sex with condoms is safe.

In the abstinence-only side of the continuum, proponents find research that shows pregnancy among youth is devastating. In his review of literature, McIlhaney (2000) finds that 30 percent of females who give birth before the age of eighteen will earn a high school diploma by the age of thirty as compared to the 76 percent of them who give birth after age eighteen. Moreover, nearly 80 percent of youth who give birth will live in poverty and support their families through welfare. Whitehead (1994) notes that children of youth run a greater risk of health and developmental problems and physical and sexual abuse. The repercussions are not favorable for adolescent fathers either. McIlhaney asserts that these youth earn an average of $2,000 less annually at age twenty-seven. Supporters of abstinence-only claim that comprehensive sex education programs are accomplishing very little to decrease the number of youth who have to contend with an unplanned pregnancy. Whitehead points out that in an eleven-year period of comprehensive sex education, New Jersey's rate of youth pregnancy occurring among unwed couples increased from 67.6 percent to 84 percent.

Proponents cite various resources that suggest that youth and society desire an abstinence-only lifestyle. One study based out of the University of Chicago surveyed adults and found 68 percent agreed that premarital sex was invariably wrong. Another study from Emory University found that of 1,000 sexually experienced female youth, approximately 85 percent expressed a desire to learn how to thwart their partner's sexual advances. In a national tabloid's survey of 1,200 youth and adults, 72 percent of the youth and 78 percent of the adults agreed with a particular proabstinence message.

Some argue that communication about sex seems to be a pillar of comprehensive sex education. They maintain that youth as young as five years old learn to talk about sex. The understanding appears to be that better communication about sex encourages youth to act more responsibly in sexual matters. Abstinence-only supporters, however, assert that no research supports this claim. Supporters maintain that teaching to influence youth's sexual behavior is ineffective. Whitehead (1994) remains steadfast in her stance that no research can claim that comprehensive sex education in the early grades increases the likelihood that youth will postpone sex.

Proponents argue that abstinence-only programs work. "Best Friends" and "Postponing Sexual Involvement" are among the frequently cited programs that have an effective record. "Best Friends" was created for the inner-city girls of Washington, D.C. In this program, youth have positive role models who teach that through abstinence from sex and drugs one can achieve a fulfilled and noble life. Youth are taught that a support network of good friends, compared to destructive ones, is essential for a successful future. They learn to plan and work toward their goals for their future and how to limit their interactions with boys to healthy nonsexual relationships. In a survey of one school system, Rowberry found that 4 percent of the "Best Friends" graduates had sex by the age of fifteen as compared to 63 percent of girls who had not been exposed to "Best Friends" (cited in Rosemond 2001). Moreover, approximately 1 percent of the "Best Friends" graduates became pregnant as compared with 26 percent of the girls in the same school system.

"Postponing Sexual Involvement" was created for youth of color who were at risk for STDs and unplanned pregnancies. This program stresses the "just say no" to sex approach. These youth have role models, essentially older popular youth, who teach them in the middle grades how to reject and refuse the sexual advances of their peers. In given scenarios, they role-play ways to resist pressure and conduct themselves responsibly. In one study of "Postponing Sexual Involvement," 24 percent of program graduates had engaged in sex as compared to 39 percent who were not included in the program.

With over two thousand programs in school districts in forty states, an organization called Choosing the Best is one of the leaders of abstinence-only curriculum. This organization provides three programs—WAIT (Why Am I Tempted), Choosing the Best (CTB), and Choosing the Best LIFE—that stress abstinence until marriage as the key to a fulfilled, grounded life composed of healthy, meaningful relationships. The programs are composed of four to eight sessions that teach the difference between love and sex, that coital sex is reserved for marriage, how to have meaningful relationships, and developing assertiveness skills to establish proper boundaries. Youth are informed through videos and slides about STDs, AIDS, and the risks of "Safe Sex." They learn from medical experts and hear from their contemporaries who are struggling with an unplanned pregnancy. Choosing the Best asserts that studies from the Institute for Research and Evaluation and Northwestern University School of Medicine find that their programs have an impact on the sexual behavior of their graduates. The Northwestern study found that 75 percent of these graduates chose abstinence until marriage and 60 percent of the sexually active graduates indicated a return to abstinence.

In summary, proponents on this end of the spectrum favor abstinence from sex until marriage. Their principal tenet is that comprehensive sex education and the "Safe Sex" campaign of the eighties decade have failed and that an abstinence-only curriculum can change the sexual behavior of youth. With this type of fervor, why then should opposition exist? Some argue that comprehensive sex education continues to be politically successful because its advocates have a well-organized campaign to persuade parents and schools.

Comprehensive Sex Education

In the continuum of sex education, the liberal end represents the goals of comprehensive sex education. Most programs on this end are more permissive of youth having sex. The goals support abstinence from sex as the best choice for youth; however, the goals are not rooted in abstinence-only. Most programs are founded on the tenet that sex education should teach youth that sexuality is a positive aspect of life, and as such youth need the wealth of sexual knowledge—inclusive of sexual development, affection and intimacy, interpersonal and decision-making skills, body image, and gender roles—to achieve a lifetime of sexual health. Debra W. Haffner, president of the Sexuality Information and Education Council of the United States (SIECUS) and champion of comprehensive sexuality education, writes of the goals:

> This education has four primary goals: to provide young people with accurate information about sexuality, to give them an opportunity to develop their values and increase self-esteem, to help them develop interpersonal skills and to help them exercise responsibility in their relationships. The ultimate goal is the promotion of adult health. (Haffner 2000, 80)

Prominent organizations such as the American Medical Association, the American Public Health Association, the National Council of Churches, and the National School Boards Association defend the comprehensive approach. A host of other organizations endorse SIECUS and the principle that youth should strive for abstinence. However, they believe that the social dynamics of contemporary youth inevitably lead many to become sexually active. In one survey of high school youth, for instance, between 40 and 45 percent had had sex at least once and were likely to have sex again. As such, proponents believe that youth need the skills to discriminate between healthy sexual behaviors and potentially destructive ones.

To achieve a sexually healthy lifestyle, youth must acquire a positive and comfortable attitude about sex. Frank and fact-based discussions about topics once considered taboo are essential. Abortions, condoms, masturbation, oral sex, and homosexuality are among the topics to be found in comprehensive sex education programs. Elia (2000) adds that comprehensive sex education programs should address "biological, sociocultural, psychological, and spiritual dimensions of sexuality drawing 'from the cognitive domain (information); the affective domain (feelings, values, and attitudes); and behavioral domain (communication, decision-making, and other relevant personal skills'" (342).

Unsurprisingly, a vast array of topics can be found within the domains. Consequently, this faction maintains that for sex education to be truly comprehensive, it must be pervasive in the schools. A foundation of skills are introduced in kindergarten and developed with age-appropriate materials and discussions throughout the grades. Defenders argue that sex education should be considered as fundamental as reading, writing, and math. When it is, youth develop the attitude that sex is to be embraced as a quality of life. Youth also learn to respect their own bodies and the bodies of others, and so proponents expect the incidences of sexual harassment and sexual coercion to decrease.

Proponents also argue that abstinence-only programs are not effective. Research supports that abstinence-only programs do increase the knowledge of youth and change their sexual behavior. Kirby (2000), however, points out that most of the research has measured the short-term effects of such programs. The work by Kirby suggests that the impact of abstinence-only on their graduates is short lived and the message of abstinence diminishes with time. He claims that only five studies have measured the impact programs have had on the initiation of sex. Of these, none has shown a significant effect on their graduates. Haffner (2000) adds that a study found an increase in the number of graduates engaging in sex in one abstinence-only program. The Alan Guttmacher Institute, a nonprofit health research organization, claims that graduates of abstinence-only programs may be at greater risk for STDs and unintended pregnancies because they do not acquire the information to protect themselves. With few studies applying accurate scientific methods to substantiate the effectiveness of abstinence-only programs, proponents defend comprehensive sex education.

This faction further believes that abstinence-only proponents have a melodramatic response to the sexual conduct of youth. Comprehensive sex education supporters are not necessarily joyful or complacent about the current facts but instead are cautiously optimistic when studies suggests that the rate of sex among youth has decreased, the rate of youth using contraceptives is up, and births to youth have decreased (Rodriguez 2000). Supporters are mindful that these rates are relatively high in comparison to other industrialized nations.

This faction, moreover, reports that the sexual conduct of adults is more regrettable than that of youth. Haffner (1998) reports that half of all pregnancies nationally are unintended with 75 percent of those occurring among adult women. Youth use condoms more consistently than young adults and are more likely to use them than older adults. The repercussions of sexual abuse of youth by adults are serious and lifelong. In one survey, 40 percent of youth who became pregnant reported rape as their only incidence of intercourse. In another, 60 percent of youth reported that an adult was the father. It also appears that adult males are to blame for nearly all of the diseases transmitted sexually, including HIV. With this kind of information, the faction calls for a sexually healthier generation of adults. To achieve this, youth must acquire the sexual knowledge, attitude, and skills found in comprehensive sex education.

Proponents of comprehensive sex education are critical of abstinence-only programs that use scare tactics and unscientific approaches to keep youth from engaging in sex. Youth in some programs are shown photographs of people in advanced stages of STDs and are told that a sexually active life can leave them devastated. Haffner (2000) provides an excerpt from "Facing Reality," an abstinence-only program, describing the ramifications of sex as "inability to concentrate on school, shotgun weddings, selfishness, poverty, loss of faith, fewer friendships formed, loss of self-mastery, difficulty with long-term commitments, aggression toward women, loss of honesty, depression and death" (81).

Although having sex before maturity is unwise and can leave youth with a problematic future, Wiley and Terlosky (2000) argue that no research has found that having sex will leave youth psychologically and physically desperate. These proponents of a comprehensive curriculum further assert that being married does not immunize one from the possibilities of STDs, unintended pregnancies, or emotional devastation.

"No sex until marriage" as a policy is a source of contention between those on distant ends of the sex education spectrum. The faction that advocates a comprehensive approach remains distressed that some youth are indoctrinated to believe that marriage is the national standard for an active sex life. Haffner (1998) argues that this standard does not accurately reflect the current sexual conduct of adults. Sources reveal that many adults engaged in sex as youth. In fact, a 1996 Alan Guttmacher Institute study suggests that only 27 percent of men and 44 percent of women waited until marriage to have sex, and Haffner states that 10 percent of men and 22 percent of women report that they had their first sexual experience with their spouse. One other study supports that some adults who had sex as youth viewed their experience as having a beneficial impact on their relationships. With a reported 74 million adults classified as single (by choice, divorced, or gay) and 77 percent having active sex lives, supporters contend that it is absurd that marriage is viewed by abstinence-only supporters as the gateway to a fulfilled sexual life. Elia (2000) maintains that abstinence-only programs fail to recognize that some adults choose not to marry or cannot be legally married. Gay, lesbian, and bisexual topics are rarely included in abstinence-only programs. Consequently, some youth who may already experience feelings of awkwardness are even further isolated when it is reinforced that the societal standard for union is a heterosexual marriage with the expectation to procreate. Elia further adds that traditional sex education programs rarely provide the opportunity for youth to explore gender roles, sexism, or different views of sex.

Proponents also contend that sex education has the support of the general public. The Children's Research and Education Institute, for instance, surveyed registered voters and found that 66 percent supported sex education in the public schools, 22 percent of the respondents were opposed, and 12 percent were neutral. SIECUS claims that organizations such as the National Institutes of Health, the Institute of Medicine, and the U.S. Centers for Disease Control and Prevention support sex education programs that stress abstinence, contraception, and condom use. SIECUS and Advocates for Youth found that 93 percent of adults favor sex education in the high schools, and 84 percent would like sex education implemented in the middle schools (SIECUS 2000). Proponents argue that the support for comprehensive sex education stems from polls that indicate the public would like an array of topics discussed in sex education. The SIECUS/Advocates for Youth poll, for instance, found that approximately 70 percent of parents want youth in middle schools to learn about abstinence, puberty, STDs, and HIV and nearly 60 percent want the same population of youth to have the sexual knowledge as it relates to love, dating, contraception, and sexual orientation. Nearly 90 percent of the adults polled expressed approval of all these topics by high school. Phi Delta Kappa (1998) polled adults to determine their attitude toward public schools and found that support ranged in the ninetieth percentile for education about STDs, AIDS, and biology of reproduction; in the eightieth percentile for teen pregnancy and birth control; in the seventieth percentile for premarital sexual relations, nature of sexual intercourse, and abortion; and in the sixtieth percentile for homosexuality. SIECUS maintains that with the continued support of the National Coalition to Support Sexuality Education (composed of 115 organizations), youth will develop the skills to embrace a sexually healthy lifestyle.

Supporters argue that abstinence-only programs are not good enough. A research review of sex education programs conducted by the World Health Organization in 1993 found that the most effective programs in preventing unintended pregnancies among youth were those that stress abstinence and contraception (cited in Haffner 2000). Similar results were found in the report published by the National Campaign to Prevent Teen Pregnancy. In *No Easy Answers: Research Findings on Programs to Prevent Teen Pregnancy,* programs based on abstinence and contraception delayed sexual activity among youth or increased their use of contraceptives (cited in Haffner 2000). The report underscored that effective sex education programs were those whose graduates were taught by trained teachers in a culturally relevant context to resist peer pressure, use contraceptives, and set sexual limitations. In 1991, a task force of experienced education and health professionals created the conceptual framework for sexuality education. The framework (titled SIECUS Guidelines for Comprehensive Sexuality Education: Kindergarten–12th Grade) is considered the first national model for comprehensive sex education (Moore and Rienzo 2000). The guidelines are composed of six concepts: human development, relationships, personal skills, sexual behavior, sexual health, and society and culture. Each concept has a cluster of topics to be addressed according to the developmental stage of the youth (see figure 1.2). The 778 developmental messages are divided into early childhood, preadolescence, early adolescence, and adolescence. The topics promote the beneficial aspects of a sexually healthy lifestyle and emphasize the postponement of sex.

A review of SIECUS resources finds a bibliography of sex education curricula, including abstinence-only. None of the curricula, however, is as comprehensive as the SIECUS guidelines. To date, only one program has been developed that is truly comprehensive. (For the last five years, however, states have been encouraged to apply for federal funds to implement abstinence-only programs. Therefore, more attention has been focused on the development of sex education programs that were unit-based as opposed to comprehensive in nature). The program, Our Whole Lives (OWL), created by the Unitarian Universalist Association is based on the SIECUS and National Guidelines Task Force guidelines. Although the curriculum was created by the Unitarian Universalist and United Church of Christ, no religious references are mentioned throughout the series. Composed of five developmental levels— grades kindergarten through third, fourth through sixth, seventh through ninth, tenth through twelfth, and adults—each covers topics of human development, relationships, personal skills, sexual behavior, sexual health, and society and culture. OWL graduates learn about abortion, abstinence, body image, families, gender identity, gender roles, HIV/AIDS, homosexuality/bisexuality, love and commitment, masturbation, parents, puberty, relationships, sexual relationships, and values. The program became available only recently; consequently, no studies have confirmed its effectiveness in changing graduates' behavior. The program, however, has evoked favorable qualitative responses from Advocates for Youth, the National Parenting Association, various Planned Parenthood organizations, and sexual health author Robie H. Harris.

Figure 1.2. Concepts and Topics Addressed in the SIECUS Guidelines

Key Concept 1: Human Development
Reproductive anatomy and physiology
Reproduction
Puberty
Body Image
Sexual identity and orientation

Key Concept 2: Relationships
Families
Friendships
Love
Dating
Marriage and lifetime commitments
Parenting Concept

Key Concept 3: Personal skills
Values
Decision making
Communication
Assertiveness
Negotiation
Finding Help

Key Concept 4: Sexual Behavior
Sexuality throughout life
Masturbation

Shared sexual behavior
Abstinence
Human sexual response
Fantasy
Sexual dysfunction

Key Concept 5: Sexual Health
Contraception
Abortion
STDs and HIV infection
Sexual Abuse
Reproductive health

Key Concept 6: Society and Culture
Sexuality and society
Gender Roles
Sexuality and the law
Sexuality and religion
Diversity
Sexuality and the arts
Sexuality and the media

Source: From "Table 3. Key Concepts and Topics in a Comprehensive Sexuality Education Program," by SIECUS, 1996. In Guidelines for Comprehensive Sexuality Education: Kindergarten–12th Grade, 2nd Edition, (p. 11). Reprinted with permission.

Arguments for a comprehensive sex education abound. Proponents assert that youth need the skills and sexual knowledge to live a healthy lifestyle. To accomplish this, youth need discourse about age-appropriate aspects of sexuality as early as kindergarten. With no scientific research to support that abstinence-only programs are effective, many believe that a generation of youth are being left without sufficient skills or facts and are ultimately unprepared to manage sexual situations. Supporters contend that the public supports a sex education that includes topics of abstinence and beyond. Moreover, when experienced health, education, and sexual professionals convene to attend to sex education, programs that are comprehensive in nature are considered ideal. In ten years, however, only one program can be considered comprehensive, and its effectiveness has yet to be determined.

The section that follows is a discussion of curricula that reach beyond abstinence-only but that do not reach far enough to be called comprehensive. These programs are known as abstinence-plus.

Abstinence-plus

A small body of literature calls attention to abstinence-plus programs. These programs can be identified along the center of the continuum of sex education programs. They promote abstinence as the ideal option for youth and recognize that they should practice protected sex, but the programs do not encompass the array of instructional units to target that are proposed by comprehensive sex education programs. Proponents of abstinence-plus believe that sex education programs should focus on reducing one or more sex behaviors that lead to sex. The programs are similar to those that help youth develop the skills to manage and resist substance abuse (Kirby 2000).

Proponents such as the American School Health Association, American Public Health Association, American Alliance for Health, Physical Education, Recreation, and Dance maintain that abstinence-plus programs should be included in school health programs. Studies have found that in some instances program graduates decreased their sexual activity, delayed the onset of sex, or increased the use of contraceptives. Such programs as "Reducing the Risk," "Safer Choices," "Be Proud! Be Responsible," and "Becoming a Responsible Teen" have proven to be effective (Kirby 2000). Graduates of "Reducing the Risk" have been found to delay their onset of sex, increase their usage of condoms, or remain abstinent for eighteen months after completing the program. The program stresses abstinence but informs youth that a condom must be used if they have sex. Research suggests that "Safer Choices" is effective as well. Graduates from these programs have learned that to avoid STDs, AIDS, and unintended pregnancies, they must avoid sex. They were also taught that protected sex is far safer than unprotected sex. Studies of the program show increased usage of condoms and a reduction of unprotected sex over a thirty-one-month period. "Be Proud! Be Responsible" and "Becoming a Responsible Teen" were both designed for high-risk youth, and studies have found that their graduates delay having sex, increase their use of condoms, or reduce their frequency of unprotected sex and sex in general for over twelve months.

Kirby (2000) designated ten characteristics of effective abstinence-plus programs. In summary, effective programs include a

•• narrow focus to modify particular sex behavior(s)
•• theoretical approach with a success record in modifying other risky behaviors
•• persuasive discussion on abstinence or protected sex as sole options
•• body of accurate sexual knowledge inclusive of the risks associated with unprotected sex
•• series of interactive situations that enable youth to contend with social pressures
•• communication element that allows youth to practice refusal and negotiation skills
•• context that allows youth to actively participate
•• resource of developmentally and culturally appropriate teaching methods and materials
•• considerable time component that allows youth to implement various activities
•• team of program administrators who believe in the programs.

The term *abstinence-plus* is a relatively new rubric for the many sex education programs that promote aspects of sexuality (development, reproduction, intimate relationships, self-appraisal) in addition to abstinence. Proponents of abstinence-plus and comprehensive sex education are seemingly one in the same. The primary difference, however, is that abstinence-plus programs are considered smaller instructional units targeted at particular groups of youth. With studies to support that abstinence-plus programs are effective and the lingering doubt that abstinence-only programs do not provide their graduates enough information, proponents defend sex education. They believe that programs that are specific yet related to the larger health program cultivate positive attitudes among youth toward their personal health (nutrition, safety, substance abuse prevention), emotional health (stress reduction), community health (family life, preventative health care), and environmental health (Wiley and Terlosky 2000).

In Schools

Although the federal government does not mandate sex education, many school districts teach about sexuality. As of 1998, 93 percent of high schools offered some sex or HIV/AIDS education. This prompts the question, How do most school districts deliver sex education? Two federal acts help clarify the answer: Title X of the Public Health Service Act enacted in 1970; and PL 104–193, the Personal Responsibility and Work Opportunity Reconciliation Act of 1996 (known as Title V of the Social Security Act, or the Welfare Reform Act).

Title X appropriated $200 million yearly in family-planning funds from 1970 to 1996. Most sex education programs of this time instructed students about sexual anatomy and technique. As mentioned earlier, a faction that was unsatisfied with the results of these programs reacted by advocating congressional authorization of $250 million in grants to encourage states to teach abstinence-only. President Bill Clinton signed into law a provision that created an entitlement program for abstinence-only education. The funds, dispensed as abstinence-education grants, were offered to states whose programs promoted abstinence from premarital sex. Each year from 1998 to 2002, $50 million was available to the states with awards ranging from $78,526 to $4.9 million (Pardini 1998). The awards require the states to match 75 percent of the funds with public or private monies. Every state including the District of Columbia has applied for the funds, and as of 1999, all but two states accepted the federal funds to support 698 abstinence-only programs (SIECUS 2000).

The requirement of sex education varies from state to state across the nation. Some states mandate sex education with provisions, some without, and some have no mandate. Figure 1.3 represents the states and the District of Columbia that mandate sex education programs.

The Alan Guttmacher Institute (1999) surveyed 825 superintendents about their districtwide sex education policies and found that 69 percent implement programs to teach youth about sexuality. In the remainder, no official policy exists and individual schools or teachers make the decision to implement programs. Of the districts with a sex education policy, 35 percent teach from an abstinence-only approach with no discussions of contraceptives or only in terms of their limitations. The findings also reveal that 51 percent teach abstinence-plus, while 14 percent of the districts include abstinence as an option in a comprehensive program. The programs that schools offer seem to vary according to the geographic location of the school. Abstinence-only programs, for instance, are more likely to be found in southern states with 55 percent offered in southern school districts and 20 percent offered in the northeast. The Kaiser Family Foundation (1999) study of 313 secondary school principals produced similar results with one-third of the schools stressing that youth should wait until marriage to have sex; 58 percent of these schools offer sex education that is considered abstinence-plus. Of the

Figure 1.3. Sexuality Education in the United States

	Sex Education Required		States with Mandated Content Requirements for Sex Ed		States without Mandated Content Requirements for Sex Ed	
State	Yes	No	States must teach abstinence, no requirement for providing information on contraception	States must teach abstinence, a requirement exists for information on contraception	If sex ed provided, abstinence is required and information about contraception is not required. Specify abstinence until marriage?	If sex ed provided, abstinence and contraception is required. Specify abstinence until marriage?
AL		✓			✓, YES	
AK		✓				
AZ		✓			✓, NO	
AR		✓				
CA		✓				✓, YES
CO		✓			✓, NO	
CT		✓				
DE	✓			✓		
DC	✓					
FL		✓			✓, YES	
GA	✓			✓		
HI		✓				✓, NO
IL	✓		✓			
ID		✓				
IN		✓			✓, YES	
IA	✓					
KS	✓					
KY	✓		✓			
LA		✓			✓, YES	
ME		✓				
MD	✓					
MA		✓				
MI		✓			✓, NO	
MN	✓					
MS		✓			✓, YES	
MO		✓				✓, YES
MT		✓				
NE		✓				
NV	✓					
NH		✓				
NJ	✓			✓		
NM	✓					
NY		✓				
NC	✓			✓		
ND		✓				

Figure 1.3. *continued*

State	Sex Education Required		States with Mandated Content Requirements for Sex Ed		States without Mandated Content Requirements for Sex Ed	
	Yes	No	States must teach abstinence, no requirement for providing information on contraception	States must teach abstinence, a requirement exists for information on contraception	If sex ed provided, abstinence is required and information about contraception is not required. Specify abstinence until marriage?	If sex ed provided, abstinence and contraception is required. Specify abstinence until marriage?
OH		✓				
OK		✓			✓, NO	
OR		✓				✓, NO
PA		✓				
RI	✓			✓		
ṠC	✓			✓		
SD		✓				
TN	✓			✓		
TX		✓			✓, YES	
UT	✓		✓			
VA		✓				✓, YES
VT	✓			✓		
WA		✓				
WV	✓			✓		
WI		✓				
WY		✓				

State	STD, HIV, AIDS Education Required		Content Requirements for States with Mandated STD, HIV, AIDS Education		Content Requirements for States without Mandated STD, HIV, AIDS Education	
	Yes	No	States require abstinence until marriage, no requirements for other prevention	States require abstinence and other methods of prevention. Specify abstinence until marriage?	If provided, abstinence is required and other prevention methods are not required. Specify abstinence until marriage?	If provided, abstinence and other prevention methods are required. Specify abstinence until marriage?
AL	✓			✓,NO		
AK		✓				
AZ		✓			✓,NO	
AR		✓				

continues

Figure 1.3. *Continued*

State	Yes	No	States require abstinence until marriage, no requirements for other prevention	States require abstinence and other methods of prevention. Specify abstinence until marriage?	If provided, abstinence is required and other prevention methods are not required. Specify abstinence until marriage?	If provided, abstinence and other prevention methods are required. Specify abstinence until marriage?
	STD, HIV, AIDS Education Required		Content Requirements for States with Mandated STD, HIV, AIDS Education		Content Requirements for States without Mandated STD, HIV, AIDS Education	
CA	✓			✓, NO		
CO		✓				
CT	✓					
DE	✓			✓, NO		
DC	✓					
FL	✓			✓, YES		
GA	✓			✓, YES		
HI		✓				✓, NO
IL	✓			✓, YES		
ID		✓				
IN	✓		✓			
IA	✓					
KS	✓					
KY	✓			✓, NO		
LA	✓					
ME		✓				
MD	✓					
MA		✓		✓, NO		
MI	✓					
MN	✓			✓, YES		
MS		✓			✓, YES	
MO	✓			✓, YES		
MT		✓				
NE		✓				
NV	✓					
NH	✓					
NJ	✓			✓, NO		
NM	✓			✓, NO		
NY	✓			✓, YES		
NC	✓			✓, YES		
ND	✓					
OH	✓		✓			
OK	✓			✓, NO		
OR	✓			✓, NO		
PA	✓			✓, NO		
RI	✓			✓, NO		
SC	✓					

Figure 1.3. *Continued*

State	STD, HIV, AIDS Education Required		Content Requirements for States with Mandated STD, HIV, AIDS Education		Content Requirements for States without Mandated STD, HIV, AIDS Education	
	Yes	No	States require abstinence until marriage, no requirements for other prevention	States require abstinence and other methods of prevention. Specify abstinence until marriage?	If provided, abstinence is required and other prevention methods are not required. Specify abstinence until marriage?	If provided, abstinence and other prevention methods are required. Specify abstinence until marriage?
SD		✓				
TN	✓			✓, YES		
TX		✓			✓, YES	
UT	✓			✓, YES		
VA		✓				✓, YES
VT	✓			✓, NO		
WA	✓			✓, YES		
WV	✓			✓, NO		
WI	✓					
WY		✓				

Source: Adapted from "Sexuality Education in the Schools: Issues and Answers" by SIECUS, 2001. Adapted with permission.

principals surveyed, the majority reported that their programs are composed of abstinence as the ideal option, HIV/AIDS awareness, and STDs. Less than half discuss how to use birth control, condoms, abortion, or sexual orientation.

Although a relatively high number of districts offer sex education programs, youth's exposure to sex education is limited. Youth in grades seven through twelve receive an average of six and a half hours of sex education a year (Silverstone 1992), and less than 10 percent of all youth receive a comprehensive sex education (Haffner 2000). Sanderson (2000) explains that schools fail to offer sex education for several reasons: the assumption that sex education increases the sexual activity of youth; the priority in teaching the academic areas; and, the comfort and training level of teachers is low. Although youth may find limited exposure to sex education at school, they definitely learn about sex through parents, peers, other adults, media, and their own experiences. As the forthcoming data reveals, the sexual conduct of contemporary youth is unprecedented.

SEXUAL CONDUCT OF YOUTH

Every generation is seemingly astonished at the behavior of the generation of youth that follows. In his review of the adolescent, Strasburger (2000) explains that early philosophers were often disappointed in youth of their time. As early as the eighth century B.C., Egyptian hieroglyphics depict youth as unwise and unruly. Egyptian historian Hesiod had little regard for youth. He mentioned, "I see no hope for the future of today, for certainly all youth are reckless beyond words" (Strasburger, p. 788). Aristotle was equally unimpressed with youth of his time. He found "'in regard to sexual desire, [teenagers] exercise no restraint,' and adolescents 'are heated by Nature as drunken men by wine'" (Strasburger, p. 788).

In the United States, reaction to the conduct of youth has not changed dramatically. When the U.S. Food and Drug Administration approved birth control pills in 1960, a sexual upheaval was sparked. Hugh Hefner's *Playboy* empire promoted consensual sex, and the "Summer of Love" in San Francisco's Haight-Ashbury district brought sex, once a taboo topic, into the realm of public discussion. Many believe that these circumstances caused the rate of out-of-wedlock births and teenage pregnancies to increase drastically. President Richard Nixon reacted by creating a comprehensive family planning program under Title X of the Public Health Service Act, and in 1972 the Social Security Act was amended to mandate states to provide family planning services for youth considered sexually active.

By 1976, pregnancies among youth were described as "epidemic" by the Alan Guttmacher Institute (Koch 1998). In the 1980s, the United States had the highest teen pregnancy, abortion, and birthrates among industrialized countries. By the 1990s, some schools distributed condoms, and the surgeon general declared, "Everybody in the world is opposed to sex outside of marriage, and yet everybody does it. I'm saying, 'Get Real.'" Sex among youth has gained much national attention in the last three years. The *New York Times* (in 2000), *Newsweek* (in 1999), and *Time* magazine (in 1998) have covered the sex lives of contemporary youth in detail. Although one's youth is often considered the time to explore and engage in some risk taking, the revealing statistics of youth engaging in risky sexual behavior and the untoward consequences leave many feeling uneasy.

Statistics

To gain an understanding of the sexual conduct of youth, statistics will be provided in the following rubrics: how youth learn of sexuality; dating among youth; sexual activity of youth; and sexual orientation of youth. As a caveat, limitations exist in all studies. Some studies may have used flawed methodologies to analyze their data, had a relatively small sample, failed to assess the statistical effect sizes for significant findings, or lacked a theoretical framework. The findings of the studies discussed below are reported for their direct samples.

How Youth Learn of Sexuality

Youth learn about sexuality from various sources including their parents, peers, other adults, and the media. The Kaiser Family Foundation (1999) found that of youth from age ten to twelve and age thirteen to fifteen, 59 percent and 45 percent, respectively, had learned the most about sex through discussion with their parents. An earlier study by the foundation (1996) asked youth where they learned about pregnancy and birth control. Of the respondents, 40 percent identified school personnel, 36 percent mentioned their parents, and 27 percent indicated their peers. The Media Project, jointly sponsored by the Kaiser Family Institute and Advocates for Youth (Koch 1998), reported that 54 percent of those polled said they learned about sex and condoms from television.

Dating

The majority of youth date. Jarrell (2000) suggests that some youth begin to date as early as ten or eleven years of age. One study found that 85 percent of youth have a boyfriend or girlfriend, and over 85 percent have kissed another romantically. The Penguin Atlas of Human Sexual Behavior (Mackay 2000) reports that girls begin to date at the age of twelve or thirteen, and boys begin to date at thirteen or fourteen years.

Sexual Activity

Fifty years ago, the most common sexual experimentation among youth was petting (Haffner 1998). During this time, the sexual conduct differed among males, females, and youth of different backgrounds with regard to race, ethnicity, and social class. Today, in contrast, most youth are actively experimenting with sex and little distinction exists between the sexual conduct of different groups. Contemporary boys have their first sexual experience at the average age of sixteen. For girls, the average is seventeen (Alan Guttmacher Institute 1994). By the time youth enter ninth grade, over 38 percent are sexually active (American Academy of Child and Adolescent Psychiatry 2000). According to the 1997 Youth Risk Behavior Surveillance Report from the Centers for Disease Control and

Prevention (CDC), 48.4 percent of high school youth have had sexual intercourse, and 16 percent have had more than four partners (Kann et al. 1998).

Research seems to indicate that as youth become older the likelihood they will have sex increases. Many youth begin sexual experimentation with harmless kissing. As they get older, more than one-half progress from light petting to more intimate behaviors. Blum et al. (1997) mentioned that youth graduate from oral sex, mutual masturbation, nudity, and exposure to full sexual intercourse. One study found that by fourteen years of age, more than half of the boys in one sample had touched a girl's breast and nearly 25 percent had touched a girl's vulva (Coles and Stokes 1985). In another sample of youth, Blum and his colleagues (1997) found that of twelve and thirteen year olds, 17 percent had had sexual intercourse. As youth approach fifteen years of age, 25 percent have engaged in sex at least once (Centers for Disease Control and Prevention 1994). Of this figure, two of ten girls, and three of ten boys have had sex more than once (Singh and Darroch 1999). By the time most youth have approached age eighteen, more than 75 percent have engaged in heavy petting and nearly half have engaged in cunnilingus.

Oral sex is seemingly increasing among youth as many consider oral sex an abstinent behavior. Remez (2000) found that although accurate, reliable data cannot confirm this rate increase, anecdotal records indicate that a rise in oral sex may be attributed to the perception that oral sex is a safe form of abstinence. Gates and Sonenstein (2000) found that of fifteen- to nineteen-year-old boys, 53 percent indicated a girl had masturbated them, 49 percent had received oral sex, 39 percent had given oral sex, and 11 percent had anal sex. Schuster et al. (1998) also found that although some youth identify themselves as virgins, many have engaged in noncoital sex. In his sample of 2,026 high school youth, 47 percent reported being virgins. Of these virgins, however, 30 percent had masturbated a partner, 9 percent had heterosexual fellatio with ejaculation, and 10 percent had engaged in cunnilingus.

Although some find these figures disconcerting, some health experts are pleased to find that the percentage rate of youth engaging in sex has decreased in recent years. From 1991 to 1997 the percentage of youth having sex decreased. A review of the Youth Risk Behavior Surveillance of 1993, 1995, and 1997 indicates that nearly 53 percent of youth had sex in 1993 and 1995, but in 1997 the rate had decreased to 48.4 percent. More youth are delaying sex, and some believe that this is because of improved national educational efforts. For the first time in twenty-five years, the majority (at 52 percent) of high school youth are virgins. The increase in the number of virgins is attributed to a change in the behavior of boys in that more have elected to postpone sex than ever before. Among them, the percentage rate of virgins increased from 39 percent in 1990 to 51 percent in 1997 (Curtin and Matthews 1998). In another study of eight large city school districts, the CDC (1999) found that from 1991 to 1997 the number of high school youth who were sexually experienced decreased with time. Other research supports that the rate of youth who had more than four sex partners also decreased from 18.5 percent in 1993, to 17.8 percent in 1995, to 16 percent in 1997 (Kann et al. 1995, Kann et al. 1996, Kann et al. 1998). Although more youth are having sex at younger ages than previous generations (Koch 1998, Jarrell 2000), the percentage rate for youth under 13 years of age who have had sex has also dropped. The CDC reports that in 1995 9 percent of this age group had had sex before the age of 13. By 1997, the rate had decreased to 7.2 percent.

The question remains, Why do youth have sex? One 1986 survey set out to find the answer. The result showed that among girls, 34 percent identified peer pressure, 17 percent identified pressure from boys, 14 percent cited curiosity, and 14 percent indicated that "everyone is doing it." Of the boys, however, 26 percent identified peer pressure, 16 percent said curiosity, 10 percent mentioned "everyone is doing it," and 10 percent identified sexual gratification (American Academy of Child and Adolescent Psychiatry 2000). A third of the youth from the Media Project indicated that they engaged in sex because television situations depict youth as sexually active.

Condom Use

Many youth have learned that condom use reduces the risks of becoming pregnant and acquiring a sexually transmitted disease. Many youth consequently use condoms for protection from pregnancy and disease and use them as consistently and effectively as adults (Haffner 1998). Youth who elect to have sex are more likely to use contraceptives than their counterparts just a few years ago (Kantrowitz and Wingert 1999). Close to 70 percent of youth who engage in sex for the first time use a condom. This is significant considering that condom use among youth tripled from 1975 to 1995. In the 1997 CDC surveillance report (Kann et al. 1998), 57 percent of the youth in the sample indicated they used a condom the last time they had sex, as compared to 46 percent of the youth in 1991. A comparison of the CDC surveillance reports in the last decade reveals the rate of condom use increased from 52.8 percent in 1993, to 54.4 percent in 1995, to 56.8 percent in 1997. Although this is encouraging for some, studies have found that the rate of condom use decreases as youth have more sex, and less than half of those who use condoms use them on a consistent basis. Youth who do not use condoms are 90 percent more likely to become pregnant within a year (Alan Guttmacher Institute 1999).

Sexual Orientation

Exactly how many youth are gay or lesbian is difficult to gauge primarily because many youth do not identify themselves as such. Acquiring reliable statistics on this population of youth is nearly impossible. A small proportion of youth do self-identify their sexual orientation during their adolescence. One study of youth in seventh through twelfth grade found that 88 percent identified themselves as heterosexual, 1 percent identified themselves as homosexual or bisexual, and 11 percent were unsure of their orientation (Remafedi 1992). These findings should be interpreted with caution in that many gay and lesbian adults report that in their youth they were often confused about their sexual orientation. Few gay and lesbian adults, in fact, identified themselves as gay in their late teens; "coming out" does not happen for most until adulthood (Haffner 1998). Another study found that 5 percent of youth between the ages of thirteen and fifteen had sex with members of the same sex. Over half of these youth reported the encounter occurred when they were eleven and twelve (American Academy of Child and Adolescent Psychiatry 2000).

Repercussions

Unintended consequences are among the greatest concerns about the emerging sexuality of contemporary youth. Many youth do not realize that engaging in sex can be life altering. Youth who have sex are likely to confront a possible pregnancy, an STD, or a host of emotional issues.

Pregnancy and Births

The rate of unintended pregnancies among youth is high. Compared to the pregnancy rate of youth in the 1950s, the rate for youth today is six times higher. A million youth become pregnant each year and of these nearly three-quarters are unwed. This amounts to 10 percent of all girls between fifteen and nineteen years of age and 19 percent of all girls who have had sex (Alan Guttmacher Institute 1999). Six of ten pregnancies occurred among youth who were eighteen to nineteen years of age. Although the pregnancy rate among youth remains undoubtedly higher in the United States than any other developed nation, the rate continues to decline. According to the Centers for Disease Control (2000), a 15 percent drop in pregnancies occurred between 1991 (when 116.5 per 1,000 women became pregnant) and 1996 (when the figure was 98.7 per 1,000). The CDC report mentions that a host of factors contribute to this decline including a decrease in sexual activity, an increase in condom use, and an increased use of birth control that is injected or implanted. Many health experts maintain that this decline can be attributed more to the effective contraceptive practices (80 percent) than the decreased sexual activity (20 percent) (Alan Guttmacher Institute 1999).

The birthrate among youth, although high, is also in decline. A surge of births to youth occurred in the 1970s and 1980s with a rate that peaked at 62.1 births per 1,000 females aged fifteen to nineteen (Stodghill 1998). This rate dropped 12 percent to 54.4 births per 1,000 in 1996. Today, approximately 480,000 youth elect to give birth. Coard, Nitz, and Felice (2000) stated that youth who elect to give birth are less likely than adult mothers to be financially supported by the biological fathers, will need financial assistance, and are less likely to complete their education or to work. Moreover, youth under seventeen who give birth are more likely to have a second child within two years than are older youth and women in their twenties (Moh, 1986). For young mothers who complete their education, it is less likely they will have a second birth than the young mothers who get married (Card and Wise 1978; Furstenberger, Brooks-Gunn, and Morgan, 1987; Maynard 1996; Mott and Marsiglio 1985). Many would infer that as the birthrate declines, the number of abortions will likely increase. Surprisingly, the abortion rate among youth also declined; from 1988 to 1996, the abortion rate fell 33 percent.

STDs, HIV, and AIDS

According to the Centers for Disease Control (as cited in Koch 1998), rates of sexually transmitted diseases (STDs) are nearly 50 to 100 times higher in the United States than other industrialized nations. The rates of STDs among youth are amazingly high. Over three million cases of STDs are reported each year among youth aged ten to nineteen. In fact, sexually active youth have the highest rate of STDs of any other sexually active group, with one in four acquiring an STD (Alan Guttmacher Institute 1999). Chlamydia and gonorrhea are more prevalent among youth than among other sexually active age groups. The 1997 rate of acquiring chlamydia was highest among those younger than twenty. The rate of chlamydia infection for fifteen- to nineteen-year-old girls was 2,044.3 cases per 100,000 (Braverman 2000). Sexually active youth also account for a higher rate of gonorrhea than any other sexually active group. Although the rate of gonorrhea has plummeted 74 percent since

1975, the fact remains that 530.3 cases per 100,000 are found in sexually active youth (Braverman 2000). Sexually active girls who engage in a single act of unprotected sex risk a 1 percent chance of acquiring HIV, a 15 percent chance of acquiring the human papillomavirus that causes cervical cancer, a 30 percent chance of getting genital herpes, and a 50 percent chance of contracting gonorrhea (Alan Guttmacher Institute 1999).

Forsyth (2000a) has documented the HIV and AIDS epidemic worldwide. From a global perspective, 688,200 AIDS cases had been reported by 1998, with 410,800 people having lost their lives from the disease. The largest risk factor for men is homosexual transmission (45 percent) and for women, heterosexual transmission (38 percent). Intravenous drug use accounts for 21 percent of the male cases and 29 percent of the female cases. Among youth, the HIV and AIDS infection rate is difficult to determine because of the long incubation period of the virus. Youth can acquire the virus that causes AIDS and not know of their illness because the disease does not appear until years later. Much of the data available on youth and HIV and AIDS is therefore often approximated or available with combined age groups such as twenty-four years and younger. At any rate, the Office of National AIDS Policy (1996) reports that approximately one-quarter of all new HIV cases were acquired by youth between the ages of thirteen and twenty-one. Approximately 7,200 cases of HIV disease among those between thirteen and twenty-four were reported to the Centers for Disease Control in 1996. However, 85 percent of these youth acquired HIV perinatally from their mothers and 11 percent acquired the virus through blood transfusions (Allen et al. 1999). As youth become older, however, sexual contact becomes a more prevalent way of acquiring the virus. Of the 7,200 reported cases of HIV among individuals thirteen to twenty-four years old, 26 percent acquired the virus through heterosexual sex.

Emotional Implications

Engaging in sex often produces a host of emotional consequences. Youth are not exempt from these difficulties and must confront the emotional issues often associated with having sex. Psychologists and psychiatrists believe that many youth who have sex have not refined their emotional and cognitive skills to contend with these issues and are left emotionally vulnerable (Jarrell 2000). Girls more often than not describe their first sexual experience as unpleasant or disappointing, and when compared to boys, they more frequently indicate that they regret having had sex. In one survey, 65 percent of the girls and 45 percent of the boys expressed regret over their first sexual experience indicating they were too young to have had sex. One 1994 survey found that girls were more likely than boys to contend with the negative consequences of their sexual experience. This finding may help explain why Orr, Beiter, and Ingersoll (1991) found that sexually active girls are more likely to attempt suicide than girls who are virgins. The suicide rate for sexually active girls between the ages of twelve and sixteen is six times higher than for girls who remain virgins. Moreover, girls who are sexually active are eighteen times more likely to run away from home. Lickona (1994) outlined the untoward emotional consequences of youth having sex. Youth who have sex experience worry, regret and self-recrimination, guilt, low self-esteem, a loss of self-respect, fear of commitment, depression, and ruined relationships.

Variables Associated with Sexual Behavior

As noted earlier, a relatively high number of youth choose to be sexually active. Parents and health experts concerned with the sexual behavior of contemporary youth often wonder about the likelihood that a particular group of youth will engage in sex. More specifically they ask, "Which group of youth is more at risk for engaging in sex?" Understanding the answers to this question ultimately leads to better prevention efforts. Variables associated with sexual behavior include family structure, academic performance and athletic participation, religious affiliation, peers, socioeconomic status, gender, ethnicity, age, and other risky behaviors.

Family Structure

Research has documented a number of familial factors associated with the sexual activity of youth. Sabo et al. (1999), for instance, found that the more cohesive the family, the lower the rate of sexual activity among youth, and Althaus (1994) noted that families who imposed strict rules on their youth decreased the likelihood that youth would have sex. Indeed, parents and siblings can have a direct impact on the initiation of sex and sexual activity among youth.

Although a number of studies have failed to find a correlation between the sexual activity of youth and the absence of a father, youth from a single parent household are more likely to have early sexual intercourse than youth from households with both parents (Moore et al. 1995). In a study of African American and Latino seventh-grade youth, Raine et al. (1999) found that for boys, living in a two-parent household was positively correlated with being a virgin. The researchers explain that a two-parent household may be more stable and supportive, and two parents can monitor youth more closely than one parent can. Unsurprisingly, little parental supervision and support increase the likelihood that youth will engage in sex (Biglan et al. 1990; Walter, Vaughn, and Cohall 1991).

The sexual onset and activity of youth can be greatly influenced by mothers. This may be explained by the fact that mothers largely bear the responsibility of educating youth about sex (Jordan, Price, Fitzgerald 2000), and most youth feel more comfortable discussing sexual topics with their mothers than with their fathers (DiIorio et al. 1999). In their sample of 10,000 youth in grades seven through eleven, Dittus and Jaccard (2000) found that the sexual activity of those in the sample was significantly influenced by their perception of their mothers' disapproval of premarital sex. The more disapproving they believed their mothers to be, the less likely the youth were to initiate sexual activity. Moreover, youth who regularly communicated with their mothers were often more likely to have conservative values and less likely to initiate sexual contact.

Parent-youth communication appears to be critical in persuading youth to refrain from sex or to practice safe sex. Most parents want their youth to abstain from premarital sex, although a small number of parents (15 percent of one study) indicate they moderately oppose or remain ambivalent with regard to their youth having sex (Jaccard, Dittus, and Gordon, 1996). Although it is not always the case, research tends to suggest that the likelihood that youth will have sex decreases when they maintain good communication with their parents. Youth who talk about sex with their parents are more likely to postpone sex (Leland and Barth 1990; DiIorio, Kelley, and Hockenberry-Eaton 1999) and are more likely to use condoms and contraceptives when they practice sex (Kotva and Schneider, 1990; Miller, Levin, Whitacker, and Xu 1998). The Whitacker and Miller (2000) study of 907 youth between the ages of fourteen and sixteen found that parental communication was associated with "less risky sexual behavior, less conformity to peer norms, and greater belief that parents provide the most useful information about sex" (p 266). This is consistent with DiIorio et al. (1999) who noted that youth are less likely to engage in sex when their parents provide sexual information than when peers provide the information.

Although surveys reveal that a significant number of parents indicate feeling uncomfortable and inadequately prepared to have sex talks with youth, most believe that sex education should first be taught at home. Compound the parents' discomfort with the indication that youth are more comfortable talking about sex with their friends, it is understandable that research on parent-youth communication suggests disappointing results. Youth often report that parents provide little direct information on sex (Jordan, Price, and Fitzgerald 2000) and that parents fail to accurately assess critical sexual issues related to contemporary

youth (SADD 2000). Most sex talks address condom use and the consequences of sex such as STDs, AIDS, and pregnancy, with little discussion
focused on body development (DiIorio et al. 1999). Same gender (father-
son and mother-daughter) sex talks are often factual and values-based.
Cross-gender sex talks are more often about values than facts (Nolin and
Peterson 1992). Within families, girls tend to receive more sex talks than
boys do (DiIorio et al. 1999). This may be accounted for by the fact that
parents may perceive girls as vulnerable and want them to be informed
and armed against potentially aggressive boys. Perhaps girls are more
likely to receive a sex talk because they require a better understanding of
menstruation. DiIorio outlined the order of topics in discussions most
mothers had with their youth. Boys received instruction in the order of

(1) consequences,
(2) protection,
(3) values,
(4) abstinence.

Girls, on the other hand, received instruction in the order of
(1) abstinence,
(2) consequences,
(3) normal development,
(4) protection,
(5) values.

Ironically, mothers gave 82 percent of the girls the "no" sex talk as
compared to 61 percent of the boys.

Jaccard and Dittus (2000) maintain that some parents must exercise caution when their sex talks involve "safe sex." Surprisingly, the researchers found among their sample that parents' "safe sex" talks increased the likelihood that some youth engaged in sex.

Siblings can also influence the age of sexual initiation in some
youth. Hogan and Kitagawa (1985) found a correlation between the
early onset of sexual experiences of younger siblings when older siblings
are sexually active. This may occur because the older siblings serve as a
role model for the younger siblings or parents of the household are liberal in their views of sex (East, Felice, and Morgan 1993; Rodgers, Rowe,
and Harris 1992).

Academic Performance and Athletic Participation

Research has found that academic achievement, athletic participation,
and the type of school attended are associated with the sexual activity of

some youth. Youth who excel in school and aspire to a higher education have a reduced risk of engaging in sex (Moore et al. 1995; Ostrov et al. 1987). In their study of 26,023 youth in grades seven through twelve, Lammers et al. (2000) found that boys who experience high academic achievement were 73 percent more likely to delay intercourse than boys with lower achievement were. The study suggests that girls who excel academically are 58 percent more likely to delay sexual intercourse. In the Raine et al. (1999) study of Latino and African American youth, the findings suggest that a higher academic performance, namely A's and B's as grades, was associated with the likelihood that they were virgins. In a study of 2,829 sixth grade youth, Marin et al. (2000) found that youth who had older boyfriends or girlfriends, which ultimately increased the likelihood that they would have sex, were performing poorly academically and maintained low educational aspirations. Researchers explain that youth who do better in school may have higher self-esteem, parental support, and plans for a successful future and therefore abstain from sex to realize their goals. The American Academy of Child and Adolescent Psychiatry (2000) also maintains that youth from families that emphasize strong academic performance are less likely to have early sexual experiences.

Valois et al. (1997), determined to compare the risky behavior of youth in public high schools with those in private schools, found that the youth in the public schools largely had sex more often than their counterparts in the private schools. The researchers surveyed 5,338 youth in the public schools and 1,089 in the private schools. The results revealed that among the youth in the public schools, 70 percent of the boys and 62 percent of the girls reported having had sexual intercourse. In comparison, 32 percent of the boys and 26 percent of the girls in private schools had had sex during the same time period. In terms of the age of the onset of sex, 50 percent of the boys in public schools reported having had sex before the age of fourteen, while only 14 percent of the boys in the private schools reported having had sex before that age. For the girls in the public schools, 33 percent reported having had sex before fourteen years of age, and their private school counterparts reported 11 percent.

Athletic participation is associated with reducing the likelihood that youth will engage in sex. It stands to reason that if an athletic youth gets someone pregnant or becomes pregnant, then his or her team's chances for success are possibly ruined. Moreover, achieving athletic status is often associated with popularity, and many youth, girls in particular, may strive to preserve their status by abstaining from risky behaviors such as sex (Sabo et al. 1999). Miller, Sabo, and Farrell (1998) revealed that athletic youth reported lower sexual activity than nonathletic youth. In the Sabo et al. study, the findings suggested that the girls involved in scholastic athletics were less likely to engage in sexual activity than were girls who were not involved in sports. This is consistent with a National Educational Longitudinal Study (NELS) that found girls who were involved in scholastic athletics were 33 percent less likely to have an unintended birth than girls who were not involved in athletics (Zill, Nord, and Loomis 1995). The findings of the Sabo et al. study are reflected in the Women's Sports Foundation study that also revealed that girls who participated in sports were more likely to have lower rates of sexual activity and pregnancy (Sabo 1998). Researchers contend that athletic participation appears to enhance girls' self-esteem and increase their confidence in resisting boys' pressure to have sex. Boys, in contrast, are not as significantly affected by sports as girls are. In fact, the NELS study found that boys who participated in sports had a 38 percent greater likelihood of becoming a father by the end of their senior year than were boys who were not in sports. Sabo et al. attribute this likelihood to the fact that sports involvement for boys increases their self-esteem and may cause them to become more sexually aggressive.

Religious Affiliation

Although religion and spirituality are constructs defined differently by various researchers, studies have been conducted on the impact that church attendance, religion, and spirituality has on the sexual conduct of youth. The findings are consistent in that youth who hold religious beliefs are more likely to abstain from sex than their peers who do not (Wallace and Williams 1997). Youth who attend church (Moore et al. 1995) and youth who maintain religious convictions (De Gaston, Jensen, and Weed 1995) are less likely to engage in sex than their counterparts. Moreover, religious youth are less likely to initiate sex at an early age (Thorton and Camburn 1989; Althaus 1994; Lammers et al. 2000).

Youth who attend church regularly and identify themselves as religious generally have negative attitudes toward premarital sex (Wallace and Williams 1999). This may be explained by the fact that religious participation tends to mold the sexual attitude of youth on three levels. Werner-Wilson (1998) hypothesized that being religious is accompanied with a value-based framework that supports responsible sexual behavior among youth. Being religious, among some youth, often means a church affiliation with a social support network of youth who share and reinforce the same values. A church affiliation, moreover, provides youth with alternative social activities to encounters that could lead to sexual experimentation. In a study of the religious motivation, belief in

God, divine support, questing, and spiritual connectedness among youth, Holder et al. (2000) found that spiritual interconnectedness—defined loosely as a support network of friends in a body of faith—had a significant impact on youth abstaining from sexual activity.

Wallace and Williams (1999) indicate that on average, youth with no religious backgrounds were more likely to have sex, have more sexual partners, and have sex more often than youth who could identify with a religious affiliation. Various studies seem to affirm this. In a study of youth from Seventh Day Adventist Schools, Hopkins et al. (1998) found that youth with this religious affiliation reported having less sex (at 16.3 percent) than other youth (53.1 percent). Zelnick, Kanter, and Ford (1981) revealed that of girls between the ages of fifteen and nineteen, those who were religious and had a fundamentalist affiliation were more likely to abstain from sex than were girls who had a more liberal religious affiliation or no religious affiliation at all. Thorton and Camburn (1989) found that 78 percent of the youth who never attended church had had sex and 39 percent of the youth who attended weekly church services had had sex. The researchers also found that of the youth who indicated the importance of religion in their lives, 50 percent had engaged in sex. By comparison, 70 percent of the youth who said that religion was not an important factor of their lives had had sex. Lastly, Murry (1994) investigated the onset of sexual activity among a sample of African American girls. The findings indicated that girls who initiated sex at younger ages were more likely to have not attended church on a regular basis.

Peers

Peers can definitely influence one another. Research has documented that youth who communicate with their peers about sex may actually increase the likelihood that youth engage in sex (Holtzman and Robinson 1995), and such youth may acquire misinformation about sex and its consequences (Lees 1994). Youth, moreover, who learn of sex from their peers are more likely to have liberal sex values (DiIorio et al. 1999). Whitacker and Miller (2000) predicted that peers' influence on youth's decision to initiate sex and use a condom was reduced if youth had received "sex talks" from their parents. Their prediction was supported when the study revealed that youth conformed less to peer norms when parents discussed the implications of sex with their children. Werner-Wilson (1998) noted in his literature review that boys are more likely to succumb to peer pressure than girls. The researcher cautions, however, that studies have revealed that youth tend to create friendships with youth who hold similar values and behavior, and youth do not terminate friendships when they do not conform to their peers' pressures.

Socioeconomic Status

Most youth progress from experimental, noncoital sex and advance gradually to sexual intercourse. The likelihood that youth will engage in sex increases if they live with parents with low levels of education (Casper 1990) or a mother who works extensively (Mott et al. 1996). Lammers et al. (2000) found that youth from a high socioeconomic status or youth who resided in rural areas were less likely to initiate sex than their counterparts. Wilson et al. (1994) also found that youth from a higher socioeconomic status were more likely to use a condom than youth from lower status. The results of the DiClemente et al. (1996) study, however, revealed that sexually active urban African American youth from lower socioeconomic status were likely to use condoms consistently.

Ethnicity

The National Center for Health Statistics indicates that the birthrate for all ethnic groups of youth has dropped in recent years (cited in Koch 1998). In fact, the largest drop (21 percent from 1991 to 1996) occurred for African American youth between the ages of fifteen and nineteen. Although the declines are satisfying to some, African American and Latino youth maintain higher birthrates than other ethnic groups. African American and Latino youth are also more likely to have sex than any other ethnic group. In 1997, the Centers for Disease Control (Kann et al. 1998) reported that among 16,262 youth in grades nine through twelve, African American youth (72.7 percent) were more likely to have had sexual intercourse than Latino youth (52.2 percent) and white youth (43.6 percent). In terms of the initiation of sex, African American youth (21.7 percent) were more likely to have had sex by the age of thirteen than Latino youth (7.7 percent) and white youth (4 percent).

Of all ethnic groups, Asian and Pacific Islander American youth have the highest percentage rate of abstinence. In a study of 2,026 youth in grades nine through twelve, Schuster et al. (1998) found that a group of 186 Asian American youth were less likely than white, African American, and Latino youth to engage in sex. The study also revealed that Asian American youth have less oral sex and anal intercourse and do not substitute masturbation for sex. The researchers found that Asian American youth were more likely to use a condom at first coital intercourse (although they do not use them consistently) and have less knowledge of HIV transmission and prevention than some other ethnic groups. Perhaps these youth engage in less sex because Asian American youth tend to maintain conservative attitudes toward premarital sex as most believe that their parents and their peers would disapprove of sex before marriage (Schuster et al. 1998; Cochran, Mays, Leung 1991).

Gender

At any given point in our history, research has well documented that boys have sex more often than girls. Boys generally have more sexual partners and engage in sex at an earlier age than girls (Newman and Zimmerman 2000; Taylor et al. 1997). As mentioned earlier, the number of youth who engage in premarital sex has declined in recent years. The rate of high school girls who were sexually active in 1991 was 51 percent ("Poll Shows Decline in Sex by High School Students" 1998). In 1998, the number declined to 48 percent. For boys, the 1998 rate dropped to 49 percent from 57 percent in 1991. For the first time in our history, the number of girls having sex is approaching that of boys. In 1988, the percentage of girls having sex before the age of fifteen was 11 percent. By 1995 the percentage rate had increased to 19 percent. For boys of that age group, the percentage remained at 21 percent (Koch 1998). By 1997, national figures indicated that 30 percent of girls were sexually active by the age of fifteen and 70 percent were active by the age of eighteen (Kenney et al. 1997).

Some studies have examined the sexual strategies used by youth and have found that boys tend to emphasize relationships and spending money with less emphasis placed on love or romance (Eyre, Read, and Millstein 1997). Boys tend to use coercion such as pressuring, lying, intoxicating their partner to have sex, and using relationships and expressions of love as a manipulation. Boys are also more likely to express that sexual coercion is justifiable (Feltey, Ainslie, and Geib 1991, as documented in Werner-Wilson 1998). Girls, on the other hand, tend to hint at having sex, flirting, and letting sex happen. They desire a secure relationship more often than boys and have a dating history that is longer with older boys. Girls are more likely to express a need for intimacy as a precursor to sex than are boys. In addition, girls often assume responsibility for birth control (Eyre, Read, and Millstein 1997).

Age

Some youth begin to date at an early age. For youth who do, the likelihood that they will engage in sex is heightened. This may be explained by the fact that youth who date at earlier ages tend to have more dates that consequently lend themselves to more sexual encounters. Werner-Wilson (1998); Miller, McCoy, and Olson (1986); and Thorton (1990) have found that the number of sexual partners and the rate of sexual activity is higher among youth who dated earlier in their lives than those who dated later. Although Robinson, Tellojohann, and Price (1999) found that 7 percent of their sample of sixth graders had had sex, in another study of sixth grade youth, Marin et al. (2000) noted that 43.5 percent indicated they had a boyfriend or girlfriend who was older or of the same age. This information is critical because research has found that having a boyfriend or girlfriend at such a young age is often associated with the early initiation of unwanted sex. In a national sample, Driscoll, Moore, and Lindberg (1997) found that girls are more likely to experience unwanted sex if their boyfriend is older. In fact, of the sixth grade youth in the Marin et al. study who had engaged in sex, many of the older youth used their power and pressure to engage the younger youth into having sex. Marin et al. indicated that youth who have sex with an older boyfriend or girlfriend were more than thirty times more likely than those with no boyfriends or girlfriends to have ever had sex. This statistic is particularly alarming for girls in that Darroch, Landry, and Oslak (1999) found that they are more likely to use contraceptives inconsistently if they have sex with older boys.

Early sexual experiences are predictors of sexual frequency. Youth who experiment with sex before the age of sixteen have more sex partners than youth who initiate sex at an older age (Burack 2000), are more likely to have recent sexual partners than those who initiate sex later (Marin et al. 2000), and less likely to use a condom on a consistent basis. Robinson, Telljohann, and Price (1999) mention that regardless of race, ethnicity, and gender, early initiation of sex is associated with an increase in the number of sexual partners. As youth become older the likelihood that they will have sex increases. Lammers et al. (2000) identified three age groups of youth in a survey of sexual conduct: thirteen to fourteen, fifteen to sixteen, and seventeen to eighteen. The percentage rate of youth having sex increased as the groups increased with age. For girls, the rate increased from 16.3 percent to 36.8 percent to 55.2 percent, respectively. For boys, the rate increased from 29.3 percent to 47 percent to 60.2 percent, respectively.

Other Risky Behaviors

Youth who engage in other risky behaviors are more likely to engage in sex. Research has not clearly established whether youth that are inclined to maintain higher levels of sexual activity are most likely to engage in other risky behaviors, or if those behaviors lead youth to become sexually active. At any rate, studies have documented that smoking, alcohol, and drugs predict the sexual activity level of some youth. For instance, a correlation exists between youth who abuse alcohol and their sexual activity. Bailey et al. (1999) found that youth who were considered abusers of alcohol were more sexually active, had more sexual partners, and had (initiated) sex at a younger age as compared to youth who were regular drinkers. Newman and Zimmerman (2000) added that alcohol and drug use is associated with sexual behavior among youth, particularly among urban minority heterosexual youth. Lammers et al. (2000) also found that alcohol, drugs, and smoking are associated with the initiation of sexual intercourse for youth. Regardless of family configuration, race, and gender, smoking appears to be the highest predictor of youth engaging in sex (Robinson, Telljohann, and Price 1999). In their sample of 683 sixth grade youth in 13 elementary schools, Robinson et al. found that among the boys and girls smoking had the highest relationship with sexual intercourse. In another study of the correlates of virginity, Raine et al. (1999) sampled 523 seventh grade youth. The study revealed that the likelihood was higher that youth were virgins if they had never smoked than for youth who were cigarette smokers.

SUMMARY

This chapter has presented an overview of sexuality among youth inclusive of their sexual conduct and sex education. Many believe that youth are experiencing a sexual revolution as evidence indicates that they have sex at earlier ages with more sexual partners than previous generations. Research has documented that youth who have sex risk becoming pregnant, dealing with the emotional consequences, and acquiring a sexually transmitted disease. Despite the fact that the rate of sexual activity and pregnancy among youth is down, and the rate of condom use is up, many remain uneasy knowing that a large number of youth expose themselves to potentially life-altering consequences. Youth definitely need the skills to cope with their emerging sexuality; exactly how, when, and by whom to impart those skills remains a politically contentious debate. A conservative faction believes in abstinence-only—no sex outside of marriage, period. A more liberal faction believes that regardless of the abstinence message, youth will have sex. Therefore, youth should be encouraged to abstain from sex but learn how to protect themselves when they do have sex. The motivation behind both factions is the same—to ensure the physical and emotional well-being of youth.

REFERENCES

Alan Guttmacher Institute. 1994. *Sex and America's Teenagers.* New York: Alan Guttmacher Institute.

———. 1997. *Preventing Pregnancy, Protecting Health: A New Look at Birth Control Choices in the United States.* New York: Alan Guttmacher Institute.

———. 1999. *Teenage Pregnancy: Overall Trends and State-by-State Information.* New York: Alan Guttmacher Institute.

———. 1999. *U.S. Teenage Pregnancy Rate Drops Another 4% between 1995 and 1996.* New York: Alan Guttmacher Institute.

Allen, Harvey A., Fred L. Splittgerber, and M. Lee Manning. 1999. *Teaching and Learning in the Middle Level School.* Upper Saddle River, NJ: Prentice Hall.

Althaus, F. 1994. "Age at Which Young Men Initiate Intercourse Is Tied to Sex Education and Mother's Presence in the Home." *Family Planning Perspectives* 26(3): 142–143.

American Academy of Child and Adolescent Psychiatry. 1999. *Your Adolescent.* New York: HarperCollins Publishers.

Anderson, Kerby. 1998. "School-Based Health Clinics and Sex Education." Richmond, TX: Probe Ministries International.

Bailey, Susan L., Nancy Pollock, Christopher Martin, and Kevin Lynch. 1999. "Risky Sexual Behavior among Adolescents with Alcohol Use Disorders." *Journal of Adolescent Health* 25(3): 179–181.

Biglan, A., C. W. Metzler, R. Wirt, D. Ary, J. Noell, L. Ochs, C. French, and D. Hood. 1990. "Social and Behavioral Factors Associated with High-Risk Sexual Behavior among Adolescents." *Journal of Behavioral Medicine* 13: 245–261.

Blum, Robert W., Michael D. Resnick, Peter S. Bearman, and Karl E. Bauman. 1997. "Protecting Adolescents from Harm: Findings from the National Longitudinal Study on Adolescent Health." *Journal of the American Medical Association* 278(10): 823–932.

Braverman, Paula. 2000. "Sexually Transmitted Diseases in Adolescents." *Adolescent Medicine* 84(4): 869–889.

Bruess, Clint E., and Jerrold S. Greenberg. 1981. *Sex Education: Theory and Practice.* Belmont, CA: Wadsworth Publishing Company.

Burack, Richard. 2000. "Young Teenagers' Attitudes toward General Practitioners and Their Provision of Sexual Health Care." *British Journal of General Practice* 50: 550–554.

Card, Josefina J., and Lauress L. Wise. 1978. "Teenage Mothers and Teenage Fathers: The Impact of Childbearing on the Parents' Personal and Professional Lives." *Family Planning Perspectives* 10(4): 199–205.

Casper, Lynn M. 1990. "Does Family Interaction Prevent Adolescent Pregnancy?" *Family Planning Perspectives* 22(3): 109–114.

Centers for Disease Control and Prevention. 1994. *Pregnancy, Sexually Transmitted Diseases, and Related Risk Behaviors among U.S. Adolescents.* Hyattsville, MD: US Department of Health and Human Services.

———. 1999. "Trends in HIV-Related Sexual Risk Behaviors among High School Students—Selected U.S. Cities, 1991–1997." *Journal of School Health* 69(7): 255–257.

———. 2000. *Trends in Pregnancies and Pregnancy Rates by Outcome: Estimates of the United States: 1976–1996.* Hyattsville, MD: U.S. Department of Health and Human Services.

Coard, Stephanie I., Katherine Nitz, and Marianne E. Felice. 2000. "The Relationship between Psychological Factors and Condom Use among African-American Adolescents." *Adolescence* 35(139): 559–569.

Cochran, S. D., V. M. Mays, and L. Leung. 1991. "Sexual Practices of Heterosexual Asian-American Young Adults: Implications for Risk of HIV Infection." *Archives of Sexual Behavior* 20: 381–391.

Coles, Robert, and Geoffrey Stokes. 1985. *Sex and the American Teenager.* New York: Harper and Row.

Crisci, George S. 1999. "When No Means No: Recognizing and Preventing Sexual Harassment in Your Schools." *American School Board Journal* 186(6): 25–29.

Curtin, S., and T. J. Matthews. 1998. *Teenage Births in the United States: National and State Trends 1990–1996.* Hyattsville, MD: National Center for Health Statistics.

Darroch, Jaqueline E., David J. Landry, and Selene Oslak. 1999. "Age Differences between Sexual Partners in the United States." *Family Planning Perspective* 31(4): 160–167.

De Gaston, Jacqueline F., Larry Jensen, and Stan E. Weed. 1995. "A Closer Look at Adolescent Sexual Activity." *Journal of Youth and Adolescence* 24: 27–54.

DiClemente, R., M. Lodico, O. Grinstead, G. Harper, R. Rickman, P. Evans, and T. Coates. 1996. "African American Adolescents Residing in High-Risk Urban Environments Do Use Condoms: Correlates and Predictors of Condom Use among Adolescents in Public Housing Developments." *Pediatrics* 98(2): 269–278.

DiIorio, Colleen, Maureen Kelley, and Marilyn Hockenberry-Eaton. 1999. "Communication about Sexual Issues: Mothers, Fathers, and Friends." *Journal of Adolescent Health* 24(3): 181–189.

Dittus, Patricia, and James J. Jaccard. 2000. "Adolescents' Perception of Maternal Disapproval of Sex: Relationship to Sexual Outcomes." *Journal of Adolescent Health* 26(4): 268–278.

Donovan, Basil. 2000. "My Choice: Teenagers and the Risks of Sexually Transmitted Diseases: A Need for the Provision of Balanced Information." *Medical Economics* 77(8): 79–82.

Driscoll, A. K., K. A. Moore, and L. D. Lindberg. 1997. *White Paper: A Statistical Portrait of Adolescent Sex, Contraception and Childbearing.* Washington, DC: The National Campaign to Prevent Teen Pregnancy.

East, P. L., M. A. Felice, and M. C. Morgan. 1993. "Sisters' and Girlfriends' Sexual Childbearing Behavior: Effects on Early Adolescent Girls' Sexual Outcomes." *Journal of Marriage and the Family* 55: 953–963.

Elia, John P. 2000. "The Necessity of Comprehensive Sexuality Education in the Schools." *The Educational Forum* 64(4): 340–347.

Eyre, Stephen, Nancy W. Read, and Susan G. Millstein. 1997. "Adolescent Sexual Strategies." *Journal of Adolescent Health* 20(4): 286–293.

Farish, Heather. 2000. *The Whole Story on Sex.* Washington, DC: Family Research Council.

Forsyth, Brian. 2000a. "The AIDS Epidemic." *Child and Adolescent Psychiatric Clinics of North America* 9(2): 267–277.

———. 2000b. "HIV Infection in Children." *Child and Adolescent Psychiatric Clinics of North America* 9(2): 279–293.

Furstenberger, Frank F., J. Brooks-Gunn, and S. Phillip Morgan. 1987. *Adolescent Mothers in Later Life.* New York: Cambridge University Press.

Gates, G. J., and Freya L. Sonenstein. 2000. "Heterosexual Genital Sexual Activity among Adolescent Males: 1988 and 1995." *Family Planning Perspectives* 32(6): 295–304.

Haffner, Debra. 1998. "Sexual Health for American Adolescents." *Journal of Adolescent Health* 22: 453–459.

———. 2000. "Abstinence-Only Education Isn't Enough." In *Taking Sides: Clashing Views on Controversial Issues in Human Sexuality,* ed. R. T. Francoeur and W. J. Tavener. Guilford, CT: Dushkin/McGraw Hill.

Hartigan, John D. 1999. *The Disastrous Results of Condom Distribution Programs.* Washington, DC: Family Research Council.

Hogan, Dennis P., and E. M. Kitagawa. 1985. "The Impact of Social Status, Family Structure, and Neighborhood on the Fertility of Black Adolescents." *American Journal of Sociology* 9: 825–855.

Holder, David W., Robert H. Durant, Treniece L. Harris, Jessica H. Daniel, Dawn Obeidallah, and Elizabeth Goodman. 2000. "The Association between Adolescent Spirituality and Voluntary Sexual Activity." *Journal of Adolescent Health* 26(4): 295–302.

Holtzman, David, and Richard Robinson. 1995. "Parent and Peer Communication Effects on AIDS-Related Behavior among U.S. High School Students." *Family Planning Perspectives* 27(6): 235–240.

Hopkins, Gary L., Joyce Hopp, Helen P. Marshak, Christine Neish, and Gayle Rhoads. 1998. "AIDS Risk among Students Attending Seventh-Day Adventist Schools in North America." *Journal of School Health* 68(4): 141–145.

Jaccard, James, and Patricia Dittus. 2000. "Adolescent Perceptions of Maternal Approval of Birth Control and Sexual Risk Behavior." *American Journal of Public Health* 90(9): 1426–1430.

Jaccard, James, Patricia Dittus, and Vivian V. Gordon. 1996. "Maternal Correlates of Adolescent Sexual Behavior." *Family Planning Perspectives* 28(4): 159–165.

Jarrell, Anne. 2000. "The Face of Teenage Sex Grows Younger." *New York Times,* 2 April.

Jones, Rebecca. 1999. "I Don't Feel Safe Here Anymore." *American School Board Journal* 186(11): 26–31.

Jordan, Timothy, James H. Price, and Shawn Fitzgerald. 2000. "Rural Parents' Communication with Their Teen-agers about Sexual Issues." *Journal of School Health* 70(8): 338–344.

Kaiser Family Foundation. 1996. *What They Say Teens Today Need to Know, and Who They Listen To.* Menlo Park, CA: Henry J. Kaiser Family Foundation.

———. 1999. *Sex Education in America: A View from Inside the Nation's Classrooms.* Menlo Park, CA: Kaiser Family Foundation.

Kann, Laura, Charles W. Warren, William A. Harris, Janet L. Collins, Kathy A. Douglas, Mary E. Collins, Barbara I. Williams, James G. Ross, and Lloyd J. Kolbe. 1995. "Youth Risk Behavior Surveillance—United States, 1993." *Journal of School Health* 65(3): 163–170.

Kann, Laura, Charles W. Warren, William A. Harris, Janet L. Collins, Barbara I. Williams, James G. Ross, Lloyd J. Kolbe. 1996. "Youth Risk Behavior Surveillance—United States, 1995." *Journal of School Health* 66(10): 365–377.

Kann, Laura, Steven A. Kinchen, Barbara I. Williams, Janet G. Ross, Richard Lowry, Carl V. Hill, Jo Anne Grunbaum, Pamela S. Blumson, Janet L. Collins, Lloyd J. Kolbe, and State and Local YRBSS Coordinators. 1998. "Youth Risk Behavior Surveillance—United States, 1997." *Journal of School Health* 68(9): 355–369.

Kantrowitz, Barbara, and Pat Wingert. 1999. "How Well Do You Know Your Kid?" *Newsweek,* May.

Kenney, J., C. Reinholtz, and P. J. Angelini. 1997. "Ethnic Differences in Childhood and Adolescent Sexual Abuse and Teenage Pregnancy." *Journal of Adolescent Medicine* 21(1): 3–10.

Kirby, Douglas. 2000. "What Does the Research Say about Sexuality Education?" *Educational Leadership* 58(2): 72–76.

Koch, Kathy. 1998. "Encouraging Teen Abstinence." *CQ Researcher* 8(25): 577–599.

Kotva, H. J., and H. G. Schneider. 1990. "Those 'Talks'—General and Sexual Communication between Mothers and Daughters." *Journal of Social Behavior and Personality* 5(6): 603–613.

Lammers, Cristina, Marjorie Ireland, Michael Resnick, and Robert Blum. 2000. "Influences on Adolescents' Decision to Postpone Onset of Sexual Intercourse: A Survival Analysis of Virginity among Youth Aged 13 to 18 Years." *Journal of Adolescent Health* 26(1): 42–48.

Landry, David J., Lisa Kaeser, and Cory L. Richards. 1999. "Abstinence Promotion and the Provision of Information about Contraception in Public School District Sexuality Education Policies." *Family Planning Perspectives* 31(6): 280–286.

Lanning, B., D. J. Ballard, and J. Robinson. 1999. "Child Sexual Abuse Prevention Programs in Texas Public Elementary Schools." *Journal of School Health* 69(1): 3–8.

Lees, S. 1994. "Talking about Sex in Sex Education." *Gender and Education* 6(3): 281–292.

Leland, N., and R. P. Barth. 1990. "Characteristics of Adolescents Who Have Attempted to Avoid HIV and Who Have Communicated with Parents about Sex." *Journal of Adolescent Research* 8: 58–76.

Lickona, Thomas. 1994. "The Neglected Heart: The Emotional Dangers of Premature Sexual Involvement." *American Educator* (summer): 34–39.

Mackay, Judith. 2000. *The Penguin Atlas of Human Sexual Behavior: Sexuality and Sex Practice around the World.* New York: Penguin Putnam, Inc.

Marin, Barbara V., Karin K. Coyle, Cynthia A. Gomez, Scott C. Carvajal, and Douglas B. Kirby. 2000. "Older Boyfriends and Girlfriends Increase Risk of Sexual Initiation in Young Adolescents." *Journal of Adolescent Health* 27(6): 410–418.

Maynard, R. A. 1996. *Kids Having Kids: A Robin Hood Foundation Special Report on the Costs of Adolescent Childbearing.* New York: The Robin Hood Foundation.

McIlhaney, Joe S. 2000. " 'Safe Sex' Education Has Failed." In *Taking Sides: Clashing Views on Controversial Issues in Human Sexuality,* ed. R. T. Francoeur and W. J. Tavener. Guilford, CT: Dushkin/McGraw Hill.

Miller, B. C., J. K. McCoy, and T. D. Olson. 1986. "Dating Age and Stage as Correlates of Adolescent Sexual Attitudes and Behavior." *Journal of Early Adolescent Research* 1: 361–371.

Miller, K., M. L. Levin, D. J. Whitacker, and X. Xu. 1998. "Patterns of Condom Use among Adolescents: The Impact of Maternal-Adolescent Communication." *American Journal of Public Health* 88: 1542–1544.

Miller, K. E., D. Sabo, and M. P. Farrell. 1998. "Athletic Participation and Sexual

Behavior in Adolescents: The Different World of Boys and Girls." *Journal of Health and Social Behavior* 39: 108–123.

Moh, F. L. 1986. "The Pace of Repeated Child-Bearing among Young American Mothers." *Family Planning Perspectives* 18: 5–12.

Moore, K. A., B. C. Miller, D. R. Morrison, and D. A. Glei. 1995. *Adolescent Sex, Contraception, and Child-Bearing: A Review of Recent Research.* Washington, DC: Child Trends, Inc.

Moore, Michele, and Barbara Rienzo. 2000. "Utilizing the SIECUS Guidelines to Assess Sexuality Education in One State: Content Scope and Importance." *Journal of School Health* 70(2): 56–60.

Mott, Frank L. 1986. "The Pace of Repeated Child-Bearing among Young American Mothers." *Family Planning Perspectives* 18(1): 5–12.

Mott, Frank L., and W. Marsiglio. 1985. "Early Childbearing and Completion of High School." *Family Planning Perspectives* 17: 234–237.

Mott, Frank L., Michelle M. Fondell, Paul N. Hu, Lori Kowaleski-Jones, and Elizabeth G. Mehaghan. 1996. "The Determinants of First Sex by Age 14 in a High-Risk Adolescent Population." *Family Planning Perspectives* 28(1): 13–18.

Murry, V. 1994. "Black Adolescent Females: A Comparison of Early Versus Late Coital Initiators." *Family Relations* 43: 342–348.

Newman, Peter A., and Marc A. Zimmerman. 2000. "Gender Differences in HIV-Related Sexual Risk Behavior among Urban African American Youth: A Multivariate Approach." *AIDS Education and Prevention* 12(4): 308–325.

Nolin, M. J., and K. K. Peterson. 1992. "Gender Differences in Parent-Child Communication about Sexuality: An Exploratory Study." *Journal of Adolescent Research* 7: 59–79.

Office of National AIDS Policy. 1996. *Youth and HIV/AIDS: An American Agenda: A Report to the President.* Washington, DC: The Office of National AIDS Policy.

Orr, Donald P., Mary Beiter, and Gary Ingersoll. 1991. "Premature Sexual Activity as an Indicator of Psychosocial Risk." *Pediatrics* 87(2): 141–147.

Ostrov, E., D. Offer, K. Howard, B. Kaufman, and H. Meyer. 1987. "Adolescent Sexual Behavior." *Medical Aspects of Human Sexuality* 19(5): 28–36.

Pardini, Prisiclla. 1998. "Federal Law Mandates 'Abstinence-Only' Sex Ed." *Rethinking Schools Online* 12(4): 1–7.

"Poll Shows Decline in Sex by High School Students." *New York Times* (18 September 1998).

Raine, Tina R., Renee Jenkins, Sigrid J. Aarons, Kathy Woodward, Johnnie L. Fairfax, M. Nabil El-Khorazaty, and Allen Herman. 1999. "Sociodemographic Correlates of Virginity in Seventh-Grade Black and Latino Students." *Journal of Adolescent Health* 24(5): 304–312.

Remafedi, Gary. 1992. "Demography of Sexual Orientation in Adolescents." *Pediatrics* 89: 714–721.

Remez, Lisa. 2000. "Oral Sex among Adolescents: Is It Abstinence or Is It Sex?" *Family Planning Perspectives* 32(6): 298–304.

Robinson, K. Lynn, Susan K. Telljohann, and James H. Price. 1999. "Predictors of Sixth Graders Engaging in Sexual Intercourse." *Journal of School Health* 69(9): 369–375.

Rodgers, J. L., D. C. Rowe, and D. F. Harris. 1992. "Sibling Differences in Adolescent Sexual Behavior: Inferring Process Models from Family Composition Patterns." *Journal of Marriage and the Family* 54: 142–152.

Rodriguez, Monica. 2000. "Working Together for a Sexually Healthy America." *Educational Leadership* 58(2): 66–69.

Rosemond, John. 2001. *Teen Proofing: Fostering Responsible Decision Making in Your Teenager.* Kansas City: Andrew McNeel Publishing.

Sabo, Donald F., Kathleen E. Miller, and Michael P. Farrell. 1998. *The Women's Sports Foundation Report: Sport and Teen Pregnancy.* East Meadow, NY: Women's Sports Foundation.

Sabo, Donald F., Kathleen E. Miller, Michael P. Farrell, Merrill J. Melnick, and Grace M. Barnes. 1999. "High School Athletic Participation, Sexual Behavior, and Adolescent Pregnancy: A Regional Study." *Journal of Adolescent Health* 25(3): 207–216.

SADD. "Parents: Do Your Teens Think 'You Don't Have a Clue'? They May Be Right . . . ," http://www.saddonline.com/preleases.htm (cited December 4, 2000).

Sanderson, Catherine A. 2000. "The Effectiveness of a Sexuality Education Newsletter in Influencing Teenagers' Knowledge and Attitudes about Sexual Involvement and Drug Use." *Journal of Adolescent Research* 15(6): 674–681.

Schiller, Patricia. 1973. *Creative Approaches to Sex Education and Counseling.* New York: Association Press.

Schuster, Mark A, Robert M. Bell, Gene A. Nakajima, and David K. Kanouse. 1998. "The Sexual Practices of Asian and Pacific Islander High School Youth." *Journal of Adolescent Health* 23(4): 221–231.

Sexuality Information and Education Council of the United States (SIECUS). 2000. *Sexuality Education in the Schools: Issues and Answers.* New York: SIECUS.

Silverstone, R. 1992. "Sexuality Education in Adolescents." *State of Art Reviews: Adolescent Medicine* 3: 192–205.

Singh, Susheela, and Jacqueline Darroch. 1999. "Trends in Sexual Activity among Adolescent American Women: 1982–1995." *Family Planning Perspectives* 31(5): 212–219.

Stodghill, Ron. 1998. "Where'd You Learn That?" *Time,* June 15, 52–59.

Strasburger, Victor. 2000. "Getting Teenagers to Say No to Sex, Drugs, and Violence in the New Millennium." *Adolescent Medicine* 84(4): 787–810.

Stryker, Jeff. 1997. "The Just-Say-No Approach in Sex Ed Lacks One Detail: Evidence That It Works." *Nation* 264(23): 19–21.

Taylor, S., C. DiIorio, T. Stephens, and J. Soet. 1997. "A Comparison of AIDS-Related Sexual Risk Behaviors among African American College Students." *Journal of the National Medical Association* 89(6): 397–403.

Thorton, A. 1990. "The Courtship Process and Adolescent Sexuality." *Journal of Family Issues* 11: 239–273.

Thorton, A., and D. Camburn. 1989. "Religious Participation and Adolescent Sexual Behaviors and Attitudes." *Journal of Marriage and Family* 51: 641–653.

Valois, R., W. Thatcher, J. Drane, and B. Reininger. 1997. "Comparison of Selected Health Risk Behaviors between Adolescents in Public High Schools in South Carolina." *Journal of School Health* 67(10): 434–439.

Wallace, John M., and David R. Williams. 1999. "Religion and Adolescent Health-Compromising Behavior." In *Health Risks and Developmental Transitions during Adolescence,* ed. J. Schulenberg et al. New York: Cambridge University Press.

Walter, H. J., R. D. Vaughn, and A.T. Cohall. 1991. "Psychosocial Influences on Acquired Immunodeficiency Syndrome: Risk Behaviors among High School Students." *Pediatrics* 88: 846–852.

Werner-Wilson, Ronald J. 1998. "Gender Differences in Adolescent Sexual Attitudes: The Influence of Individual and Family Factors." *Adolescence* 33(131): 519–531.

Whitacker, Daniel J., and Kim S. Miller. 2000. "Parent-Adolescent Discussions about Sex and Condoms: Impact on Peer Influences of Sex Risk Behavior." *Journal of Adolescent Research* 15(2): 251–273.

Whitehead, Barbara D. 1994. "The Failure of Sex Education." *The Atlantic Monthly,* 55–80.

Wiley, David C., and Beverly Terlosky. 2000. "Evaluating Sexuality Education Curriculums." *Educational Leadership* 58(2): 79–82.

Wilson, M., M. Kastrinakis, L. D'Angelo, and P. Getson. 1994. "Attitudes, Knowledge, and Behavior Regarding Condom Use in Urban Black Adolescent Males." *Adolescence* 29(1): 13–26.

Zelnick, Melvin, John F. Kanter, and Kathleen Ford. 1981. *Sex and Pregnancy in Adolescence.* Beverly Hills: Sage.

Zill, N., C. W. Nord, and L. Loomis. 1995. *Adolescent Time Use, Risky Behavior, and Outcomes: An Analysis of National Data.* Rockville, MD: Westat, Inc.

Chapter Two

● Chronology of Sex Education

1870   Average age of menarche is 16.5 years old.

1872   Anthony Comstock, leader and organizer of the New York Society for the Suppression of Vice campaigns against birth control, modern art, and literature, making it impossible to distribute any information about sex.

1878   Congress passes an Act for the Suppression of Trade in, and Circulation of Obscene Literature. These provisions become known as Comstock Laws.

1887   Henry Hanchett publishes *Sexual Health: A Plain and Practical Guide for the People on All Matters Concerning the Organs of Reproduction in Both Sexes and All Ages.*

1905   Dr. Prince Morrow launches the social hygiene movement and establishes the Society of Sanitary and Moral Prophylaxis.

1917   Margaret Sanger publishes *The Case for Birth Control.*

1929   Katharine Bement Davis publishes *The Factors in the Sex Life of Twenty-Two Hundred Women.* The study reveals that 50 percent of single women and 30 percent of married women had had homosexual experiences.

1930   Average age of menarche is 14.5 years old.

1940   Illegitimate birthrate for youth ages fifteen to nineteen is 8.3 per 1000.

1950   Senate authorizes an investigation of homosexuals who work for

1950,   the government. Of those fired from the government, 91 percent
cont. were homosexuals.

Illegitimate birthrate for youth ages fifteen to nineteen is 12.8
per 1000.

1953   Hugh Hefner publishes first issue of *Playboy* with Marilyn Monroe on the front cover. Over 53,000 copies sold.

1960   Food and Drug Administration approves birth control pill, Enovid.

Illegitimate birthrate for youth ages fifteen to nineteen is 15.6
per 1000.

1961   More than 400,000 women use the pill.

1963   A community of health experts organizes Sex Information and Education Council of the United States (SIECUS) to maintain continuous open dialogue about human sexuality within the family life education framework.

More than 2 million women use the pill.

1965   The Elementary and Secondary Education Act becomes law. Title III authorizes funds for primary and secondary schools to create or enhance family life education.

1967   A teen clinic in operation through Planned Parenthood in San Francisco and Oakland provides girls under eighteen years of age sex education, contraceptives, and pregnancy and VD testing.

"Summer of Love" in San Francisco.

Births to women younger than twenty years old account for 25 percent of all illegitimate births.

1968   Illegitimate birthrate for youth ages fifteen to nineteen is 19.8 per 1000.

1969   President of the Parent Teacher Association (PTA), Elizabeth Hendryson, supports sex education. Defends the stand that sex education enhances human relations by helping youth understand and respect one another.

Gallup poll reveals that 75 percent of parents favor sex education.

Police raid Stonewall Inn, a gay bar in New York, and the gay liberation movement begins.

David Rueben publishes *Everything You Always Wanted to Know about Sex but Were Afraid to Ask.*

"The Sex Explosion" is a *Time* magazine front cover title. The article claims that Americans have more sexual freedom than ever before.

Eight states permit physicians to examine and treat minors with venereal disease without parental consent.

Seven states (Colorado, Illinois, Oregon, Tennessee, Virginia, West Virginia, and Wyoming) provide minors the right to consent for contraceptives.

Youth fifteen to nineteen years old account for 17 percent of births.

1970　Title X of the Public Health Service Act enacted for the provision of grants to nonprofit agencies to provide family planning services.

An estimated 193,000 abortions are performed.

Approximately 997,000 youth become pregnant; 656,000 elect to give birth.

1971　A national survey finds that 55 percent of school districts have a family life or sex education program.

The American College of Obstetricians and Gynecologists recommends that girls should have access to contraceptives.

Twenty-nine states permit physicians to examine and treat minors with venereal disease without parental consent.

1971,   More than 31 percent of illegitimate births are to women
cont. younger than twenty years old.

Approximately 30 percent of girls fifteen to nineteen years old
have had sexual intercourse; 25 percent have had two or more
partners.

1972   Alex Comfort publishes *The Joy of Sex*.

Commission on Population Growth and the American Future
finds that 27 percent of fourteen to nineteen year olds have had
sex.

More than 800,000 pregnancies occur among youth.

About 300,000 youth have abortions.

The Social Security Act is amended so that sexually active minors
can receive family planning services.

Federal mandate makes it unconstitutional to prohibit pregnant
and parenting youth from school.

1973   The American Psychiatric Association acknowledges that homosexuality is not a mental disease.

Of all illegitimate births, 53 percent are to youth; 35 percent of illegitimate births are to women under twenty years of age.

Abortion is legalized through Supreme Court's ruling in *Roe v.
Wade*.

Approximately 745,000 abortions are performed.

1974   National Education Association renews its formal support for
sex education.

Planned Parenthood of America establishes the Alan
Guttmacher Institute to research social health issues, promote
social understanding, and help develop public policy.

1975   A Michigan State University study finds that more youth (fourteen to sixteen years old) are having sex than in 1970.

More than one million abortions are performed. More than 378,500 youth have an abortion.

Rate of teen pregnancy is 101 cases per 1000 teens.

1976 The Alan Guttmacher Institute claims that the sexual activity among youth has been increasing. Between 1971 and 1976, a 30 percent increase was found in the number of women younger than nineteen years old who had had sex.

Approximately 43.4 percent of girls fifteen to nineteen years old have had sexual intercourse, and 30 percent have had two or more partners.

Over 235,300 out-of-wedlock births were to teenagers. African American youth have eight times more out-of-wedlock births than white youth.

Girls under eighteen can have an abortion without parental consent in twenty-five states and the District of Columbia.

1977 *Better Homes and Gardens* finds 82 percent of middle-class Americans favor sex education in the schools.

A National Institute of Education survey finds that in a sample of high school principals, only 39 percent offered a separate family life/sex education course.

1978 A Gallup poll reveals that 77 percent of Americans favor sex education, with 69 percent that support youth learning about birth control and 56 percent supporting the provision of contraceptives to youth.

Title X of the Public Health Service Act amended to include youth eligible to receive family planning services. Although youth are encouraged to involve their parents in their decisions over contraceptives, youth can receive services without parental notification.

A *Better Homes and Gardens* survey finds middle-class Americans believe that an increase in sexual partners is caused by society's emphasis on sex and the availability of contraceptives.

1979   On the average, seven in ten women aged fifteen to nineteen had some form of sex education in school.

The Alan Guttmacher Institute reports that in a sample of parents, 98 percent said they needed help with teaching their children about sex. Some 72 percent stated that their children had some form of sex education. The study revealed that the youth wanted to have sex education in a self-contained course.

Study finds that 84 percent of parents want to teach their children about birth control. Only 7 percent state that schools should be responsible for this aspect of sex education.

The Alan Guttmacher Institute reports that of fifty-two pregnant youth, 65.8 percent did not want the pregnancy. Of these, 85.5 percent did not use contraceptives. When asked why they did not use birth control, 43 percent said they did not expect to have sex.

Nearly 1.3 million youth receive family planning services.

The average age of first coitus for metropolitan youth is 16.2 for girls and 15.7 for boys. Study reveals that 17 percent of girls and one-quarter of boys in a sample had planned their first coitus.

Nearly 49.8 percent of girls fifteen to nineteen years old have had sexual intercourse.

1980   Kentucky, Maryland, New Jersey, and the District of Columbia mandate sex education.

Two high schools in St. Paul operate a health clinic. As a direct result of the clinic's services, the school's pregnancy and fertility rate drop by 40 percent and 23 percent, respectively.

The Alan Guttmacher Institute finds that the rate of premarital sex among metropolitan youth increased from 30 percent in 1971 to 43 percent in 1976 to 50 percent in 1979. The report reveals that youth who remain unmarried despite their pregnancy has also increased from 58 percent in 1971 to 69 percent in 1976 to 70 percent in 1979.

1981   The Adolescent and Family Life Act is enacted. Communities can apply for federal grants to implement abstinence-only education programs. Programs must promote abstinence and encourage youth to give their babies up for adoption. Funds may not be used to provide information on abortions and family planning services to nonpregnant youth. Parental consent is required for all services.

Nearly 1.1 million youth become pregnant and 537,000 elect to give birth.

1982   Study finds that youth who have received sex education are no more likely to engage in sex than other youth.

Nearly 44.9 percent of girls fifteen to nineteen years old have had sexual intercourse.

1983   Study finds Latino and non-Latino groups hold similar supporting opinions of sex education.

Youth account for one-third of all abortions conducted across the nation.

Number of AIDS cases is 3,064.

1984   An Alan Guttmacher Institute study finds that 80 percent of school districts with over 100,000 students provide some form of sex education. At the junior high level, students receive five or fewer hours of sex education each year; at the senior high level, students receive six to ten hours annually. Homosexuality, gynecology exams, abortion, and masturbation are the least covered topics.

Over 1.5 billion federal dollars have been spent on family planning services through Title X.

Gallup poll finds that 91 percent of public school teachers favor sex education in the high school and 81 percent support sex education in the elementary school. The least popular area of discussion is homosexuality.

Study finds that 60 percent of women and 52 percent of men had received some form of sex education before the age of nineteen;

1984,   most of these individuals reported being sexually active before
cont.   receiving sex education.

1985   Rate of teen pregnancy is 109 cases per 1000 teens.

Gallup poll finds 80 percent of adults favor sex education in the
high school, and 55 percent support the provision of sex education at the elementary level.

1986   Study finds that gay male youth have an average number of
seven partners in a given year.

First national conference is held to address adolescent homosexuality.

Surgeon General C. Everett Koop advises communities of parents, teachers, and health professionals to teach youth to protect
themselves from AIDS. Koop requests that AIDS education begin
early at home and is reinforced in the elementary and high
school.

Study finds that 92 percent of adolescents know that AIDS is
transmitted through sexual intercourse.

The Alan Guttmacher Institute finds 80 percent of school districts provide some form of sex education.

1987   One and one-half million Americans believed to be infected with
HIV. Over 360,000 cases of AIDS in the United States, most acquired through homosexual or bisexual intercourse.

Youth thirteen to nineteen years old account for 145 AIDS
cases.

President Reagan declares AIDS "public enemy Number One."

U.S. District Court Judge finds Adolescent Family Life Act of 1981
unconstitutional on the grounds that it violates the Establishment Clause of the First Amendment—the separation of church
and state. Up to this point, the Department of Health and
Human Services has funded religious organizations and inadvertently "entangled" church and state.

1989   Roughly 85 percent of the U.S. public supports the teaching of sex education.

Over 60 percent of teenagers receive some form of sex education.

Seventeen states and the District of Columbia require the provision of sex education. Thirty states require AIDS education.

Study finds that 93 percent of teachers of biology, health, home economics, physical education, and nursing provide some form of sex or AIDS education.

Youth represent 1 percent of diagnosed AIDS cases.

The Report of the Secretary's Task Force on Youth Suicide indicates that gay, lesbian, bisexual, and transgender youth are two to three times more likely to attempt suicide than heterosexual youth.

1993   The American Association of University Women finds that of 1,632 youth in eighth through eleventh grade, 85 percent of girls and 76 percent of boys experienced some form of sexual harassment.

New York City public schools Chancellor Joseph Fernandez is fired for his support of the schools' provision of condoms for students.

Lamport and Andre study finds youth who are sexually active know less about AIDS than youth who are not. Study results show females know more about AIDS than males.

Study indicates that 97 percent of high school youth regularly hear homophobic remarks.

1995   Chancellor of New York City Schools Rudolph Crew approves of AIDS Education.

Dr. Ruth publishes *Sex for Dummies* and underscores that AIDS has brought an end to the sexual revolution.

Rate of teen pregnancy is 101 cases per 1,000 teens.

1996   The Personal Responsibility and Work Opportunity Reconciliation Act (the Welfare Reform Act) is signed by President Clinton. Congress authorizes $250 million (over five years) in state grants to encourage states to provide sex education that teaches abstinence-only.

National Campaign to Prevent Teen Pregnancy is organized with the mission to reduce the rate of pregnancy among youth by one-third.

A six-year-old boy was suspended from school because he kissed a classmate.

A University of Michigan study finds that of youth in eighth through eleventh grade, 68 percent of girls and 39 percent of boys have experienced some form of physical sexual contact.

1997   Study finds that 30 percent of girls are sexually active by 15 years old and 70 percent are sexually active by the age of 18.

1998   Ninety-nine Gay-Straight Alliance clubs exist in schools.

1999   LaShonda Davis wins a sexual harassment lawsuit against her school district, Monroe County Board of Education. The judgment sets precedent that schools are accountable if they deliberately ignore sexual harassment of students by students or staff.

The U.S. Department of Education disseminates *Protecting Students from Harassment and Hate Crime: A Guide for Schools.*

Six hundred gay-straight alliance clubs exist in schools.

Youth between the ages of sixteen and nineteen experienced sexual violence thirty-five times more often than persons ages fifty to sixty-four.

Of an estimated 2.9 million youth reporting maltreatment, 11.3 percent were sexually abused.

Study finds that the average age for "coming out" for gay males dropped from age twenty in 1979 to thirteen in 1998.

The Gay, Lesbian and Straight Education Network reports that 41.7 percent of gay, lesbian, bisexual, and transgender youth do not feel safe in their schools.

The American Counseling Association disseminates *Just the Facts about Sexual Orientation and Youth* to 15,000 public school superintendents.

2000   More than 800 gay-straight alliance clubs exist in schools.

Study reports that youth who are sexually abused are likely to know their abuser (in 42 percent of the cases the abuser is a parent and in 22 percent the abuser is a relative).

2001   The Alan Guttmacher Institute finds that youth who participate in sex education programs that involve parents are less likely to engage in risky sexual behavior and are more serious about abstinence than are their counterparts who do not participate in such programs.

The American Association of University Women finds that of 2,064 youth in eighth through eleventh grade, 83 percent of girls and 79 percent of boys experienced some form of sexual harassment.

Chapter Three

⮞ A Historical Perspective of Sex Education in the Twentieth Century

Trite as it may sound, learning from the past does help to better understand the present and plan for the future. Much can be learned by investigating the history of sex education. A review of the history finds that sex education began to evolve in the last century with its roots tracing back to several prominent leaders. Among them were physicians Prince A. Morrow and Max J. Exner, Columbia University Professor Maurice A. Bigelow, and activist Katharine Bement Davis. During the turn of the nineteenth century and early twentieth century, these individuals were living in a conservative time. An organization called the New York Society for the Suppression of Vice allowed Inspector General Anthony Comstock to confiscate material he believed was obscene or pornographic. Possession of any material dealing with sexual activity—nudity, contraceptives, abortion, and prostitution—was grounds for impoundment, arrest, and prosecution. The Comstock Law, which took effect in 1878, made it essentially illegal to distribute information about abortion and birth control, and open public discussion about sex nearly became obsolete. Margaret Sanger, known for her heroic work in birth control, was arrested time and again for her efforts to promote contraception. In its most conservative implementation, the Comstock Law was used to arrest storefront owners who left naked mannequins in their display windows (Melody and Peterson 1999).

In 1905, Dr. Morrow, determined to control venereal diseases (he later coined the term *social diseases*), established the American Society of Sanitary and Moral Prophylaxis that focused attention on the purportedly sinful aspects of sex. The society's initial objective was to curtail the rate of venereal diseases, but the organization eventually accepted a more liberal objective, "to promote the appreciation of the sacredness of human sexual relations, and thereby to minimize the moral and physical evils resulting from ignorance and vice" (Bigelow 1936 as cited in Kirkendall 1981).

1910s: SEX EDUCATION AS SOCIAL
HYGIENE IN MILITARY LIFE

Two organizations were formed in 1912: the American Federation of Sexual Hygiene and the American Vigilance Association. Although the latter was more concerned with eliminating prostitution (Kirkendall 1981), the two organizations eventually merged to form the American Social Hygiene Association. During this time, the National Education Association (NEA) and the American Medical Association (AMA) gathered for a conference to discuss sex education. The NEA supported the idea that sex hygiene was essential in the public schools, and the AMA announced that sex education was the primary avenue to eliminate sexually transmitted diseases. That year John D. Rockefeller Jr. suggested that the YMCA develop a bureau to study and promote sex education at universities and colleges. The bureau created a lecture series and publications for the colleges and is credited for laying the groundwork for sex education in higher education (Exner 1929).

The United States entered World War I in 1914. Sex education during that time was problem-centered with efforts aimed at preventing soldiers from having sex with prostitutes and acquiring sexually transmitted diseases (Maddock 1997). The nation was concerned with the spread of sexually transmitted diseases, and for the first time motion pictures were used as a form of sex education. The earliest sex education film, *Damaged Goods,* was created to inform the public of the consequences of syphilis (Eberwein 1999). The premise of the film was that of a bachelor about to marry. He has a sexual encounter with a prostitute before his wedding night; he acquires syphilis, passes it on to his newborn baby, and then commits suicide (Eberwein 1999). The film was commercially released and received favorable reviews. One reviewer wrote, "American boy(s) . . . should be made to see it, for they are to become the American manhood, and the cleaner physically, the better" (as cited in Eberwein 1999, 19).

Two more films of that decade, *Fit to Fight/Win* (1918/1919) and *The End of the Road* (1918), were also created to educate soldiers and civilians about venereal diseases. *Fit to Fight/Win* centered on five soldiers who had received information on venereal diseases, but only two heeded the warnings of the diseases: one abstained from sex, and the other had received a prophylactic treatment prior to his sexual encounter. After some sexual encounters, the three other soldiers were left in despair about their future. *Fit to Fight/Win* was later distributed commercially with audiences segregated by gender. The commercial distribution was short lived because the National Association of the Motion

Picture Industry and the surgeon general withdrew their support of its release. *The End of the Road,* designed primarily for women, was a story of two women: one who has received sex education from her mother, and one who has not. Both venture to New York where the woman who has not received sex education acquires syphilis, and the woman who has been educated about sex receives a marriage proposal (Eberwein 1999). The message is clear: women acquire syphilis from men, ergo women should abstain from sex until marriage. This film was also commercially short lived.

With the mission to eliminate venereal diseases, the American Social Hygiene Association helped the Committee on Training Camps Activities to educate and inform soldiers of sexual hygiene. In addition to viewing the aforementioned movies, soldiers were exposed to sexual hygiene via a stereomotorgraph, a machine that displayed photos on a two foot square screen. Soldiers viewed microscopic slides of syphilis and gonorrhea organisms, and symptoms of advanced stages of the diseases on the body of an actual soldier. A caveat reminded the viewers that the emotional consequences were equally dismal. Sergeants were responsible for sex education and many were trained to use the stereomotorgraph. Clark (1918) (as cited in Eberwein 1999) regarded the stereomotorgraph as an efficient technological teaching tool.

Margaret Sanger was legendary in this time period. Known largely as the founder of the birth control movement, she fought many professionals who opposed contraception. Living in a conservative time and voicing support for birth control, Sanger was often persecuted. She was arrested for publishing an article in favor of birth control, arrested for speaking at public rallies, and threatened by city officials with police disruption of her meetings (Melody and Peterson 1999). Through her work, Sanger indirectly brought sex outside of procreation to public consciousness. She wrote two books—*What Every Mother Should Know* (1916) and *How Six Little Children Were Taught the Truth* (1916)—as guides for parents to teach sex to their children. She published *The Case for Birth Control* in 1917.

The American Social Hygiene Association published the organization's first professional journal. Most of the content was focused on the spread of sexually transmitted diseases, although the organization had established that education was the mechanism to be used to combat the spread of diseases. In the first issue, Garrett (1914) wrote *Sex Education for Children before the Age of Fifteen: Sex Hygiene for Children.* Most of the article described her methods of teaching about sex through nature and biology. The content was simple. She advised her readers to teach about sex outdoors whenever possible using aesthetically attractive plants and animals. She used the peanut and its embryo as an example of the development of the human embryo. She saw no harm in teaching about sex in a coeducational style and stressed the importance of using correct vocabulary to describe anatomy. The article, however, lacked the material to teach youth how to care for themselves physically or how to socially interact with one another.

In the same issue, Sill (1914), a headmaster of a Connecticut boarding school, wrote of his disapproval of sex education in the public schools. He advised that boys can live a "morally healthy" life with a minimal amount of sex education. He indicated that parents should communicate with their children, and fathers should especially have "sex talks" with their sons.

One father, Gaffney (1914), warned that youth would learn "the secrets of life" from other children. To provide youth with more accurate information, he advised that others should follow his example and have "sex talks" with their sons. He too used nature (seeds, animals, eggs, birds) as his basis, progressed to the responsibility of the mother and father, and culminated with a physiology lesson that encompassed "abuses and care of (a) person (and) (d)iseases caused by abuse and neglect" (270). Ellis (1914), principal of a Michigan high school, discussed sex education in her school. She explained that youth could elect to take a physiology course with the content centered on sex hygiene. Students first learned about reproduction of plants and animals, progressed to heredity and eugenics, then learned simple instructions on hygiene. Boys learned to respect womanhood and studied the diseases associated with having sex, and the girls learned the parameters of their interactions with boys. Ellis mentioned that most youth had not received the "sex talk" and they showed much interest in the subject matter. She stressed the importance of having teachers who "believe in (sex education) and (were) friendly with the students" (272).

In the second issue, Geddes and Thompson (1915) proclaimed that youth should receive a sex education that was "frank, unashamed, and reverent" (330). The authors stressed that youth deserve to know the facts of life in a context that clarifies their misunderstandings and misgivings. Teachers, moreover, should refrain from frightening, exciting, or providing the youth with too much information on sex. Peabody (1915) addressed a conference of the American Social Hygiene Association. As head of biology in a New York City high school, he mentioned that children inherently seek sexual knowledge and deserve the right to know the facts of life as they pertain to sex. He maintained that well-trained and devoted teachers should impart sexual knowledge to youth as early as five years old. He supported the separation of boys and girls in the biology classes to allow them to discuss sexual issues according to gender. The boys learned about menstruation, reproductive organs, human development and birth, nocturnal emissions and masturbation, sexually transmitted diseases, and attitudes toward girls. He continued by providing the results of one of the earliest surveys of boys and their sexuality. Although archaic, his study revealed that 78 percent of the boys had received sex talks from their fathers, the majority (57 percent) were not worried by nocturnal emissions, 55 percent had learned that sexual intercourse was not necessary for health, and most of the boys were appreciative of sex education. Peabody expressed that he hoped that after each sex education lesson, the boys would have a clearer understanding of reproduction, a deeper love for their mothers, a loathing for venereal disease, and a noble appreciation of girls. Most importantly, Peabody hoped the boys would abstain from masturbation.

The girls, on the other hand, learned about menstruation, human development and birth, sexually transmitted diseases, and the standard of conduct with boys. One of Peabody's teachers conducted a survey of the girls and found most had not received a "sex talk" about reproduction, menstruation, and how to behave with boys; had not been concerned about their menstruation; and were not troubled by sex. Most of the girls claimed that sex education was valuable and informative. With these results, Peabody concluded that schools bear the responsibility to educate youth about sex.

In 1916, Armstrong and Armstrong published a sex education pamphlet entitled *Sex in Life: For Boys and Girls from Twelve to Sixteen Years.* The authors designed a single coeducational pamphlet so that youth could learn one another's physical development. The puberty stage is described with details of physical body development and rules youth must follow to prepare for adulthood. Some of the rules are substantiated; others seem ludicrous. For instance, girls are instructed to not bathe in cold water during their menstruation and to stand erect with their chests forward. Youth are admonished to avoid constipation because the extra feces would produce abnormal problems for boys, and girls would experience pain when the uterus gets misaligned. They also advised, "Another thing to be careful about is the clothing you wear near (genitalia). Nothing rough, starched, or binding should be worn" (336). Although the authors stressed the importance of love in finding a faithful friend and mate, much of their content is harsh. For example, "You are no longer a baby, but twelve is rather an unattractive age in boys and girls. You are probably awkward and homely" (332).

Cady (1917) published an article entitled *How Shall We Teach: The Normal Schools and Colleges and the Problem of Sex Education.* The article stressed that sex education was critical but the current provisions failed to inform youth about their sexuality. She discussed the responsibilities of parents, teachers, schools, and churches and acknowledged that most were unprepared to impart sexual knowledge. As a result, youth continued to receive inaccurate, "vulgar" information from their peers. She suggested that sex education should be integrated throughout the school curriculum, and research should be conducted to determine how sex education is being implemented across the nation.

A 1919 report from the U.S. Department of Labor, Children's Bureau supported the need for sex education. The author of the report, Leigh, underscored the need for a standardized, national organization and policy on sex education. He admitted that sex education was initially targeted at soldiers to reduce the incidence of venereal diseases but realized that soldiers would have been better informed if they had learned the information in their schooling. He wrote, "the worries and doubts and brooding imposed on boys and girls of the adolescent period as a result of lack of simple knowledge is a cruelty on the part of any society that is able to furnish that instruction" (264). He cited two studies to emphasize that boys and girls generally get their impressions of sex at an early age (nine and a half for boys, eleven and a half for girls) and that the source of the information is often "improper and (from) unreliable sources." He believed that youth crave sexual knowledge, and it is the responsibility of the parents, the public libraries, and schools to impart that knowledge.

1920s: SEX EDUCATION IN THE PUBLIC EYE

A review of the *Journal of Social Hygiene* finds that health professionals during the 1920s had determined that sex education should be integrated into the public school curriculum. Many journal articles and other news items considered integrating sex education into the curriculum. More studies were conducted to assess the rate of sex education implementation and survey the knowledge and behavior of youth.

Curtiss (1920), a high school English teacher, published an article entitled *Sex Instruction through English Literature*. She stressed that English teachers have the responsibility to teach sex education directly or indirectly through classical literature. In the article the author cited various pieces of classical literature and questioned the impact that story lines could have on the behavior of some youth if those pieces were not discussed at great length. She encouraged teachers to know the material that youth were reading and surmise how youth could possibly become affected by reading the material. Curtiss provided an example: *The Girl Philippa,* by Robert W. Chambers, is about a young spy who dances undercover at a cabaret. She falls in love with an American artist twice her age, and after he realizes she is pure, he falls in love with her. The story ends with the artist learning that Philippa is a princess; they marry, and live happily ever after. Curtiss wondered, however, whether young girls would become disgusted with the idea of dancing in a house of ill repute, or would the story "arouse unwholesome curiosity or even a spirit of investigation?" (266).

An abbreviated selection of Meyer's (1920) *Suggestions of Modern Science Concerning Education* appeared in the journal. No particular aspects of science were addressed, although the author underscored the need for parents to be trained to impart sexual knowledge to their children. The Isenberger (1920) report included more specifics for science. His committee of Chicago biology teachers responded to the *Cardinal Principles of Education* published by the National Committee on Reorganization of Secondary Education. His committee outlined seven objectives to be accomplished through the teaching of biology. "Worthy home membership" (436) was the rubric assigned for topics as they related to sex education. The components included:

- •• the position that the biological sciences teach, as no other subject can, fundamental knowledge and relationships of sex
- •• home and family as the ideal fundamental unit
- •• education for fatherhood and motherhood
- •• a natural and biological approach, a wholesome attitude toward sex and reproduction secured in mixed classes without offense
- •• the facts of sex and reproduction being considered a normal part of knowledge
- •• the stance that all pupils in the high school should receive this instruction (436)

White (1920), of the United States Public Health Service, published an article calling attention to the production of motion pictures to enhance the teaching of sex education. He believed that the films could be introduced in kindergarten and shown up to high school progressing from a "molding" phase to "teaching" phase. The films would be based on nature with the main characters visiting zoos and farms and leading up to elements of botany, geology, zoology, and so forth. All aspects of the film would be discussed frankly and in the context of beautiful images, moral characters, and ideal conduct. By using the films, White believed, professionals could ensure that youth would learn by the examples in the films and no longer worry about teachers' qualifications.

The Status of Sex Education in Public Educational Institutions published by Harris (1921) set out to determine how higher education institutions delivered sex education. The Harris study found that most Normal Schools of Education provided sex education integrated throughout the curriculum. Some of the schools taught sex education through courses such as "Health Problems," "Educational Hygiene," and "Mothercraft Training." Harris found that 35 percent of 228 schools were preparing teachers of sex education to teach facts through a biological approach, 40 percent of the schools were providing some form of sex education, and 25 percent had no form of sex education. When the question was posed whether sex education should be provided in the normal schools, only eight of the schools were opposed. Harris reaffirmed that the public largely supported teachers being trained to deliver sex education. She also found that South Carolina, Massachusetts, Connecticut, and Utah were progressive and sex education was required at the elementary or secondary grade level. In South Carolina, for example, a sex manual had been developed and was used with lectures at all grade levels. Harris underscored the need for the training of teachers in sex education as higher education professionals and the general public deemed it necessary.

The United States Bureau of Education and the United States Public Health Service (1921) reported the results of their survey in which 6,488 schools were asked if they provided sex education. The results showed that 53.8 percent of schools did not offer sex education. Of the schools that offered sex education, most provided information delivered through pamphlets, exhibits, or short lectures. *Keeping Fit,* the exhibit and pamphlet, was used for boys. Girls were given the pamphlet *Healthy Happy Womanhood* and were shown the exhibit *Youth and Life.*

Maurice Bigelow became the editor-in-chief of the Journal of Social Hygiene in 1922. The earliest news piece of this year alluded to the results of the Van Buskirk and Van Buskirk (1922) survey of sex education in Cincinnati schools and the public's reaction. The researchers found that most people favored sex education. In the same issue, Sandiford (1922) stressed the need for schools to implement sex education programs that taught youth correct sexual information and encouraged them to maintain a healthy attitude toward sex. The author stressed the need for qualified teachers and described the teachers who should not teach sex education as:

- those who cannot talk calmly and dispassionately on the subject

➻ those with an abnormal outlook on life, who are too readily influenced by psychopathic literature

➻ insufficiently informed people who tend to stress the abnormal in their presentation because of hasty preparation

➻ those who are pessimistic as a result of unfortunate personal experiences

➻ those of flippant attitude and questionable ethical behavior who cannot command the respect of their pupils (351)

The film *The Gift of Life* was produced to educate youth about sex with much of the content promoting healthy grooming behaviors (Eberwein 1999). A pointer moves around the screen to underscore the reproductive system and the consequences of venereal diseases while the narrator advises the audience. For boys, for instance, the film recommends:

> athletics, abundant outdoor life, wholesome companions, lots of good fun, constant occupation, the determination that will help a boy who has acquired the habit of masturbation ("self-abuse") to overcome it and repair any harm it may have done. . . . Masturbation may seriously hinder a boy's progress toward vigorous manhood. It is a selfish, childish, stupid habit. (cited in Eberwein 107)

The film indirectly reinforced gender roles and the belief that sex should be reserved for procreation.

In 1923, Achilles conducted a large-scale study on the effectiveness of particular sex education pamphlets. He investigated eight groups (three groups of youth were seventeen and younger) and their change in sexual behavior after reading one of thirteen sex education pamphlets. The groups read the pamphlets, and three days later they answered a series of questions. The study revealed that better educated groups found the pamphlets "efficient"; most of the groups had a favorable opinion of the pamphlets; most men believed the pamphlets had a good effect on them; and 66 percent benefited from reading the pamphlets, with fifteen-year-old boys reporting the highest rate of benefit (98 percent). The study asked boys if the material had changed their opinion regarding seminal emissions, masturbation, continence, and venereal diseases. Girls were asked if their opinion had changed regarding menstruation and the process of reproduction. Exactly how their opinions might have changed is difficult to determine because the sample did not qualify how, yet the authors reported that most of the sample did not change their opinions. The sample was also asked if they changed their behavior after reading the pamphlet, and 61 percent of the men and 49 percent of the women answered in the affirmative. This led Achilles to conclude that pamphlets should continue to be distributed.

The same year, Van Buskirk (1923), the executive secretary of the Cincinnati Social Hygiene Society, detailed the group's efforts to stop prostitution and the spread of venereal diseases. Over 10,000 members of the Cincinnati Federation of Mothers' Clubs enrolled in a lecture series called *Sex Education in the Home*. The course outlined the need for sex education in the home, sex education in early and late childhood, gender needs, and progress in social health. The mothers were overwhelmingly appreciative of the lectures and found them beneficial. To enhance the comfort level of Cincinnati's teachers' and refine their knowledge of sex education, *Problems of Sex Education* was offered at the University of Cincinnati. The course included the biological, physiological, hygienic, sociological, and psychological aspects of sex and a discussion of venereal diseases. More than 90 percent of the students enrolled in the course were practicing teachers. An additional 3,000 teachers enrolled in the Ohio State Department of Health's summer institute, *Social Hygiene Education—A Part of a General Health Program*, to learn new methods of teaching sex education. The society emphasized the need for teachers who would underscore the positive aspects of sex instead of teaching about diseases and use constructive teaching methods.

In her address to the National Conference of Social Work, Florence Richards (1923) emphasized that the terms *sex education* or *sex instruction* should be used instead of *sex hygiene*. She emphasized that World War I had taught health professionals that sexual promiscuity was a problem; medical and legal professionals had found that matrimonial problems were often rooted in misunderstandings of sex; and parents had failed to provide their children with sex education. For these reasons she described how sex education could be addressed in the high school curriculum. In social studies for instance, youth could learn about the biographies of great men and women, the menace of venereal diseases, gonorrhea as a depopulating factor, and syphilis as a source of insanity and degeneration. In the all-girls high school Richards administered, seniors took the "Course in Domestic Sanitation, Home Nursing, and Sex Education." The girls learned about everything from human development to prostitution to social propriety. Richards had never received a complaint from parents, and the girls were eager and anxious to learn about sex. She concluded that sex education was necessary for the greater good of society.

In 1925, New York City's Division of Visual Instruction and Division of Venereal Diseases joined to create the film *The Science of Life*. Over 40,000 youth watched the film to learn about sex hygiene. That same year more than 10,000 New Jersey youth listened to sex education lectures given by Dr. Eugene L. Swan and Dr. Edith Hale Swift of the American Social Hygiene Association. Some school officials initially opposed the lectures, but they eventually recognized the benefits and accepted the lecture series in their schools. Maurice A. Bigelow (1925) spoke at the Annual National Social Hygiene Conference and established his twenty-one points of social hygiene. They included the following.

- Point One: Social hygiene encompasses the social health and welfare of various communities.
- Point Two: The goal of social hygiene is the development of the physical, psychical, and social well-being.
- Point Three: Sex education and social hygiene are rubrics for research and teaching.
- Point Four: The delivery of sex education and social hygiene includes all measures.
- Point Five: The terms *sex education* and *social hygiene* should be used instead of *sex studies.*
- Point Six: Sex education should be an integral part of the school curriculum.
- Point Seven: Social hygiene education enhances the study of biology and vice versa.
- Point Eight: People learn to control their sexual impulses through social hygiene education.
- Point Nine: People learn the standard of sexual conduct and how to behave sexually through social hygiene education.
- Point Ten: Sex education should help youth develop an open mind and respectful attitude toward sex, acquire sexual and healthful knowledge, and enhance personal relations.
- Point Eleven: Problems can occur if sex education is unavailable—ill attitude toward sex, and/or uncontrolled/vulgar sexual behavior.
- Point Twelve: Social hygiene education has proven beneficial with incidence of prostitution and illegitimacy down, vulgarity "out of fashion," and more successful marriages.
- Point Thirteen: Youth will learn the vulgar aspects of sex from other unreliable sources if they are not given sex education.
- Point Fourteen: Sex education must be progressive and integrated with character and health education.
- Point Fifteen: Sex education is not temporary instruction.
- Point Sixteen: Biology should be used as the earliest form of sex instruction.

➥ Point Seventeen: English literature is valuable in teaching about sex.

➥ Point Eighteen: The normal, healthy, positive, and moral aspects of sex should be taught, not immorality or abnormality.

➥ Point Nineteen: Social hygiene education should stress moral practices and relationships.

➥ Point Twenty: Although sex education benefits thousands, it does not solve the problems for all people.

➥ Point Twenty-One: Social hygiene education protects, preserves, extends, improves, and develops the nuclear family.

In 1926, Hughes published his study of boys and their sexual experiences. The study was conducted in North Carolina with the boys selected from high schools, prep schools, and working mills, their ages ranging from fifteen to twenty. The boys were shown the exhibit *Keeping Fit* and then asked to complete a questionnaire. Of the 1,029 boys who completed the questionnaire, 65 percent attended high school, 28 percent attended prep school, and 7 percent were mill workers. The study found that sex entered the boys' consciousness as early as nine years old and as late as sixteen. The majority of the boys (78 percent) reported that they began thinking about sex primarily as a direct result of conversations with other boys, and 236 boys reported that this had a bad effect on them. Approximately 85 percent of the boys indicated they masturbated with the average frequency of six times per month. Most boys began to masturbate at 14 years of age, and most began to masturbate because of conversations with other boys. A sweeping 94 percent of the boys found *Keeping Fit* to be an effective means of sex education, and 86 percent reported that they had benefited from viewing the exhibit. Hughes concluded that sex enters the consciousness early primarily as a result of talking to other boys. As a result, boys are bound to be educated about sex—from reliable, accurate sources such as schools and parents, or from unwholesome, inaccurate sources such as their peers.

In 1927, the Department of Parental Education of the Women's Cooperative Alliance of Minneapolis reported that parent advisers phoned 6,730 mothers of junior high school youth to provide them with facts to help them acquire a better attitude toward sex education. Nearly 1,500 mothers were interviewed; 92 percent were appreciative of the information and 45 mothers refused the information. A series of sex education lectures and materials was then created specifically for the mothers. That year the United States Public Health Service outlined the content of an ideal sex education course for teachers. The outline stressed that teachers should teach sex education in the academic areas when opportunities present themselves, and never in a course with sex education as the sole content; and they should refrain from teaching sex education through single lectures, but could use *Keeping Fit* and *Youth and Life* for "emergency" situations.

In 1928, an Alabama county made a concerted effort to train high school and elementary school teachers to teach sex education and motivated them to establish a permanent sex education program. The Alabama State Department of Education and the American Social Hygiene Association taught the teachers how to integrate sex education into the curriculum and created a sex education manual for the elementary teachers. In a popular magazine of the time, *Children, the Magazine for Parents*, the general secretary of the Family Society of Philadelphia, Karl de Schweinitz (1928), informed parents that they must teach their children about sex. He stressed the need for parents to model a wholesome attitude toward sex and to impart sexual knowledge when their children ask questions. He explained that preadolescence is the best time for sex talks because these youth are not as emotionally charged as adolescents are.

At the 1929 convention of the New York State Congress of Parents and Teachers, the organization agreed to increase efforts to provide more social hygiene education and stressed the need for a statewide program that would foster character building, ideal sexual conduct and wholesome relationships, and parenthood. Edith Dixon (1929) of the Institute for Child Welfare encouraged parents to free themselves of embarrassment and inhibitions when talking about sex with their children. She stressed that parents should be direct with their children and answer their questions truthfully. For the first time, the terms *sex education* and *sex instruction* were distinguished. Dixon wrote, "Sex instruction is the telling of facts about sex. . . . Sex education, like other education, is a developing process in which the child must grow and mature both in his ideas of sex and in his attitude toward it" (82). During this time the *Christian Register* (1929) announced that the Unitarian Sunday School Society held its annual meeting and declared that sex education material should be prepared for their youth in church schools. The society declared: "We believe that sex education should have a part in our program. We deplore ignorant and bigoted censorship of honest and scientific attempts to teach the sex side of life. We recommend to our officers the preparation of such material as may be suitable for our use in teaching this subject" (424).

The Medical Women's International Association gathered in Paris for their 1929 convention. The association maintained that sex instruction should be provided to youth, but not under that title; be given to young children by their parents; be available for parents and teachers;

include discussions of ethical conduct and control of sexual impulses; and include discussions of sexual diseases by medical doctors. As the decade came to a close, Exner (1929) published an article entitled *Progress in Sex Education*. He described how over a span of twenty years, the sex education movement had become organized and had slowly transformed the attitude from sex the "ignoble and shameful" to sex the wholesome and natural. He captured four principles that became commonly accepted by the movement.

- Sex education is rooted in helping youth develop a wholesome life with accurate knowledge and sound experience.
- Sex education should be one and the same with character education where youth are encouraged to grow into fine citizens who exercise ideal sexual conduct.
- Sex education should be progressive, be developmentally appropriate, and go beyond discussion of facts.
- Sex education should be integrated into the curriculum with discussions of sex as they relate to academic content at hand.

The Executive Committee of the Federal Council of the Churches of Christ in America met in December and concluded that parents were primarily responsible for educating youth about sex. The Committee felt that because many parents were not prepared well enough to offer sex education, the Council would collaborate with the International Council of Religious Education to create and promote social hygiene classes for parents (along with home training of children and religion in the home).

1930s: SEX EDUCATION AND THE WHOLESOME ATTITUDE

In 1930 Alicia Barker-Ellsworth reported on her work with girls in sixth through ninth grade. A series of personal and social hygiene lectures were provided for 800 girls. The lectures included How to Advertise Mother; Home, the Backbone of Our Nation; and How to Be Beautiful. As was common of this genre, the lectures began with discussions of reproduction among insects, animals, and plants and progressed to human sexuality. Barker-Ellsworth described how she spoke about nature but did not elaborate on her human sexuality material. The girls were told that they existed because their parents were healthy and clean and were discouraged from harmful petting. Her lectures evidently benefited the community as she indicated, "Is it any wonder that after one year of this healthy information sex problems in this school were reduced greatly and obscene pictures and stories disappeared from the closet and basement?" (111). Barker-Ellsworth was among the pioneers who believed that parents should be the first providers of sex education and that discussions of sex should start early.

The YMCA (1930) surveyed YMCA branches to determine the forms of sex education provided to boys across the country. The results found that forty-four of sixty-three branches promoted some form of sex education with most delivered through interviews, lectures, and literature. Twenty branches offered services for parents, and thirty branches waited for parents to ask for services. Forty-eight branches mentioned that more sex education should be offered to boys. The findings led the national YMCA to articulate their needs: more training for their branch directors; sex education classes for parents; and organization of better sex education resources for their clients.

Under the leadership of President Hoover, the planning committee of the President's White House Conference on Child Health and Protection (1930) prepared a report that underscored the essential elements of social hygiene. The Committee outlined the following points.

- Youth should learn that sexuality is vital to self-development and happiness, and a healthy sexual lifestyle ultimately contributes to the welfare of society.
- The community of parents, school, and social groups must collaborate to ensure that youth protect themselves from unwholesome and unhealthy sexual lifestyles.
- Sex education literature and material should be made available for homes and schools so that youth learn about sex at all stages of development.
- Experienced professionals and health experts should study sex education and serve in advisory capacities to various health agencies.
- Youth should learn about sex directly rather than learning from biology, allegories, or metaphors.
- Parents need their own sex education and should be encouraged to educate their youth about sex.
- Sex education should emphasize modesty and social ideals.
- Youth should learn to protect themselves from venereal diseases.
- Higher education institutions should provide social hygiene training for teachers.

In 1931, the American Social Hygiene Association emphasized that teachers needed help in acquiring the skills to teach sex education. That summer, twelve universities offered sex education courses to practicing teachers. The association claimed that the summer courses were generally well attended, and the testimony of the teachers seemed to indicate that they had a much better understanding of sex as a result of taking the courses. Sherbon (1931) surveyed 313 female graduates of the University of Kansas to determine whether the biology of reproduction should be taught in the public schools. The graduates were divided into three groups: the most recent graduates; alumni of ten to twenty years; and alumni of twenty years or more. Of those surveyed, 71 percent of the most recent graduates, 71 percent of the middle group, and 46 percent of the older group supported the teaching of the biology of reproduction. This led Sherbon to conclude, "this most important function of life should receive the same candid and exhaustive treatment in educational curricula as any other subject" (516).

In 1932, the editor of the *Journal of Social Hygiene* wrote, *Is There a Formula of Sex Education?* He provided a series of elaborate charts created by Galloway to outline: what knowledge and skills youth need to acquire (habits, preferences, and attitudes) during their first twelve years of life; what youth aged twelve to fifteen should possess; and what youth should have attained by the age of eighteen. That same year, Jones stressed that the church bears some of the responsibility for talking about sex with its congregation. He felt that the clergy should know as much as possible about the social dynamics of sex. All too often, the clergy were not adequately prepared to discuss sex, and Charters (1932) believed that the church should educate its community about sex. He outlined how and when the church could deliver sex education: through preaching and the midweek service, the preliminary conference with young people about to be married, young people's discussion groups, parents' groups, lectures, lecture-discussion meetings, clinics, office conferences, individual service as special personal needs arise, book lists, a library, and pamphlet service (477).

Charters stressed that churches should especially provide sex education courses for parents so they could learn how to discuss sex from a spiritual point of view. Through these courses, parents could learn sex facts and how to teach their children to maintain a "true" attitude toward sex, and indirectly develop their own healthy attitude. Several sex education pamphlets were distributed by church denominations.

In 1932, the Illinois Biology Teachers Association surveyed seventy-six biology teachers to determine if sex education was adequately provided statewide. Fifty-seven of the teachers answered in the affirmative with most of the them teaching sexual facts. Most of the teachers supported sex education and favored teaching it through an integrated approach. Most of the teachers were unaware of the principals' and parents' attitude toward sex education. The Women's Cooperative Alliance of Minneapolis (1932) conducted a study on children's sex questions. In their house-to-house visits of 981 homes, the researchers gathered 1,763 questions asked by 563 boys and 546 girls. Boys asked the most questions at five and nine years old, and girls asked the most at five, ten, and thirteen years old. The questions were classified into gender differences, human reproduction, birth, body functions, and marriage. This led the alliance to conclude that youth should receive sex education at an early age. Earp (1933) delivered a speech before the World Federation of Education Association about her experiences as a faculty member at an Ohio college. Her work on sex education began when students demanded a course on social hygiene. Although the students had enough credits for graduation, many wanted to know more about sex. She taught sex education for six years and learned that most of her students knew more about the sexual reproduction of animals and insects than they did about human reproduction. No one protested, and, in fact, other organizations asked her to lecture to their members. Earp concluded that her lectures were valuable because the students learned about sex and how sex related to their personal lives.

In 1934, Villon published a study of fifty upper-middle-class families to determine parents' attitudes and practices of sex education. The findings revealed that the parents unanimously supported sex education for children, as many of them had inadequately taught their children about sex. Villon wrote, "Instruction was meager, delayed and hampered by fears and emotions" (166). This led the author to conclude that parents were in need of sex education. That same year, the American Social Hygiene Association published *Points for Parents to Remember* (see figure 3.1). The points were based on the contributions of sex education leaders Benjamin C. Gruenber, William A. White, Thomas W. Galloway, and Helen W. Brown.

In 1936, Smith described the curriculum at Benton Harbor High School, much of which focused attention on natural beauty and helping youth understand themselves in relation to life and society. Students had field experiences in natural settings, enabling teachers to elaborate on nature and relate human sexuality whenever possible, and students were simultaneously taught the value of developing long-term healthy friendships. Sex education pamphlets complemented their experiences, and all youth were encouraged to learn about the opposite sex. The faculty used calf embryos, a five-month-old human fetus, and human

Figure 3.1. Points for Parents to Remember, Circa 1934

1. Do you realize that it is usual and healthy for an intelligent child to be curious about sex? If he does not ask you questions, he will probably get his information elsewhere.
2. Do you realize that if you are embarrassed when children ask you questions about sex, they will feel it at once and will think that there is something mysterious and even wrong about the subject?
3. Do not let your children grow up with any false shame about any part of their bodies.
4. A young child asks exactly what it wants and needs to know at the time. Each question should be answered simply and frankly. But in the case of a child under eleven, do not make your answer a starting point for an explanation of matters which have not so far puzzled him.
5. The birth of another child is obviously an excellent opportunity for teaching the older children about sex.
6. Where possible, all children should be allowed to keep and look after animals. This is an important part of sex education, particularly in the case of an only child.
7. It is most important that an only child should have many natural opportunities of observing the differences between himself and people of the opposite sex at a very early age. This will prevent unnatural curiosity later on.
8. If your child is over eleven, and has not asked questions such as "Where do babies come from?" you should stimulate his interest in such subjects and answer his questions frequently.
9. Adolescence is the time when the sex glands begin their work and affect the child's life. He is then neither child nor adult and will probably find life difficult. Shyness and self-consciousness are natural at this age, and you should not expect too much from him at home or let yourself be disappointed if he does not do well at school.
10. In very young children, masturbation (or self-stimulation) is quite common, and you should not be alarmed at this habit. If it is not made to seem important by your anxiety, it will probably disappear. Older children will get over it equally easily if you help them by showing them that you understand their difficulties and by giving them as many outside interests as possible. Remember that the child should never be punished for masturbation.
11. Do you realize that however useful talks from teachers or books written by experts may be, your child's attitude to sex will be based on your own? If your own attitude is good, you are the best teacher he can have.

Source: From "Sex Education and the Parents' Point of View," by the American Social Hygiene Association, 1934. In *Journal of Social Hygiene,* 20(3): 258.

twins in amniotic sacs as tools to teach about reproduction. Engaged and married alumni were encouraged to return and discuss their experiences with the students. Smith insisted that by integrating sex education, the teachers were helping create a foundation for a satisfying lifestyle for their students.

The December 1938 issue of the Journal of Social Hygiene was devoted entirely to the sex education of youth. Maurice A. Bigelow entitled his introductory piece *Sex Education in America Today.* He noted that sex education literature of prior decades had focused attention on genital hygiene and that most material related to the aspects of sex considered vulgar. Times had changed. Bigelow had witnessed the growth of the field of sex education. That year, health experts recognized that sex education was critical at home, school, and church. Libraries now carried books and pamphlets on sex education, and youth learned about more than venereal diseases in sex education. Sex education had replaced the term social hygiene because social hygiene was thought of as the control of venereal diseases, and sex education had moved far beyond the teaching of venereal diseases. Parker (1938) published an extensive outline of lectures focused on sex education for parents. Her outline included a foundation lecture complete with information on methodology in the home, school, and church; biological facts to impart to youth with discussions on all living organisms; adolescent physical and emotional development inclusive of sexual impulses; and material on syphilis, gonorrhea, and prostitution. Much of her outline seems liberal in that parents were encouraged to talk to their children about sex at opportune times and that sex education should begin as early as infancy. Upon closer inspection, however, the material is often conservative. Sex, for instance, was strictly tied to matrimony. Parker espoused sex being reserved for marriage if one was to live a satisfied and secure life. When she talked about masturbation, she started off with a liberal tone and ended with a conservative one. She wrote, "Masturbation is a common experience; will not cause feeble mindedness nor insanity. . . . The habit, if excessive, may impair physical and mental energy; if continued, may impair ability to adjust in marital relationships" (559). And when she discussed petting, she wrote, "This misunderstanding (of petting) is often responsible for situations in which unwanted pregnancy takes place and leads to the temptation of criminal abortion, hasty marriage, or desertion of an unmarried mother. . . . Few men desire to marry a girl who is known to be an 'easy petter'" (560).

The December 1939 issue of the *Journal of Social Hygiene* was dedicated to sex education in the schools. Galloway's work in sex education was published posthumously. Up to his death, he maintained that sex had been considered taboo for too long and that society must accept sex as a vital component of human life. He maintained that sexual curiosity was natural for children and that humans have sexual impulses that must be dealt with "frankly and constructively." He defined sex education beyond factual information, biological sciences, and fear of venereal diseases. Sex education, he believed, was to be thought of in terms of psychology—the sexual emotions, habits, and behaviors of society. Moreover, sex education was to be considered something deeper and more spiritual. The goals of sex education were twofold: to eliminate vulgar and "exciting" perceptions of sex; and to produce clean behavior among youth. Parents were to be the first and best teachers of sex education, and schools would assume the responsibility in the curriculum and extracurricular activities.

Warner (1939) of the Wisconsin State Board of Health studied how 7,399 boys learned about sex. Most of the boys received their sex education through biology classes, fathers, *Reader's Digest*, State Board of Health, and other boys. Because 2,492 boys replied that neither parent had talked to them about sex, Warner concluded that schools should continue to offer youth sex education. Chase (1939) stated reasons that schools should share the sex education responsibility: more opportunities present themselves with teachers who can provide accurate information; parents may not fully understand human development and underestimate their child's sexual maturity; and parents are often poorly informed. Chase, headmaster of a day school for boys, surveyed the boys' fathers about their approval of sex education and found 66 percent supported sex education, 4 percent did not, and the rest did not respond. The teachers at the school read *Growing Up* and *Being Born* in small groups and then answered the boys' questions. Chase believed his school and students had achieved a wholesome attitude toward sex. Stohlman (1939) published *Sex Education in the Public Schools of the District of Columbia*. The schools during this time provided sex education in the primary grades (first through eighth) through science, and in the high schools through home economics. Youth slowly learned about the development and reproduction of plants and animals, and by high school, youth learned good habits, leisure activities, child-care and development, and social standards. Goldberg (1939) described the difficulty of getting New York City teachers trained in sex education. After an arrangement was made with the College of the City of New York to offer sex education for practicing teachers, very few registered for the course. Goldberg later learned that the teachers didn't register for the course because school officials had disapproved of the course and dismissed the opportunity. Another course was later created, and thirty teachers registered for the course. The outline of the course follows:

- The Social Hygiene Movement and Sex-Character Education
- Biological Foundations of Sex-Character Education
- Organic and Psychic Development of the Child
- The Family and Its Changing Forms
- Sex Hygiene: Individual and Social
- Educational Problems: (A) The Younger Child
- Educational Problems: (B) Older Boys and Girls
- Essential Characteristics of the Adolescent Girl
- How Schools May Aid in Sound Sex Education of the High School Girl
- Endocrinology and Sex Problems among Children
- Psychiatric Problems
- Medical Aspects of Syphilis
- Medical Aspects of Gonorrhea
- Summary of the Sex-Character Education Movement
- Next Steps in Social Hygiene and Sex-Character Education: Current Needs and Opportunities in New York City. (343)

1940s: MORALITY AND THE POSITIVE ASPECTS OF SEX

Kirkendall (1940) wrote *Building a Program on Sex Education for the Secondary School.* Much of the content of the article reinforced the sentiment of the 1930s—sex education is a lifelong process whereby youth should learn of sex in their classes in a natural progression with academics reinforcing its instruction. Kirkendall discussed what he believed were the four essentials of sex education for the high school student. For the first time an author described what was meant by the development of "wholesome attitudes" toward sex among youth:

- Sexual manifestations are natural and normal physical and psychological phenomena. Everyone must react in some way to sex, and one is normal if one experiences some urge toward sexual expression.
- Sex may be discussed openly, objectively, and at length, and still wholesomely. An interest in questions relating to proper adjustments is to be regarded as an indication of a normal development and an approach at least, toward good sexual adjustment. Complete and detailed discussions of sex

adjustments are desirable since only in this way can adequate knowledge and information be gained.

•➤ Social conventions concerning sex, in many cases, exist for good reasons. It should be the purpose to examine these reasons, and when they are found to be well based, a proper respect for these conventions should be observed.

•➤ Lewdness and obscenity at all ages, and under all conditions should be disapproved. (308)

Kirkendall mentioned that the sex educator must facilitate youth's adjustment to their sexual urges. In sex education, youth could learn to "control and order" their urges as they related to masturbation, homosexuality, and heterosexual relations. Sex education would be the vehicle to inform youth about those urges and help them adjust to them in the most satisfactory way. Kirkendall never stipulated that youth should refrain from those urges. He explained, "Too often there is the tendency to dwell on the perversions, abnormalities and morbidities of sexual adjustment. When this occurs it is simply another way of fostering, and for the time being satisfying, a sexual maladjustment" (309).

The New York Statewide Study Committee (1940) published its report *The School's Responsibility in Social Hygiene*. The report defined sex education as a course that should encompass facts, attitudes, conduct, and should be an inseparable aspect of youth's education. The goal of sex education would be to teach youth how to endure lifelong "wholesome, full, and satisfying" relationships with one another. Parents, schools, churches, and social agencies would collaborate to ensure that youth would receive sex education. The committee stressed that those who taught sex education would have to be emotionally mature and have correct sexual understanding. In other words, these teachers were to be the sexually well-adjusted models for the youth. Also in 1940, the Supervisors of Health Teaching of New York gathered for their annual meeting and created a questionnaire to study sex education in the state. The survey was made up of eighty-eight items to examine school variables and their influences on the development of a wholesome attitude toward sex. The questions were focused on physical facilities, the subject areas, extracurricular activities, school medical services to the physical health, parent and community education, and counseling. Although the findings of such a study would have proven beneficial, no record of the study was found.

The Education Committee of the New Jersey Social Hygiene Association endorsed the 1930 White House Conference report on the goals of sex education and cited Galloway: "Sex education is much more a matter of mind and spirit than of biology and physiology—more a matter of interpretation of facts and inspiration to ideals than of instruction alone" (Lesher 1941, 375). They added, "sex education is an inseparable part of the education of the total personality" (375). The committee established four principles to adhere to in sex education programs: underscore the positive aspects of sex and develop an appreciative understanding; introduce sex education early and integrate it in the subject areas; never offer courses under the rubric of sex education or social hygiene; and never provide sex education via lectures from health experts. Goldberg (1941) investigated sex/character education in twenty-one private schools in New York City. Sex education was offered in a variety of ways in these schools. Most of them introduced sex education through biology, physiology, or nature study, and in one school, sixth grade youth were required to buy and care for a pair of rabbits and their offspring. Many of the schools offered sex education to older youth through isolated courses such as Elementary Ethics, Social Hygiene, Introduction to the Problems of Marriage, and Human Relations in America Today. Many of the schools reported that they encountered few problems among their youth with regard to sex. One school noted than in their thirty-three-year history, only three cases of venereal disease were found. Two seniors in another high school contracted venereal diseases and this event forced the school to thoroughly examine all students twice a year. In Cleveland in 1941, the Family Health Association and the faculty in a local senior and junior high school collaborated to offer sex education to their youth. In high school, youth studied about sex in a course entitled, "Personal Regimen." The course was based largely on questions the youth had had prior to its implementation. In junior high, sex education was provided to all girls through a series of lectures entitled, "Social Hygiene."

In 1942, Zillmer and Larsen surveyed 3,300 Wisconsin girls to determine their opinions of sex. The authors chose Wisconsin primarily because social hygiene instruction had been implemented throughout the state since 1918 and parents, faculty, and students were apparently accepting of sex education. The study revealed that girls did not support phoning a boy for a date (1 in 27 said it was okay) or becoming engaged in high school (although it was a popular trend during the war). Nearly 67 percent reported that their mother had answered their questions about sex, and 5.5 percent reported that their fathers had provided some sex education. Other girls reported girlfriends, books, magazines, older sister or aunt, doctor/nurse, movie, church, and boyfriend as sources of information on sex. Fully 94 percent thought that sex education should be offered in high school, and 96.5 percent stated that they would teach their own children about sex when the time was appropriate. The authors were concerned by the fact that 75 percent felt that their community lacked enough social entertainment. Although this is not explained, one could infer that this concern was based on the fact that without a social outlet, youth could engage in sexual experimentation. The authors also asked whether the girls preferred to be married or to have a career. Of the girls who made a choice, 80 percent favored marriage; only one said she wanted both.

Carlson (1943) described the library's role in providing sex education resources to the public. Rarely did health experts write about the library as a source of sex education. Carlson reviewed all the sex education material then available in the New York City public library. The most frequently circulated resources were: *Adolescence, Your Experiment in Living, Attaining Womanhood; Healthy Babies Are Happy Babies, The Wonder of Life, A College Textbook of Hygiene, Maternity Handbook, A Marriage Manual, Being Born, Everyday Problems of the Everyday Child,* and *The Questions Girls Ask.* The following criterion was provided for evaluating sex education material:

- The content must be written in nontechnical terms so that readers comprehend the material.
- An expert in the field must author the book.
- The book must be beneficial to the reader.
- The book must discuss sex as a natural, normal part of life.

During that year, the District of Columbia's Board of Education formally accepted a course for all high schools in the district. The course outline included: *Anatomy and Physiology, Instincts, Adolescence and Its Problems, Dangers of Disease,* and *Marriage and Its Responsibility.* Teachers of the course were to have frequent conferences to ensure the "development of a proper attitude in the pupil concerning personal responsibilities for his health, happiness, and citizenship as a worthy member of the community" (551). That year marked the first time sex education was on the cover of a major newspaper, the *Evening Star,* Washington, D.C. The headline read *What Is Sex Education?* Everett (1943) wrote that the aim of sex education was twofold—to teach youth about the constructive and destructive aspects of sex. From the constructive stand, sex education should promote a happy, healthy marriage and parenthood. From the destructive stand, sex education was necessary to avoid the "evil results of uncontrolled or mismanaged sex life" (615). This included venereal disease, prostitution, illegitimacy, vulgarity, and unsuccessful marriages. Everett then stated what he believed were the tasks of sex education:

1. Developing an open-minded, serious, scientific, and respectful attitude toward all problems of human life that relate to sex;
2. Giving that knowledge of personal sex hygiene that makes for the healthful and efficient life of the individual;
3. Giving that knowledge of personal responsibility regarding the social and eugenic aspects of sex as affecting the individual life in relation to other individuals of the present and future generations—in short, the problems of sex instinct and actions in relation to society;
4. Developing an appreciation and understanding of family life
5. Teaching very briefly, during adolescence, the essential hygienic and social facts regarding the destructive venereal disease; and dealing with them as with other communicable diseases in college hygiene and in lectures to adults. (615)

The Social Hygiene Committee of Philadelphia Public Schools, which met in 1943, reported the essential phases of a comprehensive social hygiene education (1945):

- The Whole Living Phase provided youth with a variety of experiences in social living.
- The Instructional Phase provided vital hygiene information that emphasized that sex is normal and natural.
- The Counseling Phase informed youth that they could receive help if and when they needed it.
- The Special Service Phase provided youth with medical assistance.

In the same year the Institute for the Control of Syphilis of the University of Pennsylvania, the Department of Public Health, and the Philadelphia Public Schools cosponsored an intensive sex education workshop series for teachers and school counselors of Philadelphia. The outline was published in the *Journal of Social Hygiene* with information that detailed the topics, speakers, and lecture titles. The workshop divided the lectures into five weeks: *Family Background for Social Hygiene, Growth and Development of the Child, Public Health and Medical Aspects, Area of Community Relations,* and *Public School Procedures.* Nothing was documented after the workshops were held to indicate if they were beneficial.

In 1944, the American Social Hygiene Association made note of the significant stride made by the U.S. Public Health Service and the U.S.

Department of Education, Division of Physical Education when a consultant was appointed Senior Specialist in Health Education in the Office of Education. This consultant, along with another appointee, would devote some of their time to sex education. In Alabama, the State Superintendent of Education and State Health Officer (1945) cosponsored a conference on sex education. Various groups discussed the creation of courses for teachers in the state's Normal Schools and outlined sex education courses in high schools and colleges. A health center in Birmingham had created a program to study what was then called the Negro community.

In the summer of 1945, more than twenty-two universities documented that they were to offer some form of sex education to teachers across the country. The workshops ranged from the problems of youth to counseling to parenthood, sex adjustments, and human relations. The Cincinnati Public Schools offered a sex education course entitled, "Pre-Induction Course for High School Students" for the many youth who were planning to join the military (Dicerson 1945). Nearly 500 youth were dropping out of school every month to enlist. Health experts had found that many of these youth had no knowledge of sexual hygiene and had become infected with a venereal disease when they were in the military. The course comprised mental hygiene, physical fitness, social hygiene, and venereal diseases. Boys were given the sex education pamphlet, *Straight from the Shoulder,* and girls were given *Health for Girls.* All were provided *Syphilis Can Be Cured.* The youth apparently appreciated the course because of the 572 evaluations, 75.8 percent rated the course as highly valuable and 86.4 percent thought the course had influenced their behavior. One seventeen-year-old said, "Because before or just after I got in the army I was determined to have intercourse. Now I'm determined to wait and get something good that I won't be ashamed of" (214). Another seventeen-year-old wrote, "This class has shown that there is no 100 percent safety, and in order to live a clean and healthful life we must have no sexual intercourse except with one's wife" (214). That same year, the Cincinnati Social Hygiene Society joined local PTAs to offer sex education for parents. The sex education program, the *Home Study Course,* involved groups of parents meeting weekly for six weeks. As many as 60 parents per group learned how to talk to their kids about sex through topics ranging from the common questions children ask to emotional health and problems of adolescence. In Lesson Six, for instance, the parents discussed

➡ development and function of the male and female sexual system

•• fullest individual satisfaction in sexual relations
•• the psychology of intimacy
•• why premarital relations are unsound
•• ideals of marriage
•• sound conceptions of courtship and engagement
•• the signs of being in love
•• the premarital examination
•• making a good start in marriage (219)

The PTA of the District of Columbia (1947) held its thirty-fourth convention and, in their resolution to the Congress, outlined the social structures responsible for sex education. The parents were to assume responsibility for the intimate aspects of sex, the church would cover moral and ethical behaviors, and the school would impart the scientific elements of sex. Goldberg (1947) studied sex education in forty communities across the country. Eighty-four superintendents responded to questions about sex education in their districts. Sex education was implemented in a variety of ways. Most high school students received some form of sex education. Some students studied sex through health, biology, home economics, social studies, personal counseling, and human relations courses such as *Family Relationships and Responsibilities* and *Family and Community Life Education.* One school provided the students with "intercultural education," and two others provided students with courses on dating and marriage. One-quarter of the respondents answered that they provided human relations material for their junior high school students. Few elementary schools had any form of sex education.

In 1948, the Cleveland Health Museum held a two-day institute on sex education for teachers. Teachers listened to discussions on *The Maturing Boy and Girl Growing Up in the Community, Adolescent Growth,* and *Character Education and Personality Development.* In 1948, as part of their professional development, Baltimore teachers were offered two courses and a workshop on sex education—*Sex Education: One Phase of Human Relations, Methods and Materials,* and *Workshop in Sex Education* (American Social Hygiene Associetion 1948). The National YMCA met for its 1949 annual convention and focused its attention on sex education for rural areas. Because many of these communities lacked sex education and some encountered problems with the Army camps of World War I and II, groups of women appealed to various social organizations and PTAs for information and training. The women eventually became trained and, in turn, educated their children about sex. The state of Michigan (1949) became the second state to make legal provisions for sex education. (Oregon became the first in 1945.) School districts with student populations of 3,000 or more could provide sex education under health education, physical education, or sex hygiene. The law, however, stipulated that teachers of sex education were prohibited from discussing, teaching about, or offering advice on birth control (American Social Hygiene Association 1949).

1950s: SEX ESSENTIAL TO THE WHOLE PERSONALITY

Kirkendall (1951) emphasized the need for society to embrace sex education and develop the right attitude toward sex. In his address to the Kansas City Social Hygiene Society, he mentioned that society needed to reappraise their attitude toward sex and move from the seemingly conservative attitude of the time to one that regarded sex as a standard element of the personality. For the first time in that century, a health expert stated that sex should be considered in terms of pleasure and satisfaction and as a vehicle for communication. Ironically, Kirkendall didn't elaborate on this subject other than to allude to the fact that these were legitimate aspects and should be recognized as such. He also discussed sex as a natural part of everyday living, and this view meant that sexual impulses should not be ignored and/or subdued. Sex was to be accepted and talked about freely and objectively.

Sweeney (1952) discussed the partnership to be created among parents, church authorities, and school officials. Much of the content of her article reflected the desires of health experts of the 1940s—a comprehensive sex education beginning in the first grade with youth receiving social hygiene instruction from teams of caring, understanding, and qualified individuals. The New Jersey Department of Education (1952) reported its work toward sex education. The Department had implemented a comprehensive program entitled, "Education for Human Relations and Family Life" throughout the state. Youth from kindergarten through high school learned their respective roles in the family and their parents' roles and were taught how to develop and maintain meaningful relationships in their families and with their peers.

In 1953, Hoyman discussed the implications of sex education in Oregon schools. Oregon youth in grades seven to twelve learned about the human body, personal hygiene, and communicable diseases and took in their senior year a course that prepared them for marriage and family life. Teachers could not teach or talk about birth control, venereal disease prophylaxis, sex techniques, and sexual perversions. Hoyman explained that not only was it illegal to talk about birth control, but he and others feared that talking about birth control or prophylaxis might send the message that adults approve of youth engaging in sex. School administrators feared that discussing sexual techniques might "stimulate" some youth to experiment with sex. Teachers were prohibited from discussing homosexuality or "other perversions" because many believed that doing so would pique the interests of youth and develop in them "morbid" and "neurotic" behaviors. Hoyman advised that youth should learn "that some persons do not develop in this way (heterosexuals) and are called sexual perverts or deviates. The students are further informed that some sexual deviates are of the criminal type and are exceedingly dangerous to small children, teenagers and even to adults" (18).

Very little research or think tank policy papers emerged in a literature search of the 1950s. The next piece of literature to discuss sex came from Stone (1958) who discussed how sex education should be taught. His recommendations were similar to those espoused throughout this chapter—provide basic biological information with a positive approach and include the societal standards for conduct. He noted that youth needed to learn that love was a critical aspect for a successful marriage. As Hoyman wrote, "Love, affection, and companionship are truly constructive forces that lead to a successful marriage" (239).

1960s: SIECUS IS ORGANIZED

Wetherill (1960) modified the adage "The family that prays together, stays together" to suit sex education, "The family that discusses personal problems lives better together" (107). Like others of his time, he believed that the community as a whole is responsible for educating youth about sex. Wetherill's San Diego community and the PTA largely supported sex education, and he found that people who didn't were those who didn't fully understand the goals of the program. Alden and Blanchard (1962) studied sex education in a rural high school. Two years prior to the study, a group of junior and senior girls asked a teacher to start a sex education class based on their three questions:

- How does one find out facts about sex when parents refuse to discuss such topics?
- How does a girl keep physical contact under control on dates, at a party in her home or anyone's home when parents or adults are not there?
- How can teenagers get parents to trust them on dates or in groups with the opposite sex? (127)

The course content was based on sexual facts and the understanding that sex was nothing disgusting or shameful, but a natural part of life. The authors wanted the youth to develop a more liberal attitude toward sex than previous generations, although questions regarding contraception were neither answered nor discussed. Of the 200 high school youth, 127 attended the program, and the course evaluations revealed that the program was beneficial. For instance, in response to the question "Is your understanding of sex better?" 122 students answered in the affirmative. Because of the perceived success and students' and parents' comments, the authors began to offer sex education to youth in sixth, seventh, and eighth grade.

Miller (1963) discussed the need for sex education in the junior high schools. For the first time in professional literature, sex was mentioned as prevalent in our culture. Miller wrote, "Everyday (youth) see movies, books, magazines, advertisements, and the like, which glorify sex and make it permissible for everyone's indulgence. 'Why not?' is an honest, sincere question that is not being answered for many youth" (221). In her attempt to persuade readers to support sex education, Miller mentioned the "learner readiness" concept. Education experts were concerned with the reading and math readiness of youth, but no one had mentioned "readiness" for sex education. Miller believed that sex education readiness should occur before youth entered high school so they would have the knowledge and understanding to make wise choices in sexual situations.

In 1964, thirty-eight reputable professionals in education, sociology, medicine, religion, and law formed the Sex Information and Education Council of the United States (SIECUS) to help promote sex education in the schools. The mission was to "establish man's sexuality as a health entity . . .to dignify it by openness of approach, study, and scientific research designed to lead toward its understanding and its freedom from exploitation. . . ." (W. Fulton 1965, 232). SIECUS would collaborate with other interdisciplinary organizations to provide education and find the best solutions for facilitating youth's acquisition of sexual knowledge and skills to make informed choices. SIECUS encompassed members of a community contributing to the framework of family life education. Wallace C. Fulton became the first president and Mary S. Calderone was the executive secretary. Peller (1965) discussed sex education for children who were three to five years old. She provided her perspective on child development along with advice for parents. She mentioned that homosexuality was caused by numerous factors. Young boys, for instance, would become homosexual if they had a weak, absent, or brutal father. So parents were advised to be figures that their children would love and want to emulate. Parents were advised to never let their young children see them sexually excited because a child might see this as violent and out of control. Parents were encouraged to let their children see other children naked, as this would allow them to see that there are other notable differences between the sexes.

In 1966, Johnson and Schutt surveyed the attitudes of Maryland school administrators and board members toward sex education. The authors found that of eighteen superintendents and sixty-seven school board members, most of them had a favorable attitude toward sex education. Nearly 84 percent approved of sex education in the public schools. Approximately 50 percent felt that sex education was urgently needed in their schools. Many of the administrators and board members thought that abortion, contraception, homosexuality, sterility and fertility, and impotency and frigidity should not be included in sex education. A Gallup poll of adults across the country found that 69 percent favored sex education in the public schools (Johnson and Schutt 1966). Half of these supporters approved of discussions of contraceptives. In 1966, the Chicago Public Schools implemented a pilot program in family life and sex education in 175 elementary and 57 high schools. The elementary school youth received sex education from their homeroom teachers through the science curriculum; the high school youth learned about sex in health education, biology, and home economics. The program was created with the family in mind where youth learned about sexual behavior in relation to the family. In the first grade for instance, students would study "Learning about Human and Animal Families," and in high school, youth would take "Living with Your Family—Teenage Relationships." Teachers and administrators were provided professional development in sex education, and parents could attend the workshops as well. Using many qualitative responses from students, teachers, administrators, and parents, Hawkins (1969) and the Chicago School Board found the program successful enough to endorse the program and expand to all schools in the district.

Schoel (1968) wrote, "Because of (youth's) fears, anxieties, uncertainties, and fallacious health information, which they have reaped from communication media and life situations, we see much promiscuity, illegitimate babies, homosexuality, sex crimes, and much rise in sexual perversion, divorces, and early teenage marriages among our youth" (129). She advocated that sex education be integrated throughout the school curriculum through a human relations or family living approach. In her experiences as a nurse, Schoel found that many youth were simply unprepared when it came to sex. Her survey of 275 girls found that the most frequently asked questions included

1. Is sex before marriage right or wrong?

2. Exactly "how far should a girl go" on a date?
3. Why doesn't our school or parents teach us how girls get pregnant?
4. Do boys have a harder time stopping their sex feelings?
5. If a boy parks the car and the girl becomes afraid, what should she do? (129)

Couch (1967) asked a group of 110 Detroit youth for their perception of sex education. The youth indicated that in order for them to succeed in marriage, relationships, and with their own children, they needed sex education. They also felt that there was very little sex education available to them and it was often provided too late in their education. Many of them supported its implementation as early as first grade. Most of the youth felt that factual knowledge and information on venereal disease, contraceptives, and sexual techniques should be included in sex education. They preferred that sex education be provided directly, as a matter of fact, without moral tones.

Levine (1967) reiterated the need for sex education. He was appalled at some social issues: the illegitimacy rate had increased from 131,900 out-of-wedlock births in 1947 to 245,100 in 1962; homosexuality was widespread and on the increase; and a sexual revolution was occurring in the United States "with a great deal more sex freedom and a great deal less restraint than that of previous generations" (31). He believed that youth were far more exposed to divorces, prostitution, love affairs, and such in the media, and he strongly felt that they needed sex education to learn how to behave appropriately. What is disturbing about his piece is his ultraconservative perspective on homosexuality. He clearly wanted youth to make the correct choice of heterosexuality and to understand the kind of people who have "deviant sexual desires and urges." He wrote, "Homosexuality should be discussed so that adolescents may have a clear understanding of its abnormality and will not easily be drawn in by deviants as so often happens" (37).

In 1969 an educational director of Christian Crusade Against Communism, J. V. Toohey, called SIECUS a "communist front apparatus designed to erode the moral fiber of youth" (Toohey 1969, 70). Various groups joined this director in a crusade to prevent the implementation of a sex education program in Tempe, Arizona. Toohey stated that sex was a natural, healthy phenomenon that occupied adult lives, and youth should have sex education to learn how to build and maintain a healthy adjustment to sex. The John Birch Society and the Christian Crusade, two strong right-wing organizations of the time, attacked SIECUS and schools that had sex education programs. Members of these groups believed that sex education created higher rates of illegitimacy, promiscuity, sexual neurosis, and so forth.

One of the first studies on sex education for youth with disabilities was conducted by Bloom (1969). Bloom found that many of these youth had no knowledge of sex whatsoever. Their parents could not bring themselves to talk about sex, and many were horrified at the idea that their youth could have the desire to marry, have sex, and have children. Even then, Bloom emphasized, many of these youth got married, had sex, and had families. In her study, sixty-four sixteen- to nineteen-year-old youth with physical and emotional disabilities were pretested with various instruments designed to ascertain their sexual knowledge and anxiety level. After a twelve-week sex education course that included discussions of human development and reproduction, interpersonal relationships, social-sex attitudes, marriage, masturbation, problems of sexual adjustment, and venereal diseases, the youth learned about sex and their level of anxiety was no higher at the end of the course.

1970s: SEX EDUCATION AND THE BACKLASH

In 1970, sex education was under continued attack. Gordon Drake of the Christian Crusade, the John Birch Society through MOTOREDE (Movement To Restore Decency), and a host of other organizations—MOMS (Mothers Organized for Moral Stability), PAUSE (Parents Against Unconstitutional Sex Education), POSSE (Parents Opposed to Sex and Sensitivity Education), POSE (Parents Opposed to Sex Education), ACRE (Associated Citizens for Responsible Education), CHIDE (Committee to Halt Indoctrination and Demoralization in Education)—denounced sex education in the schools. In 1969 Drake authored *Is the Schoolhouse the Proper Place to Teach Raw Sex,* claiming that " . . . several prominent individuals and some of the largest U.S. corporations, as well as the United Nations, were involved in the sex education plot" (Fulton 1970, 263). Many of these organizations believed that sex education was a communist plot to destroy the American moral fiber. They believed that sex education was illegal, unconstitutional, anti-Christian, and anti-God. Young (1970) used the Bible to defend sex education against this anti–sex education faction. According to Young, the Bible implied that sex was good. Verses from the Old Testament ("You are stately as a palm tree, and your breasts are like its clusters. I say I will climb the palm tree and lay hold of its branches") and the New Testament attested to this. He emphasized that God never intended sex to be merely a one-shot physical act but instead a union of two whole spirits. Essentially, sex education, if implemented correctly, would prepare youth to make this union work.

Holcomb, Garner, and Beaty (1970) surveyed Texas superintendents to determine the scale of sex education provided throughout the state. Although the majority of the superintendents mentioned that schools owe it to youth to provide sex education, 78 percent did not include sex education in their curricula. Of the schools that offered sex education, most provided sex education at the secondary level, with only 15 percent of districts having some form of delivery at the elementary level. High school youth learned about human reproduction, venereal diseases, dating, petting, divorces, gender roles, and marriage and family. Very few schools discussed homosexuality, birth control, and masturbation, and only ten schools discussed abortion. Only 9 percent of the sample offered teachers an in-service to prepare them to teach sex education. The study also revealed that superintendents from larger school districts favored sex education more often than superintendents from smaller districts. The following year, sex education was studied in Kansas. Unlike Texas, 78 percent of the schools provided sex education through the existing curricula, 1 percent provided sex education as a separate course, and 21 percent had no sex education (Gendel and Green 1971). The study also revealed that the students, teachers, and communities were generally accepting of the programs.

Kleinerman et al. (1971) investigated the sex education questions raised by seventh grade youth from a New York City ghetto school. The questions were grouped into three categories: "Why or how come . . . ," "How to . . . ," and "Should you or shouldn't you. . . ." The authors found that although the youth knew the general aspects of sex, they were largely naïve to details. One youth, for instance, asked, "What do you have to do to have sex activity and not become pregnant?" Another asked, "If you sit on a boy's lap will you become pregnant?" The study was important in that the questions were eventually used to restructure a sex education curriculum.

Levin et al. (1972) studied 277 adults' attitudes toward sex education. The adults responded to eighteen statements that related to Family Life Education. The study found that the sample largely supported sex education. In particular, they wanted their children to take sex education and believed that sex education should be offered in all public schools. The statements that received the least amount of support were those that claimed that sex education destroyed children's morals, invaded family privacy, increased children's desire to experiment, and should only be taught at home. The data revealed that people with less education tended to have more conservative and restrictive attitudes toward sex education. Thornburg (1972) investigated how girls received most of their information about sex. The 382 college students reported their initial source of information (regardless of its accuracy) about aspects of sex such as contraception, ejaculation, homosexuality, petting, and sexual intercourse. Peers provided the most information about sex, literature was cited as the second most common source, and mothers came in a close third. Mothers provided girls with information about menstruation and origin of birth, and schools contributed the most information about venereal diseases. Cook (1972) documented the progress of an Anaheim, California, program, Family Life and Sex Education. The program taught youth to define who they were and work toward the person they want to become. In this setting, the youth were taught that there is a time and place for sex within the framework of who they want to become. Cook, nonetheless, voiced his disappointment when the John Birch Society attacked the Anaheim school board for its support of sex education. The society ousted two board members and overturned the board's support for the so-called liberal sex education program. The new school board cut the education resources from 91 to 7 sex education textbooks and films and forbade teachers to discuss topics such as homosexuality, masturbation, or abortion. Although 28,000 parents wrote in support of the old program, the new program was still implemented. Bjork (1972) wrote about the growth of sex in the media; he felt that youth were acquiring a sex education regardless of what was being taught in the schools. He mentioned that one cigarette commercial depicted a man and a woman searching for a place to spread a blanket. Once the blanket had been laid out, the man lit his cigarette and handed it to the woman. Bjork responded, "But I could see the kids watching this scene and believing that an act of love had to be preceded by both parties first smoking a cigarette" (4). Bjork was also alarmed at a mouthwash commercial. Apparently a woman, who couldn't get a kiss from her date before using the mouthwash, couldn't break free from her date after she used the mouthwash.

Libby, Acock, and Payne (1974) studied 125 pairs of parents to determine how they would prefer their youth to learn about sex. The study revealed that parents strongly believed that youth should be taught about sex at home and that the school and church should supplement the teachings. In 1975, Riechelt and Werley tested 1,327 sexually active youth's knowledge of contraception, abortion, and venereal disease before and after an information session called a rap. The youth were asked to answer *true* or *false* to statements such as "A rubber should be tested before use" and "The rubber should be held around the base of the man's penis when withdrawn." The researchers found that before the rap sessions, most of the youth could answer correctly only 40 percent of the items. After the rap session, however, the rate of correct responses increased dramatically. With the understanding that youth get most of their information about sex from peers, the authors felt that teaching some youth how to protect themselves is but one way to spread information about sex. Finkel and Finkel (1975) studied the sexual knowledge and behavior of 421 boys (mean age of 16.3 years). Regardless of the youths' ethnicity, the boys received most of their information about sex from their male peers. A large percentage of the boys knew that condoms prevent pregnancies, but a smaller percentage knew that condoms offer protection from venereal diseases. Less than a third of the boys knew that his partner might still become pregnant if he withdrew before ejaculation. Approximately 69 percent of the boys were sexually experienced and 97 percent had had sex before the age of seventeen. African American boys had first experienced sex at the average age of 11.6 years of age, Latinos at 13, and whites at 14.5. Similarly to the Thornburg (1972) study, Gebhard (1977) studied youths' first acquisition of sex information. The study revealed that the youth in his sample were acquiring sex knowledge at a much younger age than previous generations, and girls were learning about sex at the same rate as boys. In the study, boys learned about condoms and homosexuality sooner than girls, and girls learned about menstruation earlier than boys. A large percentage of the youth had same-sex peers as their sex educators when it came to learning about coitus, prostitution, penile erection, condoms, and homosexuality. Mothers, unsurprisingly, were rated higher for providing girls with information on pregnancy and menstruation. Mahoney (1979) investigated the characteristics of supporters and nonsupporters of sex education. The distinguishable features between the two groups were centered on the attitudes one might have toward the family, women, and premarital sex. People who oppose sex education were those who held a traditional view of the family, thought the woman should be at home, and had a conservative view of premarital sex. Social class, attitude toward education, and political affiliation did not bear heavily on a person's attitude toward sex education.

1980s: SEX EDUCATION PROVISIONS AND SUPPORT INCREASE

To determine the extent that sex education was offered across the country, Sonnenstein and Pittman (1984) surveyed school districts in cities with populations larger than 100,000. The 90 percent response rate of the 179 school districts sampled revealed that 80 percent of the districts had provided some form of sex education. Sex education at the elementary school level was offered in 67 percent of the districts, and 76 percent provided sex education at the secondary level. Only 61 percent of the districts provided sex education at the elementary and junior and senior high level. Districts offered sex education through various titles, such as family life education, human growth and development, sex education, and health education; few of the districts offered sex education in a separate format. The study revealed that 94 percent of the districts provided sex education with the ultimate goal being that youth would acquire decision-making skills when it came to sex; the primary goal for another 77 percent of the districts was to increase students' knowledge about reproduction. Only 40 percent reported that the goal for the provision of sex education was to mitigate the teenage pregnancy rate. The topics that were covered the most included puberty, physical differences, sexually transmitted diseases, and responsibility of parenthood. The least covered topics included masturbation, abortion, gynecological exams, and homosexuality.

In 1984 and 1985, Phi Delta Kappa conducted two surveys to determine the public's and teachers' support for sex education. The study revealed that 81 percent of the teachers endorsed sex education at the elementary level and 91 percent supported sex education at the high school level. The teachers and the public strongly supported the topics of reproduction, sexually transmitted diseases, and birth control at the high school level. At the elementary level, teachers most often supported the topic of reproduction; the public favored discussion of reproduction and sexually transmitted diseases. The least supported topics for discussion in both groups were abortion, coitus, and homosexuality. The study also found that the public's attitude toward sex education was related to their level of education. The more education one had or the younger one was, the more supportive of sex education one tended to be.

Soefer et al. (1985) found that girls who experienced an early menarche were more likely to experiment with coitus. The results of their analysis were particularly beneficial in that it was established that extensive sex education should be provided at the time when most girls experience menarche. This led the researchers to advise that although sex education is necessary throughout a youth's development, at the age of twelve and thirteen, girls should especially learn of the risks associated with unprotected sex. In a literature review, Howard (1985) found that although imparting sexual facts to youth is crucial, the knowledge doesn't directly influence their sexual behavior. Instead, the most successful sex education programs are those that teach youth the skills to contend with peer pressure. She argued that most youth younger than sixteen can be pressured to engage in behavior that can produce consequences they are not yet able to handle. In her own study, Howard found that youth cite peer pressure most often when asked why they believed teenagers engage in sex. Based on these assumptions, Howard developed a sex education program for youth thirteen to fifteen years of age, Postponing Sexual Involvement (PSI). The PSI taught youth how to recognize peer and societal pressure, about the degrees of physical affection, and the skills to resist the pressure to have sex. The PSI also provided youth the opportunities to hear from older youth and practice the skills in given scenarios. Roughly 1,043 adolescents attended PSI sessions. After the session, 55 percent of the respondents reported they had become more aware of pressures to have sex; the other 45 percent already knew of the pressures; and 52 percent said they learned how to say no to the pressures. In the follow-up survey, 63 percent stated that the PSI had facilitated their strength in standing up for themselves, and 78 percent reported they would recommend PSI to a friend. The results of the PSI were favorable enough to implement the program in the Atlanta Public Schools.

Marsiglio and Mott (1986) used data on adults in their twenties provided by the National Longitudinal Survey of Work Experience of Youth to investigate the impact sex education had on their lives. The results revealed that 60 percent of women and 52 percent of men had taken a sex education course by the age of nineteen. In terms of their racial background, whites (57 percent) were more likely to have had sex education than African Americans (53 percent) and Latinos (48 percent). The analysis also found that most youth have sex before having sex education. Only 48 percent of the girls who had sex before the age of fifteen had taken a sex education course. The rate increased to 61 percent for the girls who had taken a sex education course before having sex by the age of eighteen. For boys who had sex before the age of fifteen, only 15 percent had had a sex education course. For those boys who had sex before the age of eighteen, the percentage rate was 52 percent. Overall, by the age of nineteen, 79 percent of the men and 66 percent of the women were sexually active.

Dawson (1986) studied the effects of sex education—primarily pregnancy and birth control—on the sexual behavior of girls. The National Survey of Family Growth provided data on 1,888 youth between the ages of fifteen and nineteen. The respondents were asked about their first educational introduction to the menstrual cycle, how pregnancies happen, venereal disease, and birth control. The study found that most girls received information about menstruation from their parents (83.8 percent) and formal programs (88.1 percent). Formal programs informed the girls about how a pregnancy occurs 81 percent of the time, and parents provided that information 67.3 percent of the time. Parents informed the girls about venereal disease infrequently at a rate of 39.8 percent, and formal programs educated the girls 81.0 percent of the time. In terms of birth control, parents provided the information at a rate of 53 percent, and formal programs at the rate of 68.2 percent. Between 57 percent and 67 percent of the respondents had some form of sex education before having sex. In the analysis of the data, the researchers found that education about or exposure to contraceptives and how a pregnancy occurs does not increase the likelihood that girls will initiate sex. Moreover, such knowledge and exposure influences girls to use contraceptives when they have sex.

Remafedi (1988) responded to the AIDS crisis and emphasized that youth needed AIDS education, especially young homosexual men who were sexually active. At the time of that publication, most AIDS cases were contracted during homosexual or bisexual encounters. Although youth accounted for only 145 AIDS cases, many health experts were concerned because of the fact that AIDS does not manifest itself until years later. Remafedi believed that homosexual youth could have profited the most from AIDS education but many were avoiding the programs because of their fear of the social stigma associated with being gay. He stressed that AIDS education should stretch beyond schools and into communities and outreach programs that help serve youth who do not attend school. Remafedi stressed that AIDS programs should be clear, concise, culturally sensitive, and should avoid judgmental tones.

SUMMARY

In all, we find that the impetus for sex education began in the early twentieth century. Undoubtedly, the social sentiment at the time was quite conservative, yet a few progressives longed for a mechanism to eliminate venereal diseases among adults. The surefire way for the elimination was to educate the next generation about sex. The fact that our nation entered two world wars ignited the sex education movement. Sex education was in the forefront as venereal diseases among soldiers were epidemic. The government and health experts of the time now realized that adults did not know how to abstain from sex or at the very least protect themselves from sexually transmitted diseases. Consequently, sex education literature for the next generation emerged. The material that circulated never really discussed sex in great detail. Instead youth, and some adults for that matter, learned factual elements of human anatomy through hygiene, biology, and physiology and were then instructed to refrain from sex until marriage—any sex outside of marriage was grounds for social censure. Masturbation, homosexuality, and sex for a fulfilled lifestyle were all taboo topics. Throughout the decades, the public, and parents in particular, have endorsed sex education. Each generation has largely believed that sex education is essential at home, school, and church. Although some visionaries had set out to make sex education a reality for some youth, few states required sex education, few universities trained their teachers to teach sex education, few schools offered sex education, few churches discussed sex education, and few community organizations trained parents about sex education. As early as 1919, the United States Department of Labor argued for the creation of a special federal organization to oversee national policy on sex education. This has not yet happened, although the 1964 creation of SIECUS comes close. As a controversial topic, a few groups have had disdain for sex education (some have even gone so far as to accuse the government of converting youth to communism through sex education), but for the most part sex education has been supported. The provision of sex education is contentious and perhaps always will be, but from a historical standpoint, regardless of political identity, it is safe to say that society wants youth to learn how to put sex into perspective. Each generation will always want the next generation to learn how to maintain a happy, healthy lifestyle free from sexually transmitted diseases and unwanted pregnancies.

REFERENCES

Achilles, Paul S. 1923. "The Effectiveness of Certain Social Hygiene Literature." *Journal of Social Hygiene* 9(2): 84–100.

Alden, Carl A., and Jane Blanchard. 1962. "Nurse-Teacher Relationship on the Elementary Level." *The Journal of School Health* 32(3): 127–132.

American Social Hygiene Association. 1948. "Sex Education Courses for Baltimore Teachers." *Journal of Social Hygiene* 34(7): 393.

———. 1949. "Michigan Adopts Law Providing for Social Hygiene Education." *Journal of Social Hygiene* 35(7): 346.

———. 1949. "National YMCA Holds Annual Convention in San Francisco." *Journal of Social Hygiene* 35(4): 179.

Armstrong, D. B., and E. B. Armstrong. 1916. "Sex in Life: For Boys and Girls from Twelve to Sixteen Years." *Journal of Social Hygiene* 2: 331–346.

Barker-Ellsworth, Alicia. 1930. "Sex Education in Junior High School." *Journal of Social Hygiene* 16(2): 107–112.

Bigelow, Maurice A. 1925. "The Established Points in Social Hygiene Education." *Journal of Social Hygiene* 10 (1): 2–11.

———. 1938. "Sex Education in America Today." *Journal of Social Hygiene* 24(9): 527–532.

Bjork, Robert M. 1972. "Surprise for Youngsters: Sex Education on TV." In *Sex, Schools, and Society,* ed. S. E. Fraser. Nashville: Peabody International Center.

Bloom, Jean L. 1969. "Sex Education for Handicapped Adolescents." *The Journal of School Health* 49(6): 363–367.

Cady, Bertha C. 1917. "The Normal Schools and Colleges and the Problem of Sex Education." *Journal of Social Hygiene* 3: 367–371.

Carlson, Edna M. 1943. "The Public Library and Sex Education." *Journal of Social Hygiene* 29(3): 353–370.

Charters, J. A. 1932. "The Opportunity of the Church for Sex Education." *Journal of Social Hygiene* 18(8): 477–479.

Chase, W. L. 1939. "The School's Responsibility to the Home and the Child in Sex Education." *Journal of Social Hygiene* 25(7): 321–329.

Christian Register. 1929. "Unitarians Favor Sex Education." *Journal of Social Hygiene* 15(7): 424.

Cook, Paul W. 1972. "A Great Experiment in Sex Education—The Anaheim Story." *The Journal of School Health* 62(1): 7–9.

Couch, Gertrude B. 1967. "Youth Looks at Sex." *Adolescence* 2(6): 255–267.

Curtiss, Lucy S. 1920. "Sex Instruction through English Literature." *Journal of Social Hygiene* 5(2): 263–272.

Dawson, D. A. 1986. "The Effects of Sex Education on Adolescents' Behavior." *Family Planning Perspectives* 18(4): 162–170.

De Schweinitz, K. 1928. "When? How?" *Journal of Social Hygiene* 14(9): 551.

Dickerson, Roy E. 1945. "Recent Progress in Sex Education." *Journal of Social Hygiene* 31(4): 211–216.

Dixon, E. 1929. "A Talk on Sex Education." *Journal of Social Hygiene* 10(2): 80–85.

Earp, Rosslyn. 1933. "The Sex Questions of Children." *Journal of Social Hygiene* 19(5): 279–281.

Eberwein, R. 1999. *Sex Ed: Film, Video, and Framework for Desire.* New Brunswick: Rutgers University Press.

Ellis, Grace F. 1914. "Sex Instruction in a High School: Central High School, Grand Rapids, Mich." *Journal of Social Hygiene* 1: 271–272.

Everett, Ray H. 1943. "What is 'Sex Education'?" *Journal of Social Hygiene* 29(9): 614–619.

Exner, M. J. 1929. "Progress in Sex Education." *Journal of Social Hygiene* 15(2): 80–85.

Finkel, M. L., and D. J. Finkel. 1975. "Sexual and Contraceptive Knowledge, Attitudes, and Behavior of Male Adolescents." *Family Planning Perspective* 8(6): 256–260.

Foster, Greg R. 1967. "Sex Information vs. Sex Education: Implications for School Health." *The Journal of School Health* 37(5): 248–250.

Fulton, Gere B. 1970. "Sex Education: Some Issues and Answers." *Journal of School Health* 60(5): 263–268.

Fulton, Wallace C. 1965. "Why Is There a Sex Information and Education Council of the United States? Why a New, Separate Organization?" *The Journal of School Health* 35(5): 232–233.

Gaffney, Charles E. 1914. "A Father's Plan for Sex Instruction: Instruction within the Home." *Journal of Social Hygiene* 1: 270–271.

Galloway, Thomas W. 1939. "Sex Education in Home and School." *Journal of Social Hygiene* 25(1): 26–30.

Garrett, Laura B. 1914. "Sex Education for Children before the Age of Fifteen: Sex Hygiene for Children." *Journal of Social Hygiene* 1: 257–266.

Gebhard, Paul H. 1977. "The Acquisition of Basic Sex Information." *The Journal of Sex Research* 13(3): 148–169.

Geddes, Patrick, and J. Arthur Thomson. 1915. "Sex Education." *Journal of Social Hygiene* 2: 330.

Gendel, Evalyn S., and Pauline B. Green. 1971. "Sex Education Controversy—A Boost to New and Better Programs." *Journal of School Health* 61(1): 24–28.

Goldberg, Jacob A. 1939. "Arousing Teacher Interest in New York City." *Journal of Social Hygiene* 25(7): 321–329.

———. 1941. "Sex Character Education in Twenty-one Private Schools in New York City." *Journal of Social Hygiene* 27(8): 380–391.

———. 1947. "Sex Education or Social Hygiene Education in Schools in Forty Cities." *Journal of Social Hygiene* 33(9): 421–444.

Gruenberg, B. C. 1938. "Sex Education in Secondary Schools: 1938." *Journal of Social Hygiene* 24(9): 527–532.

Harris, Vivian H. 1921. "The Status of Sex Education in Public Educational Institutions." *Journal of Social Hygiene* 7(2): 167–180.

Hawkins, Barbara A. 1969. "How One City Teaches Sex Education and Family Life." *The PTA Magazine* 63(10): 24–26.

Holcomb, J. David, Arthur E. Garner, and Harper F. Beaty. 1970. "Sex Education in Texas Public Schools." *Journal of School Health* 60(10): 563–566.

Howard, M. 1985. "Postponing Sexual Involvement among Adolescents." *Journal of Adolescent Health Care* 6(4): 271–277.

Hoyman, Howard S. 1953. "Basic Issues in School Sex Education." *The Journal of School Health* 23(1): 14–22.

Hughes, W. L. 1926. "Sex Experiences of Boyhood." *Journal of Social Hygiene* 7(5): 262–273.

Isenberger, J. 1920. "Biology in High Schools." *Journal of Social Hygiene* 5(3): 435–438.

Johnson, Warren R., and Margaret Schutt. 1966. "Sex Education Attitudes of School Administrators and School Board Members." *The Journal of School Health* 36(2): 64–68.

Jones, J. P. 1932. "Should Sex Be Discussed from the Pulpit?" *Journal of Social Hygiene* 18(3): 177–178.

Kirkendall, Lester A. 1940. "Building a Program of Sex Education for the Secondary School." *Journal of Social Hygiene* 26(6): 305–320.

———. 1951. "Sound Attitudes Toward Sex." *Journal of Social Hygiene* 37(6): 241–251.

———. 1981. *Sex Education in the Eighties: The Challenge of Healthy Sexual Evolution.* New York: Plenum Press.

Kleinerman, Gerald, Michael Grossman, James Breslow, and Rene Goldman. 1971. "Sex Education in a Ghetto School." *The Journal of School Health* 61(1): 29–33.

Leigh, R. D. 1919. *The Need for Sex Education.* Washington, DC: U.S. Department of Labor.

Lesher, Mabel Grier. 1941. "An Approach to Sex Education in Schools." *Journal of Social Hygiene* 27(8): 373–378.

Levin, Barbara B., Joel R. Levin, and Donald N. Lange. 1972. "A Peek at Sex Education in a Midwestern Community." *The Journal of School Health* 62(8): 462–465.

Levin, Milton I. 1967. "Sex Education in the Public Elementary and High School Curriculum." *The Journal of School Health* 37(1): 30–39.

Libby, Roger W., Alan C. Acock, and D. C. Payne. 1974. "Configurations of Parental Preferences Concerning Sources of Sex Education for Adolescents." *Adolescence* 9(33): 73–80.

Maddock, J. W. 1997. *Sexuality Education in Postsecondary and Professional Training Settings.* New York: Hawthorne Press, Inc.

Mahoney, E. R. 1979. "Sex Education in the Public Schools: A Discriminant Analysis of Characteristics of Pro and Anti Individuals." *The Journal of Sex Research* 15(4): 264–275.

Marsiglio, W., and F. L. Mott. 1986. "The Impact of Sex Education on Sexual Activity, Contraceptive Use and Premarital Pregnancy among American Teenagers." *Family Planning Perspectives* 19(4): 151–161.

Melody, M. E., and L. M. Peterson. 1999. *Teaching America about Sex: Marriage Guides and Sex Manuals from the Late Victorians to Dr. Ruth.* New York: New York University Press.

Meyer, Adolph. 1920. "Science and Sex Education." *Journal of Social Hygiene* 5(3): 390.

Miller, H. A., and R. S. Breakey. 1940. "Sex Education in Lansing Schools." *Journal of Social Hygiene* 26(7): 329–330.

Miller, Susan E. 1963. "Sex Education Is a Must in the Junior High School Curriculum." *The Journal of School Health* 33(5): 221–222.New Jersey Department of Education. 1952. "An Approach in Schools to Education for Personal and Family Living." *Journal of Social Hygiene* 38(2): 56–67.

New York Statewide Study Committee. 1940. The School's Responsibility in Social Hygiene Education. *Journal of Social Hygiene* 26(10): 297–300.

Parker, V. H. 1938. "Sex Education for Parent Groups." *Journal of Social Hygiene* 24(9): 527–532.

Peabody, James E. 1915. "Sex Education in the Home and High School." *Journal of Social Hygiene* 2: 363–374.

Peller, Lili. 1965. "Sex Education of the Young Child." *The Journal of Sex Research* 1(1): 17–23.

President's White House Conference on Child Health and Protection. 1930. *Journal of Social Hygiene* 16(7): 385–430.

Reichelt, Paul A., and Harriet H. Werley. 1975. "Contraception, Abortion, and Venereal Disease: Teenagers' Knowledge and the Effects of Education." *Family Planning Perspectives* 7(2): 83–88.

Remafedi, Gary J. 1988. "Preventing the Sexual Transmission of AIDS During Adolescence." *Journal of Adolescent Health Care* 9(2): 139–143.

Richards, Florence L. 1923. "Sex Education and the Schools." *Journal of Social Hygiene* 9(6): 396–403.

Sandiford, Peter. 1922. "The School Programme and Sex Education." *Journal of Social Hygiene* 8(2): 351.

Schoel, Doris R. 1968. "Sex Education, Family Living and Human Relations—an Integrative Program That Grows with Youth." *The Journal of School Health* 38(3): 129–139.

Sherbon, Florence B. 1931. "Should the Biology of Reproduction Be Taught in the Public School?" *Journal of Social Hygiene* 17(9): 515–519.

Sill, Frederick H. 1914. "Parent-Teacher Cooperation in Individual Instruction: The Kent School Method." *Journal of Social Hygiene* 1: 266–269.

Smith, Hazel V. 1936. "A High School Educational Program in Social Hygiene." *Journal of Social Hygiene* 22(5): 219–221.

Social Hygiene Committee of the Philadelphia Public Schools. 1945. "Guiding Principles in a School Social Hygiene Program." *Journal of Social Hygiene* 31(4): 198–199.

Soefer, E. F., et al. 1985. "Menarche: Target Age for Reinforcing Sex Education for Adolescents." *Journal of Adolescent Health Care* 6(5): 383–386.

Sonenstein, Freya L., and Karen J. Pittman. 1984. "The Availability of Sex Education in Large City School Districts." *Family Planning Perspectives* 16(1): 19–25.

Stohlman, Mary H. 1939. "Sex Education in the Public Schools of the District of Columbia." *Journal of Social Hygiene* 25(7): 321–329.

Stone, Donald B. 1958. "A Basic Philosophy of Sex Education." *The Journal of School Health* 28(7): 237–240.

Sweeney, Esther E. 1952. "Partners in Sex Education." *Journal of Social Hygiene* 38(2): 49–55.

Thornburg, Hershel D. 1972. "A Comparative Study of Sex Information Sources." *The Journal of School Health* 62(2): 88–92.

Toohey, J. V. 1969. "Sex Education, Water Fluoridation and Dr. Sigmund Freud." *The Journal of School Health* 49(1): 70–73.

United States Bureau of Education. 1921. "Sex Education in High Schools." *Journal of Social Hygiene* 7(4): 471.

Van Buskirk, Edgar F. 1923. "Educational Activities of the Cincinnati Social Hygiene Society." *Journal of Social Hygiene* 9(2): 101–110.

Van Buskirk, Edgar F., and E. J. Van Buskirk. 1922. "Report of a Questionnaire upon Sex Education." *Journal of Social Hygiene* 8(2): 258.

Villon, Miriam S. 1934. "Attitudes and Practices of Parents in Sex Education of Children." *Journal of Social Hygiene* 20(3): 166.

Warner, D. 1939. "Wisconsin Boys and Sex Education." *Journal of Social Hygiene* 25(4): 200.

Wetherill, G. G. 1960. "Accepting Responsibility for Sex Education." *The Journal of School Health* 30(3): 107–110.

White, H. F. 1920. "A Motion Picture Curriculum of Sex Instruction." *Journal of Social Hygiene* 6(4): 612–613.

Young, Robert D. 1970. "Sex, the Bible and Modern Man." *Journal of School Health* 60(10): 527–531.

Zillmer, Aimee, and Ruth Larsen. 1942. "What She Thinks about It." *Journal of Social Hygiene* 27(8): 464–468.

Chapter Four

•◦ Sexual Violence against Youth: Abuse and Harassment

Youth are vulnerable. When it comes to victimization, youth are more likely to experience a sexual or physical assault than adults are (Finkelhor and Dziuba-Leatherman 1994). Many youth experience a wide range of assaults from physical neglect and punishment, to sibling assault, to sexual abuse and rape. The scope of this chapter is to investigate the sexual violence that some youth experience. For the purposes of this chapter, sexual violence is taken to mean sexual abuse and sexual harassment. Two relatively recent incidents propel the content of the chapter:

On May 1, 2001, a twenty-eight-year-old principal of a Baptist school in northwest Indiana, William "Andy" Beith, fled with one of his eleven-year-old female students across state lines. His intentions, at the time unclear, became evident upon his capture—to engage in sex with the youth. The sixth grade youth, who had become infatuated with Beith, later disclosed that she and her principal had initially had sex at a school camping trip in Michigan a week prior to their eight-day cross-country run and had sex three times during their voyage. Beith was captured and arrested for "coercing and enticing a minor" and "transporting a minor to engage in sexual activity." Years before this incident, a teenaged Beith had been arrested for exposing himself to a fifteen-year-old girl.

During the 1992–1993 school year in Forsyth, Georgia, a nightmare unfolded for fifth grade student LaShonda Davis. For five months, LaShonda was victim to one of her classmates' sexually suggestive behaviors and comments. The harassment worsened as her tormentor allegedly tried to touch LaShonda's breasts and genital area, and commented, "I want to get in bed with you," and "I want to touch your boobs." In one physical education class, the boy placed a doorstop in his pants and suggested a sexual act toward LaShonda. She pleaded with her classroom teacher, her principal, and two other teachers, but her complaints were ignored. The only action taken by the school was to reassign her a seat farther away from her tormentor and to threaten the boy. LaShonda was emotionally injured. Her grades worsened, and she contemplated suicide. Frustrated with the school's indifference, LaShonda's mother took matters to the police, and the tormentor was charged with sexual battery. The boy never denied the charges.

The sexual abuse of youth, much like that committed by Beith, is among the most repugnant acts committed in human society, the offenders receiving unrelenting social censure. Yet millions of youth are sexually abused each year. From 1980 to 1990 alone, there was a 322 percent increase in the number of reported incidents of sexual abuse. Some researchers believe that 60 million Americans are survivors of childhood sexual abuse. Although estimates of childhood sexual abuse vary, sources reveal that one in four girls and one in ten boys are victims of sexual abuse (Lanning, Ballard, and Robinson 1999). The physical and emotional manifestations of the abuse may not be readily apparent, but they are certainly indelible. Many youth are left with short- and long-term emotional scars that include depression, fear, withdrawal, anxiety, anger, hostility, and poor self-esteem.

The emotional repercussions of sexual harassment may be nearly as deep as those of sexual abuse. Youth, like LaShonda Davis, must often contend not only with their tormentors but also with school officials who fail to validate and act on the complaints that are brought to them. The American Association of University Women (AAUW) (2001) found that of 2,000 eighth through eleventh grade students, four of five youth experienced some form of student-against-student sexual harassment that included unwanted sexual advances (groping and sexual innuendoes). Some youth have had sexual rumors circulated about them, such as those suggesting they are promiscuous or homosexual. Other youth have been forced to engage in a sexual activity or have had their clothing pulled off them. Although Title IX of the Education Amendments of 1972 prohibits sexual harassment and more youth today are aware of sexual harassment policies, sexual harassment against youth committed by youth is still prevalent. The AAUW study revealed that 83 percent of girls and 79 percent of boys experienced some form of sexual harassment.

The American Academy of Child and Adolescent Psychiatry (2000) advises that the best protection from sexual abuse is to build the self-esteem of youth early in childhood and teach them to trust their instincts when it comes to physical intimacy. The same could be said about sexual harassment. Through sex education, youth can learn how to trust their instincts and protect themselves from aggressors and spot and stop the abuse and harassment from recurring. The first half of this chapter discusses sexual abuse against youth, and the second half delves into sexual harassment among youth.

SEXUAL ABUSE AGAINST YOUTH

To better understand how sexual abuse fits in the scheme of sex education, a general examination of sexual abuse among youth follows. This part of the chapter includes the definition of sexual abuse, legal issues, factual information, repercusions, and sexual abuse and sex education.

Definition

A standard definition of child sexual abuse is difficult to find. Most researchers, policy makers, and clinicians define the term according to their needs at hand. Haugaard (2000) points out that although some acts are obviously sexual abuse, such as a father fondling his ten-year-old son's genitals, other acts are far more open to interpretation, such as a father sleeping nude with his ten-year-old son. A lack of consensus exists when it comes to the term because field experts disagree with concepts of age, intent, and abuse (Haugaard 2000). When, exactly, is one considered a child? Some researchers believe those younger than eighteen years of age should be considered children; others believe that sixteen years is a more realistic limit. When deciding whether a case of sexual abuse has occurred, courts have to determine the offender's intent. However, this is often very difficult to judge and open to interpretation. Take the following example:

A boyfriend of an eight-year-old girl's mother had finished showering when the girl walked in on him. The boyfriend had inadvertently exposed himself to the child when the mother joined them and told her daughter that the boyfriend's nudity was perfectly natural. The mother briefly discussed male anatomy, and the young girl asked if she could touch the man's penis. Neither of the adults objected.

Many people find the scenario repulsive and see it clearly as a case of sexual abuse; others can understand the mother's point of view. To determine whether the adults are guilty of sexual abuse, the courts would have to determine the adults' intentions at the time of the scenario.

In the effort to define *abuse,* most believe the term should indicate that harm was inflicted, but often it is difficult to observe the harm that was done because many sexual offenders are gentle with their victims. Moreover, even the dictionary finds varied meanings for the word abuse (Haugaard 2000).

Many definitions of sexual abuse exist. The following definitions proceed from the adult focus that includes the use of a child for sexual gratification to the child-focused definition that indicates the child was violated. Sexual abuse is considered:

- "nonconsensual physical contact with a minor for the purpose of sexual gratification" (Telljohann, Everett, and Price 1997, 149)
- "the utilization of the child for sexual gratification or an adult's permitting another person to so use the child" (Walters 1975)
- "a sexual act imposed on a child who lacks emotional, maturational, and cognitive development" (Sgroi, Blick, and Porter 1982, 9)
- "when any individual—adult or child—forces, coerces, or threatens a child to have any form of sexual contact or to engage in any type of sexual activity" (Jensen and Kiley 1999, 142)
- "a betrayal of trust involving overt or covert sexual actions, direct or indirect, physical or verbal, which may include but is not limited to intercourse between a child and a trusted adult or authority figure" (Finkelhor 1980)

For the purposes of this chapter, the definition provided by Abney and Priest (1995) will be used because it appears more descriptive of sexual abuse: "the sexual manipulation and/or coercion of a dependent child or adolescent by a dominant authority figure in which the child or adolescent is unable to give informed consent" (11).

Sexual abuse generally involves a person of power dominating a youth into sexual exposure (genitalia, masturbation, pornography, and fondling), sexual contact (touching any genitals or intimate areas, fellatio), sexual conversation, or sexual intercourse (vaginal or anal penetration). Sexual abuse also includes lewd looks and the denial of privacy (Mach 1994). In most cases of sexual abuse, youth have come to trust the offender and the offender has manipulated the trust into sexual activity with the youth. Once the activity has occurred, the offender threatens the youth to maintain secrecy. Jensen and Kiley (1999) outlined various types of sexual abuse:

- incest: sexual involvement with family members
- pedophilia: the desire for sex with prepubertal youth
- exhibitionism: exposing genitalia to youth

- molestation: fondling, groping, touching, and kissing youth in a sexual manner
- statutory rape: vaginal or anal intercourse or fellatio between youth, or between an adult and a youth
- rape: forcing unwanted sexual intercourse
- sexual sadism: achieving sexual pleasure from inflicting pain
- child pornography: video, film, or photographs that depict youth in sexual activities
- child prostitution: receiving funds for engaging youth in sexual activities

Legal Issues

Although the states vary greatly in identifying, reporting, evaluating, and prosecuting criminals accused in cases of sexual abuse, youth are protected from sexual abuse in every state. The legal vernacular may vary among states, but the legislation recognizes an array of sexual offenses and protects youth from "indecent liberties," "lewd and lascivious acts," "molestation," "carnal abuse," or "corrupting the morals of minors." Graves and Sgroi (1982) described the following core elements of state laws that are used to determine criminal conduct.

Age

This element is based on the assumption that the victim is young and lacks the developmental capacity to consent to sex and that the offender is generally older and has influential power over the victim. In some states, if the offender is a minor, the law maintains that the offender has to be older with a minimum age difference between the victim and the offender. Other states do not address the age difference. In most cases, only the age of the victim is the basis for the classification of the crime. In California, for instance, a person who engages in sex with a youth who is three years younger than the offender is guilty of a misdemeanor. If the difference in the ages is more than three years, the offender is guilty of a misdemeanor or a felony. In Tennessee, an offender is convicted of statutory rape if the offender is at least four years older than the victim and the victim is at least thirteen years old but less than eighteen. If the offender is an adult, most legislation will adhere to the state's designated age of consent. If an adult has sexual relations with a minor, the adult is guilty of "statutory rape" regardless of the circumstances. The age of consent ranges from fourteen years of age, as in Hawaii, to eighteen years in Arizona.

Relationship between the participants

This element addresses the question, How was the offender related to the victim? This is the basis for incest and molestation charges, and in the instances when the offender is a parent, guardian, or custodian, the age of consent is often raised or the sentence is more severe. In Wisconsin, for instance, if the offender is not related more closely than as second cousin to the victim, the offender is guilty of a class B felony. If the offender is related to the victim, the offender is guilty of a class BC felony.

Type of Sexual Behavior

This element describes the offender's conduct with the youth. State laws address the degree of criminal behavior of an offender or the degree of sexual contact or intercourse with the victim. Most laws address exposure, fondling, sexual intercourse, and incest. New Mexico law, for instance, defines criminal sexual behavior as, "Criminal sexual contact of a minor is the unlawful and intentional touching or applying force to the intimate parts of a minor or the unlawful and intentional causing a minor to touch one's intimate parts . . . the primary genital area, groin, buttocks, anus or breast" (National Center for Prosecution of Child Abuse 1999, 39).

Degree of Force Employed

This element addresses such questions as, How was the youth handled during the alleged incident? Did the offender use force? Was the victim or a third party threatened? Was a weapon used? Generally, the standard remains that the more severe the offense, the more severe the penalty. In Virginia, sodomy and sexual penetration of a victim thirteen years old or younger is punishable by imprisonment for life or no less than five years. Yet aggravated sexual battery is punishable by imprisonment from one to twenty years and a $100,000 fine.

Corroboration

This element addresses whether the offender manipulated the victim to secrecy.

Child Pornography

Forced participation in and/or viewing of sexual photographs or films have their own set of statutes. However, some state statutes may address pornography, found under sexual exploitation, in their child sexual abuse laws.

Risk of Injury to a Minor or Impairing the Morals of a Minor

This broad, general phrase is used to raise charges of sexual abuse.

In addition to the protection youth receive in their home state, four U.S. Codes protect youth on the federal level from sexual abuse. The federal codes in full can be found in Appendix A; however, in brief the legislation defines sexual act, contact, and bodily injury and details the repercussions for those found guilty of sexual abuse of youth.

Most professionals who work with children are required to report alleged incidents of sexual abuse. Understandably, most states mandate that physicians, teachers, and day care providers—the professionals who serve children directly—report endangered youth. The states vary in their lists of other required professionals with a legal obligation to report the suspected incidents. Some states, such as Alabama include the following:

- Hospitals, clinics, sanitariums, doctors, physicians, surgeons, medical examiners, coroners, dentists, osteopaths, optometrists, chiropractors, podiatrists, nurses, school teachers, and officials;
- Peace officers, law enforcement officials, pharmacists, social workers, day-care workers or employees, mental health professionals;
- Any other person called upon to render aid or medical assistance to any child. (National Clearinghouse on Child Abuse and Neglect Information 2000, 7)

In the state of California, the list of professionals mandated to report sexual abuse is exhaustive—over eight times longer than Alabama's. In general, however, everyone has a social and moral obligation to report sexual abuse, and anyone can report suspected incidents. Those individuals who know that sexual abuse is occurring and willingly fail to report the incidents are subject to fines (for example, $1000 in Massachusetts) and/or imprisonment (of no more than a year in Rhode Island, for instance).

All states including the District of Columbia have enacted statutes that describe the procedures for reporting incidents of sexual abuse. The statutes detail the responsibilities of the parties—reporter, law enforcement, and social agencies—and the content of the report. In

Nevada, for instance, anyone who has reasonable suspicions of child sexual abuse can call the toll-free hot line at the Division of Child and Family Services. The statute then mandates that the Division transmit the information to the local law enforcement or the agency that handles protective services.

Incidence

In line with the difficulty of acquiring a consensus in a definition of sexual abuse or uniformity of a legal perspective, finding statistical information on sexual abuse among youth is just as challenging. Since no standard definition of sexual abuse exists, it is understandable that the estimates of the number of youth who are sexually abused varies. Telljohann, Everett, and Price (1997), for instance, found that studies report that 19 to 64 percent of girls are sexually abused, as are 10 to 16 percent of boys. Lanning, Ballard, and Robinson (1999) found a variation for girls ranging from 6 to 62 percent, and for boys from 3 to 13 percent. Similar results can be found in studies of adults who recall being sexually abused. Hyde and Forsyth (1997), for instance, report a variation of 15 to 38 percent for adult women and up to 10 percent for adult men. Shaw (1999) believes that one in three girls and one in seven boys will be sexually abused by the age of eighteen.

For an actual figure, the Child Maltreatment 1999 report (U.S. Department of Health and Human Services 1999) said that states received nearly three million referrals for general cases of abuse and neglect, but only 826,000 resulted in substantiated cases. Of this figure, 11.3 percent—more than 93,000 youth—were confirmed cases of sexual abuse. This is a considerably lower figure than the one proposed by Kenney, Reinholtz, and Angelini (1997) who estimate that between 250,000 and 300,000 youths are sexually abused each year, or roughly 2 to 3 percent of all children. The difference in these figures is notable because the 1999 figures are not for the number of incidents of sexual abuse but the number of victims found to be sexually abused.

Most incidents of sexual abuse among youth, up to 80 percent (Kenny and McEachern 2000), are underreported for various reasons. Some youth may not be developmentally able to understand that the violation was inappropriate and illegal. Others may be too young to verbally express what has happened to them. Some may be too embarrassed or scared to discuss the ordeal. Many have been manipulated into secrecy and threatened with violence if the secrecy is violated. In cases of incest, some youth may not want to disrupt the family dynamics. Moreover, many times when adults suspect their child has been abused, they do not report the incident because they lack the evidence to substantiate their claim. The National Center for Juvenile Justice (2000) found that between 1991 and 1996, youth (from infancy to seventeen years old) comprised 67 percent of all reported cases of sexual assault. Over half of the reported cases of rape, sodomy, fondling, and sexual assaults with objects were found among youth. Despite the effort to curtail sexual abuse, social censure of sexual abuse, and statutes of protection, researchers believe that 90 percent of the offenders are not prosecuted (Stewart 1985 cited in Everstine and Everstine 1989).

Offenders

Who are these offenders? Why would they engage in such foul behavior with youth? The assumption that most parents, teachers, and caretakers of youth have of these offenders is generally a dark one—a stranger, "a dirty old man," probably a homosexual male, who drives a dark automobile and wears dark clothing, and lures youth into a dark corner. The stereotype made up of these characteristics is a complete fallacy. Abusers know their victims. Abusers tend to be friends, neighbors, relatives, and so forth (Finkelhor 1980). Refuting common misconceptions, Hunter (1990) estimated that 75 to 95 percent of child and adolescent victims know their abusers, and most offenders commit their first act of sexual violation before they are thirty years old. Other researchers have found that up to 99 percent of sexual abuse victims knew their abusers, and some studies reveal that nearly 62 percent of the abusers are fathers or father figures (Hyde and Forsyth 1997). Hyde and Forsythe also show that most adult abusers are heterosexual, many are married with children, do not physically injure their victims, and on most occasions appear as normal and ordinary as most citizens. It is important to underscore, however, that adults who sexually abuse youth make up a heterogeneous group of characteristics—some are violent, others may be passive; some may be psychotic, others are not; some want to inflict pain, others seek mutual love from their victims; some are antisocial, others are the pillars of their church community. In other words, no set of attributes can be ascribed to these offenders other than the fact that they have a predilection for sexual activity with youth. Theories as to why adults sexually abuse youth range from offenders having unhealthy, "disturbing" relationships with their parents to having had sexually gratifying experiences in childhood (Finkelhor 1980).

   Not all sexual abuse offenders are adults. An unfortunate fact is that some youth sexually abuse other youth. Alarming evidence finds an increase in reports of sexual abuse by youth and sexual aggression among youth (Shaw 1999). Present data provided by the U.S. Department of Justice (1999) indicate that youth under the age of eleven were more likely to be sexually abused by an offender younger than seventeen than by an adult. In fact, of all sexual offenders under the age of seventeen, 43 percent abused children younger than six years of age, 34 percent abused youth between the ages of seven and eleven, and 24 percent abused those who were between twelve and seventeen years old. Of all offenders of sexual abuse reported to law enforcement, 23 percent were youth and 16 percent were under twelve years old (National Center for Juvenile Justice 2000). In Idaho, the state's attorney general passed legislation to register all juvenile sex offenders because one-third of all child sexual abuse victims were abused by a juvenile and 75 percent of these victims were under the age of eleven. These figures have serious implications because research has found that youth offenders tend to be repeat offenders. Righthand and Welch (2001) found research that reveals that nearly 79 percent of juvenile youth offenders had prior arrest records for sexual abuse. Moreover, some youth grow up to become adult offenders. The U.S. Department of Justice (1996), for instance, found that 80 percent of imprisoned criminals convicted of sexual assault committed their first sexual assault before the age of eighteen.

Youth who sexually abuse other youth know their victims. Research has found that in the majority of cases, victims of sexual abuse were acquainted with their offenders (U.S. Department of Justice 1999). The offenders may appear to be the same age and size and have similar powers of influence, but it is clearly the offender who is more intimidating and powerful than the victim. In most cases, the offender coerces the victim into sexual activity and threatens the victim with physical harm if he or she discloses the incident. Research has found that 96 percent of youth sex offenders are males (National Center for Juvenile Justice 2000), most of whom committed their first act of sexual abuse when they were thirteen or fourteen years old (Weinrott 1996). Moreover, most offenders engage in other criminal behavior, experience social incompetence, and have had prior consensual sexual experiences (Righthand and Welch 2001).

Victims

Sexual abuse among youth crosses all variable domains. Any youth, regardless of gender, socioeconomic status, culture, ethnicity, age, or physical stature can be a victim of sexual abuse. Research has found, however, that most victims are females. The National Center for Juvenile Justice (2000) reported that girls were six times more likely to be sexually assaulted than boys, and as the age of the youth increased, so did the likelihood that the victim was a girl. Age plays a factor to a degree. Most victims tend to be younger than their offenders (Righthand and Welch 2001). Although some infants have been sexually abused (Besharov 1990), preadolescents are more vulnerable to sexual abuse (Finkelhor 1980). As mentioned earlier, more than two-thirds of all reported sexual assaults were committed against youth. Of these, one-third were between the ages of twelve and seventeen, 34 percent were twelve and younger, and 14 percent were under the age of six. The National Center for Juvenile Justice figures seem to indicate that the younger the victim was the more likely it was that the youth was sodomized or assaulted with an object. The older the victim, the more likely it was that victim was raped or fondled.

The research regarding ethnicity of victims is uncertain and inconclusive. Although some research has found that youth of color are more likely to be sexually abused than white youth, other studies have revealed the opposite or found no differences in the rate of sexual abuse (Kenny and McEachern 2000). A family's socioeconomic status or income level, however, seems to play a factor in the likelihood that a youth will be sexually abused. Youth from impoverished homes are more likely to be sexually abused than those from homes who have a higher family income. The National Center on Child Abuse and Neglect (1996) reported that youth from homes whose families earned less than an annual salary of $15,000 were seventeen times more likely to experience sexual abuse than families whose average annual income exceeded $30,000.

Repercussions

Sexual abuse can leave youth with physical and emotional scars. The physical scars can be readily apparent, for instance, from a torn, lacerated, or infected vagina, a swollen or inflamed penis, or a bleeding rectum (Besharov 1990). Other times youth do not even have physical signs because they may have been fondled or coerced into fondling their abuser. At the very least, youth may complain of abdominal pain or a recurring genital rash, or they may remain completely silent. The most significant injury that youth encounter is an emotional one. Indeed, sexual abuse can leave youth with emotional scars that run deeper than physical ones. They may become disruptive and angry at home and school, lashing out at parents, siblings, teachers, and peers. Alternatively, they may become depressed and withdraw from those who care about them the most. Some youth contemplate suicide after being sexually coerced (Gidycz and Koss 1989). Researchers have found that girls who attempt suicide are more likely to have experienced sexual abuse than girls who have not (DeWilde et al. 1992).

Using seminal research as a basis, Saywitz et al. (2000) outlined the possible degrees of emotional effects. After being sexually abused, some youth may experience

- no emotional effects
- mild symptoms such as emotional distress, self-esteem and identity issues, or anxiety
- serious problems such as clinical depression, substance abuse, or aggression
- severe psychiatric disorders such as post-traumatic stress disorder (PTSD), overanxiety, or sleep disorders

As many as 55 percent of youth referred for clinical treatment have more than one diagnosis (Target and Fonagy 1996), 50 percent meet some or all of the criteria of PTSD (McLeer et al. 1992), and one-third show no signs of emotional problems (Kendall-Tackett, Williams, and Finkelhor 1993). Research has also found that some youth become sexually aggressive and coercive with other children after they've been sexually abused (Zeanah and Hamilton 1998), and some youth show sexually overt behaviors with their peers (American Academy of Child and Adolescent Psychiatry 2000). Some youth have even become prostitutes (Zigman 1999).

The effects for some youth appear to be long lasting. Research cited in Finkelhor and Dziuba-Leatherman (1994) indicates that sexually abused youth are more likely to experience a lifetime of psychiatric disorders and substance abuse than youth who are not abused. Several factors must be considered when determining the impact sexual abuse may have on youth. Hunter (1990) found the following most critical:

- the degree of violence encountered
- the age of the victim at initiation
- the duration of the abuse
- the frequency of the abuse
- the number of abusers
- the relationship of the victim and the abuser
- the way others (adults especially) responded to the abuse

In the most general of terms, the more violent and frequent the abuse, the more traumatic the experience. In that vein, the younger the victim, the greater number of people who took part in the abuse, and the closer the relationship between the victim and abuser, the more damaging the experience. Moreover, if youth are not supported after the incident has occurred, or at the very least if their allegations are not validated by adults closest to them, the more profound effect the abuse will have.

Sex Education and Sexual Abuse

With all the available information on sexual abuse among youth and the public outrage that is evoked when a youth is violated, a logical assumption would be that sex education curricula on sexual abuse abound. Ironically, the sexual education curricula commercially available do a relatively poor job at preventing sexual abuse. Beyer and Ogletree (1998) conducted a content analysis on twenty-one sex education curricula for adolescents. The researchers assessed topics of sexual coercion—date rape, stranger rape, exploitation, unwanted touch, pressure, incest, and sexual harassment—in the curricula. Depending on the number of paragraphs devoted to a sexual coercion topic, a curriculum was rated on a scale of one to five. The researchers did not evaluate the quality of the content; they simply wanted to know how often a topic was addressed in the curriculum. None of the curricula addressed sexual harassment (to be discussed in the second part of this chapter), and only three curricula—Streetwise to Sex-Wise, Values and Choices, and Life Planning Education, D.C.—addressed all of the topics of coercion (except harassment). Streetwise to Sex-Wise scored the highest rating with sixty paragraphs devoted to sexual coercion. Values and Choices scored the second highest with thirty-five paragraphs, and Life Planning Education, D.C. included thirty paragraphs on sexual coercion. Various themes were present throughout the curricula such as blame, communication, drug use, fear, premeditation, and resource help. Guilt and pressure seemed to be addressed the most throughout the curricula, date rape was addressed second most often, and exploitation scored third. The study led Beyer and Ogletree to conclude that sex education curricula must do a better job at covering all aspects of sexual coercion.

Lanning, Ballard, and Robinson (1999) sought to determine how many districts throughout the state of Texas implemented a sex education program that helped youth understand and learn how to prevent sexual abuse. The study was based on the fact that sexual abuse among youth is relatively high, teachers and school personnel are required to report suspicions of sexual abuse, and more importantly, Texas law requires schools to implement child abuse prevention programs in elementary and secondary schools. In their survey of eighty-nine large public school districts, the researchers found that more than 50 percent of the sample implemented a program. School districts that did not operate such programs stated that they were developing their own curriculum, their counselors were used for crisis intervention, or the community was too conservative for any sex education programs. Half the districts offered the program independently from the general curriculum, and the rest chose to incorporate the program in general health or guidance.

As expected, most (fifty-two) of the districts directed their program to children; surprisingly, however, thirty-seven districts provided a program for teachers, thirty-four for counselors, and twenty-eight for parents and teachers. Most of the programs included such elements as appropriate touch (a good touch versus a bad one), children's rights, how to refuse inappropriate touch, empowerment, asserting themselves by exclaiming "No," key "safe" people to confide in, and disclosure. About half of the districts implemented the programs for the duration of two days to a week with a session lasting nearly an hour. The most salient finding of the study was that less than half of the districts had an evaluation procedure, and only three districts implemented an experimental control group type of evaluation plan.

Although this study was conducted in Texas, the results underscore that although school districts throughout the nation may be required to provide sex education that enhances students' (elementary school youth, at least) awareness of sexual abuse, many districts choose not to. The districts may have bona fide reasons for not implementing such programs; however, what about all those youth who could have learned to prevent sexual abuse? The lack of implementation consistency makes it hard to quantitatively assess the benefits of the program; however, districts must make an effort to answer the questions, Is the program effective? and, How do we know?

Telljohann, Everett, and Price (1997) set out to answer those questions based on a sexual abuse prevention program in Ohio. The program, entitled Sexual Abuse Prevention Program, Third Grade Curriculum, included elements of inappropriate touching, safety procedures, disclosure, and empathy among youth who have been abused. In two one-hour sessions, the youth acquired knowledge and behavioral skills through discussions, role-playing, videos, and demonstrations. Youth practiced being assertive with "No" and had to verbally identify the adult they would contact if an abuse happened to them. An experimental control group design was applied to assess the program. About 236 third-grade youth were assigned to the experimental group and 195 to the control group. All the students were pre- and post-tested. Although the sex education program was brief, the authors found the program successful because of small increases in pre- to post-test scores. The authors pointed out that the ultimate success of a program is if it decreases the likelihood that youth will be sexually abused. A limitation of this study, the authors warned, was that it could not provide such evidence.

The literature on sex education for the prevention of sexual abuse is limited. However, most authors believe that such programs should begin in early childhood and should be integrated into the general sex education program (Herman 2000). Curricula found in the SIECUS (2001) clearinghouse (such as All about Life: Grades K–4 Caring about Myself, My Family, and My Community; FLASH: Family Life and Sexual Health Grades; The Family Education Program; and Streetwise to Sex-Wise: Sexuality Education for High-Risk Youth) that address the prevention of sexual abuse, as do most prevention programs, have certain core elements in common. Prevention programs within sex education should teach youth

- to recognize sexual abuse, teaching them to trust their instincts; if a situation feels bad, wrong, or uncomfortable, it most likely is
- the differences between good touching versus bad; affectionate versus exploitive; safe versus unsafe and secret
- that they have a right to their own bodies—no one can violate their bodies
- that keeping unwanted physical contact a secret is harmful
- the behavioral skills to prevent an incident from occurring—practicing saying "No"; articulating a plan of action if an incident occurs (i.e., running to a neighbor's house); a school counselor they can talk to
- how and to whom to disclose the incident—trusted adults, school personnel.

The Boys Scouts of America (1990) summarize it best when they teach youth the three R's: recognize, resist, and report anyone taking advantage of a youth's body.

SEXUAL HARASSMENT AMONG YOUTH

A discussion on sexual harassment among youth in schools will make up the remainder of this chapter. The content of the discussion is provided in four sections: definition of sexual harassment, legal issues, factual information, and sexual education and sexual harassment. A quote from former secretary of education Richard W. Riley captures the importance of bringing sexual harassment among youth to the forefront:

> Our schools owe students a safe environment that is conducive to learning and that affords all students an equal opportunity to achieve high educational standards. Harassment and hate crimes undermine these purposes and may cause serious harm to the development of students who are victimized by this behavior. (U.S. Department of Education 1999)

Definition

Sexual harassment garnered much attention and entered public consciousness on October 11, 1991, when University of Oklahoma Law Professor, Anita F. Hill, testified at the confirmation hearing for Supreme Court Justice Clarence Thomas. In her broadcasted testimony, the nation heard Hill describe the allegations of the sexual harassment she endured from 1981 to 1983 from Thomas, who was then her superior at the Equal Employment Opportunity Commission. The harassment took the form of continuous pleas for dates with Hill and conversations with explicit (pornographic acts depicted in films) and implicit (pubic hair on coke cans) sexual tones, all of which were unwanted by Hill. He allegedly persisted as she resisted.

This situation may appear to be far removed from the walls of classrooms across America but it is not. Sexual harassment in the classroom is very real, and many youth encounter experiences similar to or even worse than the type of harassment endured by Professor Hill. Take the following example:

In a seventh grade classroom in South Side Chicago, two boys taunted a girl in her homeroom. The boys continuously taunted her with such sexually explicit comments as "I want to sleep with you baby. Show me what you can do with my condom. Clean my ears with those nipples. Give me a pedicure with your tongue." She hated every minute of the encounters and pleaded with the boys to stop. When she told her teachers, the boys temporarily ceased in their torment, but they soon started again with different taunts. "She doesn't eat meat; she's a big, fat lesbian. Fat, ugly dyke with a bra too small." On a few occasions the boys had snapped the front and back band of her bra, and in other instances the boys had pinched her buttocks. One of the boys remarked to the whole class, "She's all that and a bag of chips." The class erupted in laughter, and the teacher actually smiled at the comment. The girl was beyond being merely bothered by the boys, she was emotionally drained, extremely embarrassed, and uncomfortable enough to miss school.

Using the example as a basis for a definition, sexual harassment among youth can best be defined this way:

Sexual harassment is undesired and offensive conduct that is sexually suggestive by means of taunts, gestures, or physical contact that is consistent and to a degree that makes a student uncomfortable and makes it difficult to participate in or enjoy the benefits of an education duly deserved.

In other words, to determine if sexual harassment has occurred among youth, one should ask:

- Was sexual conduct conveyed verbally, nonverbally, or by physical contact?
- Was the conduct unwelcome?
- Was the conduct in the form of a sexual advance or a request for a sexual favor?
- Was the student's well-being eroded to a point that participation in academic and nonacademic opportunities was limited or denied because of the conduct?

Sexual harassment can occur in any school setting from the classroom, or band practice, or on the football field. Sexual harassment can happen on the way to or from school, on the playground during recess, during the transition between classes, at the school library while doing a research paper, or off campus at scholastic competitions. Sexual harassment is not gender or age driven. A girl can harass another girl, for example by calling her a *slut*. A boy can harass another boy, for instance, by calling him "Ben Dover." A freshman can harass another student who is a sophomore, a junior, or a senior. A student does not have to report an incident for sexual harassment to exist, and harassment does not only have to affect the person for which it is intended. Sometimes the harassment becomes physical, and the harasser may embrace the victim and imitate sexual movements, use an object and prod the victim, pinch or spank the victim, or gesture oral sex by maneuvering the tongue around the mouth.

The federal government also has standards in effect to determine whether sexual harassment has occurred:

- The degree to which the conduct affected one or more students' education—This standard asks questions such as "Did the student's grades deteriorate because of the alleged conduct? Did the conduct cause the student some distress? Did the student miss school to avoid the conduct?"

•• The type, frequency, and duration of the conduct—In other words, "How consistent and severe were the patterns of conduct?" Generally speaking, the more severe the incident, the less repetitive it must be. One severe incident can create a sexually hostile environment. By that same token, one incident is not necessarily grounds for sexual harassment (for example, one student telling another that she smells nice).

•• The identity of and relationship between the alleged harasser and the subject or subjects of the harassment—This standard addresses the dynamics of the relationship between the harasser and victim. This attempts to understand whether the relationship was a romantic one, or if the harasser had influential power over the victim.

•• The number of individuals involved—Generally, the larger the number of people involved in the alleged harassment, the more intimidating and overwhelming it may be for the victim. On the other hand, taunts made by an individual to a group may be less intimidating for a victim (for instance, a boy calling a group of gay and lesbian youth "a bunch of faggot rods").

•• The age and sex of the alleged harasser and the subject or subjects of the harassment—Research tends to support that the greater the age difference between the harasser and the victim, the more intimidating it may be for the victim.

•• The size of the school, location of the incident, and context in which the incident occurred—The physical location of the incident affects the degree of harassment. If the incident occurs in public (for example, on the playground), it may be a safer experience for the victim, albeit more humiliating. Yet an incident on a school bus may be less humiliating, but the intimidation factor may be greater if the victim cannot escape from the harasser.

•• Other incidents at the school—A hostile environment can be created if one or more than one group of students continuously harasses a student (for instance, a gay youth being tormented by a group of boys in gym class, then by a different boy in his math class, and then another group during band practice).

•• Incidents of gender-based, but nonsexual harassment—This

standard addresses whether the student was teased, tormented, or physically assaulted in a nonsexual manner. This asks, "Did the youth encounter other threatening situations that were sexual and nonsexual?" An adolescent boy, for instance, because of his small stature, high voice, and proclivity for math and science may be bullied and teased by others. The incidents become more serious and the environment becomes sexually hostile when he enters gym class and some students call him "queer bait." (U.S. Department of Education 2001b)

School authorities may find some sexual taunts and banters to be standard among youth and consider those who resent them high-strung and overreactive. Many times the exchanges are excused with a comment such as "They're just being kids." However, grabbing parts of a body, writing sexual graffiti about someone, spreading sexual rumors about another, pulling off someone's clothes, forcing a kiss, flashing another, pinching, or cornering someone can be very intimidating, uncomfortable, and humiliating for some youth (Teen Voices On-line Magazine 1999).

Legal Issues

Federal law, Title IX of the Education Amendments of 1972 (P.L. 92–318), prohibits sexual harassment in schools. Title IX mandates that education programs and activities that receive federal funding cannot discriminate against youth based on gender—all youth are to be treated equally. Males and females must have equal opportunity in all aspects of academic and extracurricular programs including admissions, recruitment, and athletics, and have comparable locker rooms, bathrooms, and other facilities. Moreover, pregnant and married youth cannot be discriminated against. A distinct feature of the law is that sexual harassment is included under sexual discrimination, and a student, teacher, administrator, or school employee violates the law if he or she engages in, condones, tolerates, or allows sexual harassment to continue (U.S. Department of Education 2001a).

Sexual harassment has two forms: quid pro quo or hostile environment. The Latin term quid pro quo roughly means "this for that" or the exchange of one thing for another. This type of sexual harassment is committed when an individual asks another individual for a favor that is sexual in nature (a kiss, a date, a hug, oral sex, or sex) in return for a desirous consequence such as first chair in band, lead twirler, varsity team, a higher or passing grade, or editor of the school paper. The harasser sometimes threatens or punishes the victim if she or he does not comply. The hostile-environment form of harassment is when one party makes a second party feel uncomfortable, intimidated, or frightened in an environment where the second party has a right to be or is required to be (for instance, in a biology lab). The U.S. Department of Education (2001b) emphasizes that a hostile environment is one in which the aggressor's conduct "is so severe, persistent, or pervasive that it affects a student's ability to participate in or benefit from an education program or activity, or creates an intimidating, threatening, or abusive educational environment" (1).

School officials are morally and legally obligated to protect all youth from sexual harassment. All youth have a right to learn and work in a climate that is safe from sexual harassment. In 1981, the U.S. Department of Education, Office of Civil Rights held that in order for public schools to be in compliance with Title IX, districts must create, publish, and enforce a sexual harassment policy and outline and adhere to procedures for resolving all complaints in an equitable and timely fashion. The policy can include:

•➤ parameters of sexual harassment
•➤ examples and types of sexual harassment
•➤ statement of student rights and how rights will be protected
•➤ statement of no tolerance
•➤ reporting and investigation procedures
•➤ action follow-up
•➤ disciplinary action for the violators
•➤ steps taken to protect students from retaliation

The U.S. Department of Education (cited in Crisci 1999) recommends that the grievance procedures be clear and that the school community know the process for filing a complaint; that the investigation will be impartial; the time frames for an investigation; that all parties involved in the complaint will be notified of the outcome; that retaliation is prohibited; that the school will prevent any other harassment from recurring; and the appeal process. Schools are also required to designate an employee to ensure compliance with the law, to monitor complaints, and to coordinate the elimination of sexual harassment. To get a better understanding of how a policy might be written, a copy of St. Edward Parochial School policy on sexual harassment is provided in figure 4.1.

When a student files a sexual harassment report with a school, school officials must take immediate action. They must follow their

Figure 4.1. St. Edward School Sexual Harassment Policy

Policy Statement

The schools of the Diocese of Oakland prohibit any form of sexual harassment of students whether verbal, physical, or environmental. It is a violation of this policy for any employee or agent of the Diocese to harass a student or for a student to harass another student in a sexual manner as defined below.

Definition of Sexual Harassment

For purposes of this policy, sexual harassment is defined as including but not limited to unwelcome sexual advances, requests for sexual or physical conduct of a sexual nature directed toward a student under any of the following conditions:

- Submission to, or toleration of, sexual harassment is an explicit or implicit term or condition of any services, benefits, or programs sponsored by the Diocese
- Submission to, or rejection of, such conduct is used as a basis for an academic evaluation affecting a student
- The conduct has the purpose or effect of unreasonably interfering with a student's academic performance, or of creating an intimidating, hostile, or offensive environment
- Submission to, or rejection of, the conduct is used as the basis for any decision affecting the individual regarding benefits and services, sponsored by the Diocese

Student-to-Student Sexual Harassment

The policy prohibits student-to-student sexual harassment whenever it is related to school activity or attendance and occurs at any time including, but not limited to, any of the following:

a. While on school grounds
b. While going to or coming from school
c. During the lunch period whether on or off campus
d. During, or while going to or coming from, a school-sponsored activity.

Any student who engages in the sexual harassment of another student is subject to disciplinary action including verbal warnings and reprimands, counseling, suspension, and expulsion.

Employee to Student Sexual Harassment

Employee-to-student harassment is prohibited at all times whether or not the incidents of harassment occur on school property or a school sponsored event.

To prevent sexual harassment, amorous relationships between a student and an agent or employee of the Diocese are strictly prohibited.

Any employee or agent of the Diocese who participates in the sexual harassment of a student is subject to the disciplinary action including, but not limited to, verbal warnings, letters of reprimand, transfer, re-assignment, suspension without pay, and dismissal.

continues

Figure 4.1. *Continued*

Retaliation

The Diocese forbids retaliation against anyone who reports sexual harassment or who participates in the investigation of such a report.

Grievance Procedure

The Diocese has adopted administrative procedures for filing sexual harassment complaints. A copy of the formal complaint procedure is contained in the Diocese of Oakland School department's Administrative Handbook. At an informal level, complaints may be reported to a school counselor, the principal, or assistant/vice principal. Formal written complaints may also be filed at the office of the principal or designee. Complaints should be presented in written form to the principal.

Source: From "St. Edward School Sexual Harassment Policy" by Archdiocese of Oakland, 2001. Reprinted with permission.

---

adopted procedures to address the alleged incident and "eliminate the effects of the harassment on the victim and other students, and prevent the harassment from recurring" (U.S. Department of Education 1999,1). Schools cannot ignore an incident and must provide evidence that prompt action was taken to mediate the situation. In addition to the implementation of a sexual harassment policy, public schools are strongly encouraged to take proactive measures to ensure a safe, anti–sexual harassment environment. In other words, schools should make a concerted effort to create a secure learning climate that is free from sexual harassment. In *Protecting Students from Harassment and Hate Crimes,* the U.S. Department of Education indicates that schools can create secure environments by supporting and promoting diversity among their learning community. To achieve this, schools should monitor their environments, identify student and parent concerns, hold recurring staff training on sexual harassment, implement curricula that teaches respect for all, and encourage mediation programs among students. Ultimately, all students need to understand that a violation of a youth's civil rights through unwelcomed sexually suggestive taunts, gestures, or physical contact will not be tolerated.

When complaints of sexual harassment have been substantiated, Hughes (1999) recommends the following for the betterment of the harasser, the victim, and the school:

- Separate the victim from the harasser—One of the two should be transferred to a different classroom or school. The victim should have no contact with the harasser whatsoever.

⊷ Have counseling available for both parties—The harasser should learn the harmful effects of harassment and learn to respect the rights of others. The victim will need some guidance to an emotional recovery.

⊷ Hold conferences for parents—The harasser's parents need to understand the penalties imposed for continued harassment. They should be encouraged to reinforce that sexual harassment damages the school climate and one's spirit. The victim's parents need validation that their youth will no longer suffer in a hostile environment.

⊷ Take disciplinary action—The harasser should be disciplined with suspension, detention, or denial of certain privileges. The harasser could be expelled for more severe situations. The local law enforcement should be notified for situations that border on criminal acts.

⊷ Assess climate where the harassment occurred—School officials should make an effort to help the silent victims. Counseling services could be made available for any youth who witnessed the harassment. If required, youth should be afforded tutoring services and the opportunity to make up missed work.

⊷ Prohibit retaliation—The victim and witnesses should feel certain that the harassment is eliminated and that no form of retaliation will occur.

A school district's failure to acknowledge and remedy a sexually hostile environment or curtail sexual harassment leaves it liable for monetary damages. The Supreme Court ruling in *Gebser v. Lago Vista Independent School District* established the precedent that schools are liable if they have "actual knowledge" and are "deliberately indifferent" to sexual harassment (Crisci 1999). According to Mann and Hughes (1998), the Gebser case involved a fifty-three-year-old male public school teacher who had a continued affair with a fifteen-year-old female student. The teacher and the student were caught having sex; the teacher was arrested, fired from his job, and eventually lost his teaching credentials. The student confessed she knew the affair was inappropriate but did not know how to end it. School administrators had no knowledge of the teacher and student affair. Although federally mandated, the school district never instituted a sexual harassment policy. The district did not even make an effort to instill an antiharassment spirit in its schools. When the youth's mother sued the district for monetary damages, the court ruled in the district's favor because of its apparent lack of knowledge. Essentially, a school's legal burden in cases of sexual harassment does not rest on the innocence or culpability of its employees or students but in how the school responds to and resolves the complaints.

This brings to mind the matter of two cases: *Davis v. Monroe County Board of Education* and *Nabozny v. Podlesny.* The case of LaShonda Davis, one of the narratives at the beginning of this chapter, reached the Supreme Court after the District Court and Court of Appeals found that a "district is not liable under Title IX for failing to prevent sexual harassment among students" (Crisci 1999, 7). The Supreme Court overturned the rulings and sided with Davis because the school had reacted with an apparent indifference to Davis's ordeal. In the Jamie Nabozny case, the Seventh U.S. Circuit Court of Appeals ruled against the district, Ashland School District, because school officials knew of and were indifferent to Jamie's plight. Based simply on the fact that Jamie was gay, he was harassed to the point of being pushed into a urinal and urinated upon. His tormentors even gestured raping him in a classroom. The school did little about his complaints, and the harassers received no serious disciplinary action. Moreover, some school officials trivialized his ordeal, responding, "that is what is expected when one is gay." Nabozny settled out of court for $900,000.

Factual Information

Serious incidents of sexual harassment occur in our nation's schools every single day. School administrators, teachers, and students—girls and boys alike—know what it is, know that it exists, and can readily describe instances vividly (Stein 2001). To organize the following factual content, answers will be provided to a series of questions associated with sexual harassment.

How Many Youth Experience Sexual Harassment?

Although research on sexual harassment among youth is scant, the results have shown that a relatively large number of youth experience some form of sexual harassment. In a nonscientific survey conducted through a mainstream magazine popular among girls, *Seventeen,* Stein, Marshall, and Troop (1993) found that girls as young as nine and as old as nineteen had been sexually harassed. Of the 4,200 respondents, 92 percent of girls between the ages of twelve and sixteen were harassed. In one of the earliest national scientific studies on sexual harassment, the American Association of University Women (AAUW) (1993) found that of 1,632 students in grades eight through eleven, 85 percent of the girls and 76 percent of the boys had encountered some form of sexual harassment. Among the youth, four out of five had experienced sexual harassment. Another study of youth in similar grades found that 68 percent of the girls and 39 percent of the boys experienced some form of physical contact that was of a sexual nature (University of Michigan 1996). The most current AAUW (2001) study of 2,064 youth (in eighth to eleventh grade) found that 83 percent of the girls and 79 percent of the boys report having experienced some form of sexual harassment. These percentages should be interpreted with caution, however: it is difficult, if not impossible, to ascertain an accurate, or near accurate, count of the number of youth who are harassed because school districts poorly maintain accounts of sexual harassment among youth, youth prefer not to report sexual harassment, and the definition of sexual harassment is imprecise (Schwartz 2001). Nonetheless, research is consistent—sexual harassment is common among youth.

Who Is Harassed Most Frequently?

Sexual harassment among youth is not discriminatory. Most youth are likely to be sexually harassed, regardless whether they attend urban or suburban schools (American Association of University Women 2001). Although boys are more likely to initiate harassment toward girls, girls *do* harass, and boys *do* get harassed. In a study of 1,000 youth in junior and senior high schools, Shakeshaft et al. (1997) found that youth perceive boys to harass boys and girls alike. The researchers noted that boys tend to be more direct about their harassment than girls, and girls generally harass boys to counter the initial harassment. Girls most often targeted were those considered physically mature and those considered unattractive. Boys often harassed girls about their weight with slurs such as "fat cow," and for the physically mature girl, boys often made sexual overtures toward them, spread sexual rumors about them, or called them "slut." Boys who were harassed were those considered effeminate or those who did not fit the masculine student mold. They were called "queer" or "sissy" or any name associated with a feminine feature. Many boys feared being labeled gay and worked hard to associate themselves with the norm.

Although the 1993 AAUW study found that more girls experience sexual harassment more often than boys (one in three girls as compared to one in five boys), the number of boys who reported they were sexually harassed (either "often or "occasionally") increased to 56 percent in 2001 from 49 percent in 1993 (AAUW 2001). When ethnicity is considered, white, African American, and Latino girls are sexually harassed at

similar rates although white girls experience a higher rate of sexual harassment (87 percent, 84 percent, and 82 percent respectively) (AAUW
1993). Among boys, African American boys (81 percent) report a higher
incidence of sexual harassment than white (75 percent) or Latino boys
(69 percent) (AAUW 1993). Some studies have found that nearly 90 percent of gay and lesbian youth are more likely targets of sexual harassment (Schwartz 2001).

Girls seemed to be more affected by sexual harassment than boys
were (AAUW 1993, 2001). They were more likely than boys were to feel
self-conscious, embarrassed, less confident, and more likely to change
their behavior because of the experience. The girls were more likely than
boys to report that they would become "very upset" if they experienced
any of the fourteen accounts of harassment described in the AAUW
(2001) study. The only account of sexual harassment that affected the
boys to the same degree was if they were called "gay." Findings such as
these lead many experts to believe that homophobia begins at an early
age and is reinforced throughout adolescent development.

What Type of Harassment Is Most Common?

Most youth experience student-on-student sexual harassment. In other
words, peers and fellow schoolmates are the harassers (Stein, Marshall,
and Troop, 1993). A small percentage of school personnel harass youth.
The number of youth harassed by school personnel dropped from 18
percent in 1993 (American Association of University Women) to 7 percent in 2001 (AAUW). The AAUW (2001) study also found that most sexual harassment is nonphysical. In fact, 76 percent of youth have experienced this form of sexual harassment, and 58 percent have encountered
a physical harassment. This is consistent with Shakeshaft et al. (1997)
who found that most of the sexual harassment observed in their study
was verbal and impromptu.

Where Is Sexual Harassment Most Likely to Occur?

Sexual harassment is more common in junior and senior high school
but has been reported in elementary school (Schwartz 2001). The American Association of University Women (AAUW) (2001) found that more
than 35 percent of the youth reported they experienced some form of
sexual harassment in elementary school. Sexual harassment is rarely
concealed; most instances occur directly in sight of other youth and
adults (Stein 2001). More than half of the physical and nonphysical incidents of harassment occurred in the classrooms, and 71 percent of the

physical harassment (64 percent nonphysical) occurred in the hallways. This may very well explain why some youth expect this behavior as a normal part of the school culture (Shakeshaft et al. 1997).

Why Does Sexual Harassment Occur among Youth?

To a large degree, sexual harassment is an issue of power and far less an issue of sex. The person who is being harassed is generally less powerful than the person who is being harassed, and the harasser apparently appreciates the sense of dominance associated with harassing another. Schwartz (2001) believes that harassment continues among youth because society ultimately fosters the idea that males can communicate with females in an inappropriate fashion. Family dynamics and media images can model the attitude that emotionally overpowering a girl is socially acceptable. In most recent years, the advertising and entertainment media has portrayed females as objects of the dominant, macho male, and this reinforces certain behavior among youth. Schwartz also theorizes that girls in the classroom can threaten a boy's sense of dominance, and he may attempt to reassert his superiority through threatening, sexually-based behavior.

What Effect Does Sexual Harassment Have on Youth?

The impact of sexual harassment can score deeply into a youth's emotional, social, and physical well-being. Youth can experience a host of destructive problems as a direct result of being sexually harassed. Youth can feel "sad and worthless" to "powerless" (Shakeshaft et al. 1997, 24). The following real-life comments capture how harassment affects some youth:

- "It made me feel cheap. . . ."
- " . . . made me feel really bad."
- "It was like fighting an invisible, invincible enemy alone. I didn't have a clue as to what to do to stop it. . . ."
- "I felt really alone and stupid."
- " . . . I still felt it was my fault and I still do a little bit."
- "I feel very terrible."
- "I also felt embarrassed and mad. . . ."
- "I grew angry, sad, and I had wanted to get back at him. . . ."
- "Being harassed makes me angry and I feel degraded." (Stein 2001, 3–6).

Many youth feel humiliated, vulnerable, hopeless, isolated,

angry, frustrated, depressed, and anxious. They miss school, cut classes, suffer academically, and become introverted, embarrassed, and self-conscious (American Association of University Women 1993). Youth may attempt to thwart their harasser's behavior by "ignoring it, rationalizing it, fighting it, changing behavior, or becoming part of a group" (Shakeshaft et al. 1997, 24). Regardless of their adopted strategy, the harassment will leave youth emotionally, socially, or physically wounded.

Sex Education and Sexual Harassment

Youth must learn to resist sexual harassment. If school communities do not embrace the challenge to teach resistance, many youth will develop into adults believing that sexual harassment is socially permissible and acceptable. As unfortunate as it already is, some youth grow up to believe that they have to overpower and disrespect certain people and assert their dominance through degradation. Many of them learn this behavior at school and/or from role models. Stein (2001) calls schools "the training grounds for domestic violence." To this effect, many youth, girls in particular, are often violated by sexual harassment and expect school authorities, or adults in general, to understand their plight or at the very least validate their experience. When school officials trivialize the situations, as they seemingly do (Stein 2001), or do nothing to stop the harassment from occurring, girls begin to feel much "like battered women who are not believed or helped by the authorities and who feel very alone and abandoned." Furthermore, what effect does this acquiescence have on the harassers and observers? Their beliefs are reinforced and/or they learn that sexual harassment is appropriate, or at the very least, tolerated. Imagine, the shock for youth like LaShonda Davis and Jamie Nabozny who believed that security, comfort, and support was available from school officials only to realize that their complaints were trivialized and dismissed. The harassers, targets, and observers learn a potent lesson—it is permissible to degrade, disrespect, and insult.

Sex education is an avenue for youth to learn to respect one another. School communities should collaborate to ensure that a school climate is free of sexual harassment. In most recent years, schools have made significant strides to educate students about sexual harassment. The American Association of University Women's (1993) study, for instance, found that 26 percent of students reported their school had a sexual harassment policy. Eight years later, their study found that the number had increased to 69 percent. These kinds of gains are noteworthy; however, instituted policies have had minimal impact on curbing the conduct of some youth (CNN.com 2001).

Approaching sexual harassment through sex education involves the establishment of a secure school climate by raising the school's awareness about sexual harassment, defining appropriate student behavior, and monitoring student behavior (Shakeshaft et al. 1997). This deed can only be accomplished by members who are deeply committed to maintaining an institution free of sexual harassment. Although schools are responsible for implementing a sexual harassment policy, a written policy without spirit is hardly beneficial to anyone. In order for the rate of sexual harassment to decrease, youth must be made aware of the policy, believe in it, and know that their role models and peers act in accord with it. Sexual harassment should never be trivialized, and youth need to fully understand the short- and long-term implications of harassment. Shakeshaft et al. believe that youth can learn about the implications of sexual harassment through projects and assignments that teach appropriate and acceptable behavior. To complement this effort, schools can teach from a nonsexist curriculum and address sexual harassment in various academic areas. All youth should educate one another about their views of harassment. As with all teaching, sex education material should be meaningful, relevant, and age- and grade-appropriate (Schwartz 2001).

Schools should not only identify the behaviors considered inappropriate and intolerable; they should teach youth the behaviors that are appropriate and expected. One researcher found that sexual harassment thrives in climates where women are devalued (Howard 1991). The same holds true for youth. When a school climate fails to value students' worth, sexual harassment will run rampant. Through sex education, students can learn that they are valuable and contribute value to the learning community. They can collaborate to inform the learning community to respect one another's boundaries and define questionable, uncomfortable, and unwanted behavior. Youth can then hear each other depict the behavior that is considered hurtful and harmful and learn to substitute that behavior with one of respect and support. As such, youth will learn to distinguish sexual harassment from banter, innocent flattery, or flirting (Steineger 1997 cited in Schwartz 2001). Essentially, youth become sensitive to one another's views and learn to foster respect and tolerance for diversity (U.S. Department of Education 1999).

Teachers can use sex education to build students' self-esteem and teach them certain skills to contend with sexual harassment (Schwartz 2001). Strengthening the self-worth of youth makes them more confident and less likely targets of sexual harassment. Seemingly, confident youth who encounter sexual harassment are more likely to find fault in the harasser and take action to defend themselves or report the incident. Moreover, a youth who has a healthy sense of self-worth is unlikely to find pleasure in degrading the self-worth of another. Through sex education, youth can also learn the skills to best interact with one another. Girls can learn how to communicate assertively, and boys can learn to honor girls' boundaries and respect them for the contributions they make to a community. Youth can begin to better understand one another when they discuss aspects of sexual harassment such as sex roles, stereotypes, and sexual discrimination. The discussions can be made more effective through resources provided by local and national organizations that serve victims of sexual violence (Schwartz 2001).

The learning community should ensure that everyone lives up to expectations in terms of countering harassment. School personnel should learn about sexual harassment and how to model nonsexist behavior in and outside of the learning community (U.S. Department of Education 1999). This type of professional development can train teachers to detect sexual harassment, how to handle a situation as equitably as possible (support the victim, consult the harasser, report the incident, address observers) (Schwartz 2001). The U.S. Department of Education (1999) recommends that school officials survey their students to determine if sexual harassment occurs in their schools. Students, teachers, and administrators should attend to any complaints and remedy problematic situations immediately. All members of the learning community need to know that their secure learning climate is cultivated when serious consequences befall anyone who models disrespectful behavior. When harassment has occurred, everyone who was involved (victim, harasser, witnesses) should be able to provide their account of the situation and how the situation has affected them (Schwartz 2001). Counseling or guidance should be available for anyone who requests such services. The disciplinary action should fit the situation—neither too severe nor too mild—and include provisions that the harasser(s) receive some antiharassment remediation.

Commercial sex education programs have done a relatively poor job at addressing sexual harassment. The Beyer and Ogletree (1998) study of twenty-one sex education curricula investigated such topics as date rape, exploitation, incest, and so forth and also included sexual harassment. Although three of the curricula ranked high on six topics of sexual coercion, none devoted a single paragraph to sexual harassment. This led the researchers to conclude, "Even if schools have a written sexual harassment policy, it is important to explore the concept of sexual harassment and clarify what it is, how to prevent it, and how to deal with it if it occurs" (374). Moore and Reinzo (1998) sought to determine the degree of compliance among Florida schools with the Florida Department of Education's (DOE) sexual harassment guidelines. In 1992, the DOE had developed guidelines and sample policies that encouraged schools to institute a clear policy condemning sexual harassment, a process that encourages youth to report sexual harassment, programs to ensure awareness, and a process for handling all cases. Of sixty-seven school districts and the Florida School for the Blind, fifty had a policy in effect, and the remaining few were developing or considering a policy. The results of the study found that most of the districts developed policies similar in scope to the policy provided by the DOE. Basically, the districts had used the provided policy as a template. Although the policies included important elements such as a philosophy statement, definition, specific behaviors, and sanctions for harassers, many of them fell short of other critical elements such as an appeal process, available services, and student school rights and responsibilities. Many mentioned they promoted their policies in their schools through the student code of conduct, flyer distribution, and general discussions. Overall, however, the awareness promotion and attempts to include sexual harassment in the curricula was minimal.

Several years have elapsed since both of those studies, and more sexual harassment material is commercially available for the benefit of youth and their learning communities. The SIECUS (2001) bibliography finds twenty-six curricula specifically designed for sexual harassment. Many of them have been developed as recently as 1998. Judging from the following titles, districts should take notice:

- *Sexual Harassment, Work, and Education: A Resource Manual for Prevention,* Paludi and Barickman, 1998
- *Classrooms and Courtrooms: Facing Sexual Harassment in K–12 Schools,* Stein, 1999
- *Confronting Sexual Harassment: What Schools and Colleges Can Do,* Brandenburg, 1997
- *Protecting Students from Harassment and Hate Crime: A Guide for Schools,* U.S. Department of Education, 1997
- *Sexual Harassment: It's Not Academic,* U.S. Department of Education, 1997
- *Sexual Harassment: "This Doesn't Feel Right!"* Havelin, 2000

Most of these feature definitions of sexual harassment; identification, prevention, protection, and intervention techniques; meaningful and relevant scenarios; policy guidance; and a host of references and resources. Take, for example, *Flirting or Hurting? Sexual Harassment in Schools* (Stein 2001). In this program, youth in sixth through ninth grade can watch and respond to a series of dramatized scenarios to learn of sexual harassment. Not only do students learn about their rights and facts associated with sexual harassment, they are able to interact with one another throughout the program to explain how they perceive (flirtatious or hurtful) behavior. After a scenario, youth answer "Agree" or "Disagree" and a series of related questions. The learning experience is ultimately in their responses. They teach each other why certain behavior is unacceptable and how they should treat one another. These interactive sessions are the impetus for youth to change their behavior. That change leads to a safer learning environment.

SUMMARY

Sexual violence among youth is pervasive. Ignoring, trivializing, or dismissing the fact that many youth encounter some form of sexual violence does not make the problem disappear. Two real-life events were described at the beginning of the chapter; another will end it.

In 1998, a thirteen-year-old female student from a reputable Boston school was sexually assaulted on her way home from school. In broad daylight, on a subway train, four male classmates cornered her and tied the cords of her backpack to a pole. They taunted her with sexual comments, fondled her breasts and buttocks, and tried to tear off her top. As much as she could, she fought back by kicking and screaming. Of the ten or so student witnesses, only one came to her aid, but he could do little to protect her. All four boys were arrested and arraigned on indecent assault and battery charges. The boys' ringleader had previously harassed the girl.

Much of the attention from this event focused on the fact that the City of Boston failed to provide appropriate security and questioned why others wouldn't come to the girl's defense. The greater issue, however, is one of respect and the lack thereof. The boys seemingly had not learned that certain behaviors are unwelcomed, unwanted, and offensive or how to respect the boundaries of others. Considering the fact that sexual violence is a widespread problem, the best that schools can do is provide youth with a sex education that nurtures their self-esteem and teaches them the skills to respect and interact with one another. The worst they can do is continue to turn their backs on the youth who need them most.

REFERENCES

Abney, V. D., and R. Priest. 1995. "African Americans and Sexual Abuse." In *Sexual Abuse in Nine North American Cultures*, ed. L. Fontes. Thousand Oaks, CA: Sage.

American Academy of Child and Adolescent Psychiatry. 2000. *Your Adolescent.* New York: Harper Collins Publishers.

American Association of University Women. 1993. *Hostile Hallways: The AAUW Survey on Sexual Harassment in America's Schools. Bullying, Teasing, and Sexual Harassment in School.* Washington, DC: AAUW.

———. 2001. *Hostile Hallways: Bullying, Teasing, and Sexual Harassment in School.* Washington, DC: AAUW.

Besharov, D. J. 1990. *Recognizing Child Abuse: A Guide for the Concerned.* New York: The Free Press.

Beyer, Christine E., and Roberta J. Ogletree. 1998. "Sexual Coercion Content in 21 Sexuality Education Curricula." *Journal of School Health* 68(9): 370–375.

Boy Scouts of America. 1990. *Boy Scouts Handbook, Tenth Edition.* Irving, TX: Boy Scouts of America.

Brandenberg, Judith B. 1997. *Confronting Sexual Harassment: What Schools and Colleges Can Do.* New York: Teachers College Press.

CNN.com, "Report Finds Sexual Harassment Common at School" *http://www.cnn.com/2001/fyi/teachers.ednews/06/06/school.harassment/index.html* (cited July 12, 2001).

Crisci, George S. 1999. "When No Means No: Recognizing and Preventing Sexual Harassment in Your Schools." *American School Board Journal* 186(6): 25–29.

DeWilde, E. J., I. C. Kleinhorst, R. F. Diekstra, W. H. Wolters. 1992. "The Relationship between Adolescent Suicide Behavior and Life Events in Childhood and Adolescence." *American Journal of Psychology* 149(1): 45–51.

Everstine, Diana S., and Louis Everstine. 1989. *Sexual Trauma in Children and Adolescents: Dynamics and Treatment.* Levittown, PA: Brunner/Mazel.

Finkelhor, David. 1980. *Sexually Victimized Children.* New York: The Free Press.

Finkelhor, David, and Jennifer Dziuba-Leatherman. 1994. "Victimization of Children." *American Psychologist* 49(3): 173–183.

Gidycz, C. A., and M. P. Koss. 1989. "The Impact of Adolescent Sexual Victimization: Standardized Measures of Anxiety, Depression, and Behavioral Deviancy." *Violence and Victims* 4(2): 139–149.

Graves, Patricia A., and Suzanne M. Sgroi. 1982. "Law Enforcement and Child Sexual Abuse." In *Handbook of Clinical Intervention in Child Sexual Abuse*, ed. S. Sgroi. New York: The Free Press.

Haugaard, Jeffrey J. 2000. "The Challenge of Defining Child Sexual Abuse." *American Psychologist* 55(9): 1036–1039.

Herman, Judith L. 2000. *Father-Daughter Incest.* Cambridge: Harvard University Press.

Howard, Sharon. 1991. "Organizational Resources for Addressing Sexual Harassment." *Journal of Counseling and Development* 69(6): 507–511.

Hughes, William. 1999. "School Liability for Student Sexual Harassment." *American Secondary Education* 28(2): 23–26.

Hunter, Mic. 1990. *Abused Boys: The Neglected Victims of Sexual Abuse.* New York: Fawcett Columbine.

Hyde, Margaret O., and Elizabeth H. Forsyth. 1997. *The Sexual Abuse of Children and Adolescents.* Brookfield, CT: The Millbrook Press, Inc.

Jensen, Rita A., and Therese J. Kiley. (1999). *Teaching, Leading, and Learning: Becoming Caring Professionals.* Boston: Houghton Mifflin Company.

Kendall-Tackett, K. A., L. M. Williams, and David Finkelhor. 1993. "Impact of Sexual Abuse on Children: A Review and Synthesis of Recent Empirical Studies." *Psychological Bulletin* 113: 164–180.

Kenney, Janet W., Cindy Reinholtz, and Patti J. Angelini. 1997. "Ethnic Differences in Childhood and Adolescent Sexual Abuse and Teenage Pregnancy." *Journal of Adolescent Health* 21(1): 3–10.

Kenny, Maureen C., and Adriana G. McEachern. 2000. "Racial, Ethnic, and Cultural Factors of Childhood Sexual Abuse: A Selected Review of the Literature." *Clinical Psychology Review* 20(7): 905–922.

Lanning, Beth, Danny J. Ballard, and James Robinson. 1999. "Child Sexual Abuse Prevention Programs in Texas Public Elementary Schools." *Journal of School Health* 69(1): 3–8.

Mach, Kathleen F. 1994. *The Sexually Abused Child: A Parents' Guide to Coping and Understanding.* Williamsburg, MI: Family Insights Books.

Mann, Richard L., and William Hughes. 1998. "Sexual Harassment: The Supreme Court Speaks." *American Secondary Education* 27(2): 28–31.

McLeer, S. V., E. Deblinger, D. Henry, H. Orvashel. 1992. "Sexually Abused Children at High Risk for PTSD." *Journal of the American Academy of Child and Adolescent Psychiatry* 31: 875–879.

Moore, Michele J., and Barbara Reinzo. 1998. "Sexual Harassment Policies in Florida School Districts." *Journal of School Health* 68(6): 237–242.

National Center for Juvenile Justice. 2000. *Sexual Assault of Young Children as Reported to Law Enforcement: Victim, Incident, and Offender Characteristics (NCJ 182990).* Washington, DC: National Center for Juvenile Justice.

National Center for Prosecution of Child Abuse. 1999. *Child Abuse and Neglect: State Statutes Elements (Number 35: Sexual Offenses).* Alexandria, VA: National Center for Prosecution of Child Abuse.

National Center on Child Abuse and Neglect. 1996. *Child Maltreatment 1994: Reports from the States to the National Center on Child Abuse and Neglect.* Washington, DC: National Center on Child Abuse and Neglect.

National Clearinghouse on Child Abuse and Neglect Information. 1999. *Child Abuse and Neglect: State Statutes Elements (Reporting Procedures).* Washington, DC: National Clearinghouse on Child Abuse and Neglect Information.

———. 2000. *Child Abuse and Neglect: State Statutes Elements (Mandatory Reporters of Child Abuse and Neglect).* Washington, DC: National Clearinghouse on Child Abuse and Neglect Information.

Paludi, Michele A., and Richard B. Barickman. 1998. *Sexual Harassment, Work, and Education: A Resource Manual for Prevention,* 2d ed. Ithaca, NY: Cornell University Press Services.

Righthand, S., and C. Welch. 2001. *Juveniles Who Have Sexually Offended: A Review of the Professional Literature (NCJ 184739).* Washington, DC: U.S. Department of Justice.

Saywitz, Karen J., Anthony P. Mannarino, Lucy Berliner, Judith A. Cohen. 2000. "Treatment for Sexually Abused Children and Adolescents." *American Psychologist* 55(9): 1040–1049.

Schwartz, Wendy. 2001. "Students Sexually Harassing Students." *Choice Briefs* 8: 1–9.

Sexuality Information and Education Council of the United States (SIECUS). 2001. *Sexuality Education Curricula.* New York: SIECUS.

Sgroi, Suzanne M., Linda C. Blick, and Frances S. Porter. 1982. "A Conceptual Framework for Child Sexual Abuse." In *Handbook of Clinical Intervention in Child Sexual Abuse,* ed. S. M. Sgroi. New York: The Free Press.

Shakeshaft, Charol, et al. 1997. "Boys Call Me Cow." *Educational Leadership* 55(2): 22–25.

Shaw, J. A. 1999. "Practice Parameters for the Assessment and Treatment of Children and Adolescents Who Are Sexually Abusive of Others." *Journal of the American Academy of Child and Adolescent Psychiatry* 38(12): 55–76.

Stein, Nan. 1999. *Classrooms and Courtrooms: Facing Sexual Harassment in K–12 Schools.* New York: Teachers College Press.

———. 2001. *Violence in Schools: Gender and Sexual Harassment; Schools as the Training Grounds for Domestic Violence.* Wellesley, MA: Wellesley College Center for Research on Women.

Stein, Nan, N. Marshall, and L. Troop. 1993. *Secrets in Public: Sexual Harassment in Our Schools: A Report on the Result of a* Seventeen *Magazine Survey.* Wellesley, MA: Wellesley College Center for Research on Women.

Steineger, M. 1997. Preventing and Countering School-Based Harassment: A Resource Guide for K–12 Educators. Portland: Northwest Regional Educational Laboratory.

Target, M., P. Fonagy. 1996. "The Psychological Treatment of Child and Adolescent Psychiatric Disorders." In *What Works for Whom? A Critical Review of Psychotherapy Research,* ed. A. Roth and P. Fonagy. New York: Guilford Press.

Teen Voices On-Line Magazine, "Know Your Rights: Student-on-Student Sexual Harassment," *http://teenvoices.com/issue9_2/fl.htm* (cited November 11, 1999).

Telljohann, Susan K., Sherry A. Everett, and James H. Price. 1997. "Evaluation of a Third Grade Sexual Abuse Curriculum." *Journal of School Health* 67(4): 149–153.

University of Michigan. 1996. *Abolishing Harassment.* Ann Arbor, MI: University of Michigan.

U.S. Department of Education. 1999. *Protecting Students from Harassment and Hate Crimes: A Guide for Schools.* Washington, DC: U.S. Department of Education.

———. 2001a. *Sexual Discrimination: Overview of the Law.* Washington, DC: U.S. Department of Education.

———. 2001b. *Sexual Harassment Guidance: Harassment of Students by School Employees, Other Students, or Third Parties.* Washington, DC: U.S. Department of Education.

U.S. Department of Health and Human Services. 1999. *Child Maltreatment 1999.* Washington, DC: U.S. Department of Health and Human Services.

U.S. Department of Justice. 1985. *When the Victim Is a Child: Issues for Judges and Prosecutors.* Washington, DC: National Institute for Justice, U.S. Department of Justice.

U.S. Department of Justice. 1996. *Child Victimizers: Violent Offenders and Their Victims (NCJ 158625).* Washington, DC: U.S. Department of Justice.

U.S. Department of Justice. 1999. *Juvenile Offenders and Victims: 1999 National Report.* Washington, DC: U.S. Department of Justice.

Walters, D. 1975. *Physical and Sexual Abuse of Children: Causes and Treatment.* Bloomington: Indiana University Press.

Weinrott, M. R. 1996. *Juvenile Sexual Aggression: A Critical Review.* Boulder, CO: Center for the Study and Prevention of Violence.

Zeanah, Paula D., and Martha L. Hamilton. 1998. "Staff Perceptions of Sexuality-Related Problems and Behaviors of Psychiatrically Hospitalized Children and Adolescents." *Child Psychiatry and Human Development* 29(1): 49–64.

Zigman, Mary. 1999. "Under the Law: Teen Prostitution in Kensington." *Critique of Anthology* 19(2): 193–201.

Chapter Five

❖ Sexual Orientation: Gay, Lesbian, Bisexual, and Transgender Youth

For a great part of our history, homosexuality has been perceived as nonexistent and has been kept hidden from society. For most of the twentieth century, whenever homosexuality was investigated or discussed, it was qualified in the pejorative with homosexuals considered sick, abnormal, unnatural, perverted, and an abomination to society. It was not until 1972, for instance, that the American Psychiatric Association stopped categorizing homosexuality a psychiatric illness. Significant events in the last thirty or so years have brought homosexuality out of the social closet. The Stonewall Riots of 1969, the advent of AIDS, a more accepting entertainment industry, recent debates over whether homosexuals can become heterosexual, the homosexual gene, homosexuals in the military, and the Boy Scouts' ban of homosexuals are a few of the events that have made homosexuality a prominent current issue.

Through events such as these, many believe that society is becoming more tolerant and accepting of homosexuality than ever before (Adams 2001). A recent *Journal of Sex Research* study found that men and women are having more homosexual sex than ever before, and some researchers believe that this is happening because the nation is more tolerant of diverse sexual values (Butler 2001 cited in Adams). Because of this, some believe that more youth are coming to terms with their homosexuality and choosing to come out to their peers at school. Some of these youth may feel more comfortable with their homosexuality considering that a federal law protects them from harassment and requires that their schools ensure them a safe learning environment. Some districts, such as one in Honolulu, Hawaii, have further enacted policies that offer specific protection for homosexual youth. These kinds of policies have made it possible for some youth to create and maintain school clubs that celebrate their diversity. The Gay, Lesbian, Straight Education Network estimates that since 1989, over 800 gay-straight alliances have been formed in public and private schools throughout the nation (GLSEN 2001b). The alliances are student-based, curricular clubs whose mission is to eliminate sexual orientation discrimination and homophobia.

Some youth are not fortunate enough to live in a community that tolerates, let alone celebrates, homosexuality, and some youth have to remain silent about their homosexuality. Some take serious abuse. Take the following examples:

Adam Colton attended San Marin High School outside of San Francisco. The seventeen-year-old had come out of the closet in September 1999 and founded the Gay-Straight Alliance club. Shortly thereafter, Adam was victim to senseless abuse. He was attacked by some youth outside of a store, some youth wrote warnings on his car and his driveway, and he was victim to countless taunts, threats, and rumors. One particular day, while on school grounds, Adam was so severely attacked that he required hospitalization. He was beaten and the word *FAG* was cut into his stomach and arm. Adam had informed the school's principal of the harassment and attacks, but the principal did little to curb the violence.

On June 18, 2001, in Cortez, New Mexico, Pauline Mitchell reported her sixteen-year-old son, Fred C. Martinez, missing. On June 23, her son's bludgeoned body was found near a canyon. Fred died of a blunt instrument trauma to the head. Some consider the murder a hate crime because the murderer, eighteen-year-old Shaun Murphy, had bragged to his friends that he had "beat up a fag." Fred was openly gay and considered transgender since he was known to carry a purse and wear make-up at school. Because of his sexual orientation and gender identity, Fred endured continued harassment at one high school and transferred to another to find similar problems. Although school officials stated they did what they could to help Fred, his mother believes that they did little to ensure him a safe learning environment. His mother stated, "Violence was a common part of his life, and as I learn more, I know that this was a crime based on anger and hate" (GLSEN 2001a, website).

As one high school club coordinator stated, "Every week a new kid comes to our group talking about being beat up, spit on, harassed, not only by other students but by the administration" (Keesing 2000). Although the nation may be more tolerant of homosexuality, many homosexual youth still find themselves in violent environments. An April 12, 2001, report finds an 8 percent increase in antigay hate crimes from 1999 to 2000 (National Coalition of Anti-Violence Programs cited in the Advocate Report 2001). The Gay, Lesbian, Straight Education Network found that students hear antigay comments twenty-six times a day and teachers do nothing 97 percent of the time (cited in McIntosh 2001). Some school officials even model the antigay behavior. Gay and lesbian youth have countless stories that indicate that school officials do little to eliminate the violence or offer them protection. One gay youth, George Loomis, had his Spanish teacher comment, "Only two kinds of men wear earrings, pirates and faggots, and there isn't any water" (McIntosh 2001).

All youth need to be respected. U.S. Surgeon General David Satcher summed it up best when he announced that schools, parents, and communities must teach youth to approach sexual orientation with a mature and thoughtful attitude. Satcher recognized that harassment can leave gay and lesbian youth with mental anguish and that sexual orientation cannot be changed (cnn.com 2001). More importantly, he stated, "We have a responsibility to be more supportive and proactive than judgmental" (cnn.com 2001). This chapter will discuss issues as they relate to youth who are gay, lesbian, bisexual, or transgender. The issues are divided into the following: Terms that Describe the Population at Hand; Historical Perspective on Homosexuality; Legal Issues; Demography: Who Are Gay, Lesbian, Bisexual, and Transgender Youth? What Do They Endure? Schools for Gay, Lesbian, Bisexual, or Transgender Youth; Sex Education and Sexual Education Orientation; and Summary.

TERMS THAT DESCRIBE THE POPULATION AT HAND

Various rubrics are used, sometimes interchangeably, to discuss non-heterosexual persons. For the record, the following terms will be used throughout the chapter when addressing youth who have a sexual predisposition that differs from that of heterosexuals. The following terms are associated with sexual behavior or sexual identity:

Homosexual

The term describes those who have romantic or sexual desires for persons of the same sex, or those that engage in consensual sex with members of the same sex. German journalist Karl Maria Kertbeny initiated the term in 1868 when he wrote a letter indicating his opposition to an antisodomy law in Eastern Europe. He used the term *homosexualitat*, sexual desires between members of the same sex, in contrast to sex of the norm, or *normalsexualitat* (Fone 2000).

Gay

In the most general use of the term, gay is considered a descriptive of homosexuality (Hirsh, Kett, and Trefil 1993) that represents the social lifestyle of homosexuals or the modern homosexual community. At times, *gay* includes homosexual men and women, and other times the term is used exclusively to identify homosexual men. The publication manual of the American Psychological Association (1995) suggests that the term *gay* precede a gender to specify groups of people (for example, *gay men, gay women*).

Lesbian

The term denotes homosexual women. *Lesbian* is derived from the birthplace of Sappho, an ancient Greek poet. Sappho was homosexual and from the island of Lesbos.

Bisexual

This term describes those who have sexual attraction, romantic desires, or coitus with both genders.

Transgender

This describes persons who are "biologically normal persons whose core gender identity is the opposite of the anatomic sex" (Westheimer 2000, 268). These individuals may feel more comfortable being the opposite sex and to this end will cross dress and/or seek to become the opposite sex. Such persons may have no deep attachment to their physical body and often describe themselves as trapped within the wrong gender.

Queer

In the 1920s and 1930s the term was used by homosexual men to distinguish themselves from other derogatory labels such as pansies, fairies, and so forth (Fone 2000). The term eventually became unpopular among homosexuals, and mainstream society used the word to offend and disparage homosexuals. In the last fifteen years, the term has again become more acceptable to describe persons who are gay, lesbian, bisexual, or transgender.

Sexual Orientation

The term describes the sexual value, identity, or behavior of an individual as an inborn, innate, and unchangeable feature. The term is often preferred over the term sexual preference (American Psychological Association 1995).

Sexual Preference

The term denotes that an individual has a choice in the matter when it comes to his/her sexual value, identity, or behavior.

As the historical perspective will find, these persons have endured a longtime social stigma and have been ridiculed with such monikers as *faggot* or *dyke*. They now deserve to be regarded with respect, and proper terminology should be used to identify them.

HISTORICAL PERSPECTIVE ON HOMOSEXUALITY

Homosexuals have not had an easy time in society. Historically, they have been ostracized, discriminated against, threatened, intimidated, tormented, harassed, arrested, imprisoned, beaten, raped, and killed. They have been targets of witch-hunts, and often unfounded, untrue information has been circulated about them. Moreover, many have lost their ties with family members, relatives, and close friends simply because they were not heterosexual. Gay, lesbian, bisexual, and transgender persons have yet to be afforded the rights and privileges that heterosexuals enjoy. Homophobia, fear and/or hatred of homosexuality, still exists in modern society. In his book, *Homophobia*, Fone (2000) writes, "Indeed, in modern Western society, where racism is disapproved, anti-Semitism is condemned, and misogyny has lost its legitimacy, homophobia remains, perhaps the last acceptable prejudice" (3).

A review of the last 100 years finds that homosexuality has largely been considered unhealthy and abnormal. In 1911, a city vice commission mentioned that homosexuals were members of a cult and they engaged in "nauseous and repulsive" practices (Fone 2000). One 1911 sex education manual, *Confident Chats with Boys*, warned, "Never trust yourself in bed with a boy or a man . . . . They (homosexuals) are only waiting to teach boys to help them in self-abuse or something far nastier" (cited in Fone, 372). Society in the early 1900s came to believe that homosexuals were degenerates who should be eliminated (Robinson 1914, cited in Fone) and often weak, powerless, and a menace to society (Abrams 1918, cited in Fone). In a 1921 manual, *A Textbook of Sex Education*, Gallichan discussed homosexuality in a chapter entitled *The Psychopathology of Sex*. Homosexuality was considered as perverse as exhibitionism and sadism, and homosexuals were considered as wicked as those with tendencies to visit houses of "ill fame." Although homosexuals are described as beings who are responsible for their fate, Gallichan reported that homosexuality was a common phase for youth. He called this period a temporary aberration in that youth rarely develop into homosexuals (Gallichan 1921). In 1926, Joseph Collins published *The Doctor Looks at Love and Life*. The popular text suggested that people were born homosexuals and that 3 out of 100 men were homosexual (Melody and Peterson 1999). Collins admitted that he knew well-adjusted and balanced homosexuals. These acquaintances must have been influential because he believed that homosexuals should be pitied and treated as social misfits. He ultimately believed that medical science would eventually be able to tailor the nervous system and eliminate the deviants known as homosexuals.

Sex in Childhood by Groves and Groves (1933) discussed homosexuality in the chapter devoted to *Psychic and Social Abnormality*. Homosexuality was perceived as the most severe sexual abnormality. They wrote, "Born a male, he has the characteristics and desires of a female; born a female, she exhibits thoroughly masculine sex impulses. Happiness under such circumstances is not to be had" (222). The authors believed that homosexuality was caused by masturbation. The logic behind their assertion was that youth who habitually masturbate developed a deep self-love and ultimately projected this onto members of their own sex. Thus, they advised that youth should be discouraged from masturbating. That same year, La Forest Potter published *Strange Loves: A Study in Sexual Abnormalities*. He warned, "Do you know that their number is constantly increasing? The strange power they wield over normal people is almost unbelievable" (Fone 2000). Potter believed that parents should make strides to ensure that their youth do not become homosexual. He warned that if parents observe their children acting peculiarly—boys effeminately and girls in a masculine way—they should take their children for "gland stimuli" or "endocrine treatment." He also outlined signs to look for to spot homosexuals—men tended to have girlish features with a soft, delicate, white (powder-free) skin, and a "gracefully round" physique. Homosexual women, on the other hand, were mannish, skilled at seduction, and often demonstrated "deep voices and facial hair" (Fone 2000). Potter professed that homosexuals could be cured if they got married but those who could not be cured should be restrained or killed.

Richmond (1934), in *An Introduction to Sex Education*, declared that homosexuality was wrong in and of itself, and that to complicate matters, homosexuals liked to seduce young boys and girls into their sexual practices and then continue to have their way with them. He described them as people who " . . . are notoriously fickle, and go from one affair to another, so that one person may corrupt a dozen youth. . . . The homosexual personality has an affinity for drugs and alcohol, probably as a means of escape from the consciousness of social stigma, and not infrequently we find the homosexual plying a trade in drugs, so that he is the center of a vicious circle in very truth of homosexuals and drug addicts, with all the attendant degradation and crime" (288). In a 1943 sex education manual entitled, *When Children Ask about Sex,* the Child Study Association of America addressed whether parents should inform their children of the "ugly, sordid" side of sex in which homosexuality was included. They wrote, "It is much better to admit frankly that such things (as homosexuality) happen and discuss with young people why there are these evils" (13). In *Basic Issues in School Sex Education,* Hoyman (1953) also believed that youth go through temporary stages of homosexuality. He encouraged teachers to discuss homosexuality with youth, but not to the point of creating "morbid curiosity." Teachers were to be frank with students and should explain that some people develop into sexual perverts known as homosexuals. He recommended, "The students are (to be) further informed that some sexual deviates (such as homosexuals) are of the criminal type and are exceedingly dangerous to small children, teen-agers and even to adults" (17).

In 1948, Alfred C. Kinsey published *Sexual Behavior in the Human Male.* The text, which became known as the Kinsey Report, outlined a series of studies on homosexual men and essentially concluded that society's perceptions of homosexuals were stereotypes. Kinsey found that among American males, 50 percent had experienced some arousal by other men, nearly one-third had had a homosexual encounter that resulted in an orgasm, 4 percent were bona fide homosexuals, and one out of eight males had been homosexual for a three-year period. Kinsey wrote:

> Persons with homosexual histories are to be found in every age group, in every social level, in every conceivable occupation, in cities and on farms, and in the most remote areas of the country. . . . In large city communities . . . an experienced observer may identify hundreds of persons in a day whose homosexual interests are certain. (cited in D'Emilio and Freedman 1997, 292)

By the middle of the century, a gay culture began to evolve, and society reacted with a vengeance (D'Emilio and Freedman). In the late forties, the House Un-American Activities Committee, largely known for finding and destroying those considered American communists, targeted homosexuals. Homosexuals were perceived by the political control as perverts who were as dangerous as communists. In 1950, most of those fired from the government were homosexuals. In fact, an executive order considered homosexual men and women "moral perverts" and too pathological for employment with the federal government. These alleged sexual perverts were legally prohibited from working for the government. The FBI also kept a close watch on homosexual organizations and their members, and some states required the registration of those convicted of homosexual-related crimes (Melody and Peterson 1999). It was fairly common for police to target particular organizations and pressure them into naming persons considered homosexual. Florida Governor Farris Bryant publicly announced, "This office is doing everything it can to control or wipe out homosexuality" (cited in Melody and Peterson, 119). During this time, police in metropolitan areas habitually arrested homosexual men and women by the hundreds. Even in Boise, Idaho, fourteen hundred people were interrogated and pressured to name homosexuals whom they knew. Newspapers routinely printed the names, addresses, and occupations of those arrested for homosexual conduct (D'Emilio and Freedman). For much of the 1950s and 1960s homosexuals were persecuted, and police frequently raided gay and lesbian bars. Laws were stacked against homosexuals and this made it very difficult for them to function openly in society. Until 1967, for instance, in New York City, the State Liquor Authority mandated that bartenders refuse service to those believed to be nonheterosexual (Clendinen and Nagourney 1999). Indeed, homosexuals were denied nearly all access to political power, and their civil liberties were withheld.

On June 27, 1969, things changed for homosexuals, and thereafter gay, lesbian, bisexual, and transgender people entered public consciousness on a broader scale. When a Manhattan police precinct raided and arrested thirteen patrons of a Greenwich Village gay bar known as the Stonewall Inn, the patrons had had enough of the city's so-called cleaning, and they fought back in what became known as the first gay riot. Some media made light of the situation with headlines that read, "Homo Nest Raided, Queen Bees Are Stinging Mad" and the "Great Faggot Rebellion" (Clendinen and Nagourney 1999), but the *Village Voice* ran a story, albeit with a humorous tone, with a headline that captured the historical event, "Gay Power Comes to Sheridan Square" (Fone 2000). Other media giants such as *Time* and *Newsweek* did not cover the event until October (Lipkin 1999). The riot continued the next day, but only four people were arrested. The maxim "Gay Power" was scrawled throughout Greenwich Village, and a social movement was born. Although two organizations had formed in the fifties to fight for gay and lesbian rights—the gay men's Mattachine Society and its lesbian counterpart, Daughters of Bilitis, the New York City gay and lesbian community united as the Gay Liberation Front (GLF). The GLF declared liberation for all gays and lesbians:

We are a revolutionary homosexual group of men and women formed with the realization that complete sexual liberation for all people cannot come about unless existing social institutions are abolished. We reject society's attempt to impose sexual roles and definitions of our nature. (cited in D'Emilio and Freedman 1997, 321)

The GLF substantiated the phrase "coming out." Initially used among homosexuals to acknowledge one's homosexuality to another, "coming out" became their political tactic. The public declaration became associated with gay and lesbian pride and symbolized the bravery to confront possible censure.

The gay movement grew in the early seventies. The GLF fought and staged riots against such giants as the American Psychiatric Association. David Reuben (1969) had just published *Everything You Always Wanted to Know about Sex but Were Afraid to Ask,* and mainstream society learned, once again, that homosexuals could be fixed with the right psychiatrist. Many commonly believed that homosexuals could be cured, and research continued in electric shock therapy, castration, and lobotomies. However, by 1973, things were beginning to change. Nearly 800 gay and lesbian organizations had formed, and the American Psychiatric Association no longer listed homosexuality as a mental disease. The government no longer barred gay men and lesbians from federal employment. Some states lifted sodomy from the penal codes. Police harassment decreased drastically, and gay men and lesbians were becoming political candidates. With all this, the communities of gays, lesbians, bisexuals, and the transgender began to proliferate. This is not to say that society took this lightly. Anita Bryant, a fundamentalist Christian former beauty queen and spokesperson for Florida orange juice, proclaimed, "They can only recruit children, and this is what they want to do. . . . Some of the stories I could tell you of child recruitment and child abuse by homosexuals would turn your stomach" (cited in D'Emilio and Freedman 1997, 347). In addition, TV minister Jerry Falwell believed, "So-called gay folks just as soon kill you as look at you" (cited in D'Emilio and Freedman, 347).

In the eighties, the community of gays, lesbians, bisexuals, and the transgender suffered a setback. In 1980 a devastating, fatal illness swept through communities of gay men. Called the "gay cancer" and the "gay plague," the disease became known as AIDS. The number of persons taken by AIDS increased at alarming rates: 225 deaths in 1981, 1,400 by 1983, 15,000 by 1985, and 40,000 by 1987 (cited in D'Emilio and Freedman 1997, additional statistics are provided in Chapter Two). AIDS had a definite impact on society. Now, as we know, AIDS no longer is the gay man's disease; the disease has taken the lives of infants, toddlers, youth, adolescents, senior citizens, men, and women, regardless of nationality, ethnic background, or social status. Some believe that AIDS brought the community of gay, lesbian, bisexual, and transgender persons together to combat the disease and help those who acquired it. Lipkin (1999) wrote, "In the face of social condemnation and early governmental and scientific indifference, gay people organized to save themselves. . . . Perhaps never before have lesbians and gay men collaborated so closely with one another as service-providers, fund-raisers, and lobbyists." (97). Others believe that AIDS caused gays and straights alike to think in terms of safe sex. Through media coverage of AIDS, society was forced to acknowledge that a whole vibrant community coexisted with them. Moreover, for the first time in history, youth were learning about AIDS and gays, abstinence, safe sex, and the dangers of unprotected sex. The gay community became increasingly visible in that decade with such historical events as the 1980 Democratic party including gay rights in its platform; Wisconsin becoming the first state in 1982 to uphold gay civil rights; the hundred thousand protesters marching at the 1984 Democratic convention; the 1986 Supreme Court ruling that no Georgian has the constitutional right to gay sex; the 200,000 plus gathering for the 1987 AIDS awareness and quilt display in Washington, D.C. (Lipkin 1999).

Through the nineties, mainstream society was exposed to gay men and lesbians through the media coverage and debate over whether gays could openly serve in the armed forces, gay marriages, the gay gene, and the Boy Scout ban on gay men as leaders. Moreover, gay and lesbian communities were becoming more prominent. In Chicago, for instance, Census 2000 found a 300 percent increase in the number of same sex couples living in the metropolitan area (Guerrero and Sweeney 2001). Society is becoming increasingly used to gay, lesbian, bisexual, and transgender persons. Through mainstream television programming, society is exposed to more and more gay characters and situations. Up until five years ago, only two prime time shows featured a gay theme: *Soap* and *Family*. Prime time TV today is apparently diverse. The October 6, 2000, issue of *Entertainment Weekly* ran a special report entitled "Gay Hollywood 2000" with a story insert that read "Is Your TV Set Gay?" When Ellen DeGeneres's character on her show *Ellen* announced before 36.2 million viewers that she was a lesbian, the closet door was opened. Although DeGeneres suffered the cancellation of her show after that episode, she recovered and started a new series that won a People's Choice best new comedy award in 2002. She also hosted the Emmy awards in 2001. In the 2000 TV season line-up, thirteen gay characters had ongoing roles. Doctors, lawyers, adolescents, students, cartoon characters, parents, and more have all been represented as gay or lesbian. As Svetkey (2000) writes, "gay characters are so common on television, so unexotic, that their sexual orientation has become all but invisible to most viewers" (26).

What does this history have to do with gay and lesbian youth today? In all, youth are exposed to gays and lesbians more than ever before. Prior to the nineties, the struggles of gay, lesbian, bisexual, and transgender youth took a back seat to other causes of gay adults, and youth were often invisible within the gay community (Ryan and Futterman 1998). In fact, the court systems had reviewed almost no cases involving schools, gay youth, and sexual discrimination until the mid 1990s (Buckel 2000). But now, these youth are more aware of gay and lesbian causes. They have begun to realize that there are others like them, and they know they have civil rights and needs that cannot go unmet. As Ryan and Futterman have indicated, "Lesbian and gay youth face the same health and mental health challenges as their heterosexual peers, with the addition of social and health challenges associated with having a stigmatized identity" (xi). School officials and teachers are obligated to meet their needs, nurture their development, and help them become well-rounded, healthy, and stable adults.

Legal Issues

Gay, lesbian, bisexual, and transgender youth are here to stay, and some believe that these groups of youth will only become larger and far more noticeable given the fact that schools are legally obligated to protect them from harassment, torment, or assault. The growth is apparent according to the Gay, Lesbian, and Straight Education Network. In 1998, 99 groups of Gay-Straight Alliances existed. A year later the number increased to 600. Currently, more than 800 Gay-Straight Alliances exist nationwide (Jones 1999). Regardless of how a school or community may feel about addressing sexual orientation in the classrooms, ignoring this population of students is no longer an option. In fact, school districts are beginning to see an increase in the number of lawsuits related to sexual discrimination against gay, lesbian, bisexual, and transgender youth (Jones).

Title IX strictly prohibits this type of discrimination. As mentioned in chapter 4, Title IX of the Education Amendments of 1972 (P.L. 92–318) prohibits schools from discriminating against youth based on their gender. The premise of the law is simple—treat all youth equally, regardless of their gender. Thus, boys and girls should have equal access to academics, extracurricular activities, athletics, and so forth in order for schools to continue to receive federal funds. A distinct feature of the law, however, is that all youth are protected from sexual harassment of any kind. Although Title IX does not legally prohibit sexual-orientation discrimination, the law is applied to cases where youth may have been targets of unwanted sexual conduct or victims of a sexually hostile environment. Simple name calling such as "a bunch of fags and dykes" demoralizes a school's spirit, but it is not grounds for a Title IX lawsuit (unless it is recurring and the school fails to take action). When a teacher tells a gay youth, "All of your troubles would come to an end if you would just hang your sissy act in the closet, join a sports team, and act more like a man," it is sexual discrimination according to Title IX. (Such comments are also a violation of the First Amendment).

Title IX is not the only legal avenue available for youth to challenge harassment or discrimination. Buckel (2000) has outlined four laws often used in the court system when these youth have experienced sexual harassment or violence in school.

Equal Protection Clause of the U.S. Constitution

This clause mandates that schools cannot arbitrarily or intentionally choose to provide a safe environment for one group of youth and not another. All youth, gay or straight, are entitled to function in a safe environment. The American Counseling Association (1999) clarified, "public officials may not impose discriminatory burdens or unequal treatment on gays and lesbians because of the public's animosity towards them" (8). Youth have been denied equal treatment, for instance, when school officials fail to protect gay boys because they believe that boys can fend for themselves.

State and Local Civil Rights Protections

Some states, cities, and counties impose civil or human rights laws that make sexual orientation discrimination illegal. Attorneys may hold schools accountable to these laws if they fall within their jurisdiction. As of May 2000, eleven states prohibited sexual orientation discrimination: California, Connecticut, Hawaii, Massachusetts, Minnesota, Nevada, New Hampshire, New Jersey, Rhode Island, Vermont, and Wisconsin.

State Tort Law

Tort law is applied when personal injury has occurred. If a school principal trivializes and ignores a lesbian youth's plea for help, for instance, and the youth encounters harassment or violence at school, this law can be used against the school if the youth was harmed by the principal's negligence.

Criminal Law

Regardless of the state, a youth is subject to legal action when he or she assaults another. If a child has been assaulted, his or her parents can take action into their own hands and notify police, file a complaint, and have the assailant prosecuted.

Attorneys for Lambda Legal Defense and Education Fund (2001) have alluded to the fact that a number of gay, lesbian, bisexual, and transgender youth are treated unjustly simply because of their sexual orientation. As such, some attorneys believe that schools should be punished severely when they fail to protect these youth. This sends a message to other schools: protect all youth equally or risk financial rebuke. Cases similar to *Nabozny v. Podlesny* are erupting in California, Illinois, Minnesota, Missouri, New Jersey, and Washington (Buckel 2000). A recent case involves a Nevada youth, Derek Henkel.

Derek was in ninth grade when he chose to come out of the closet on a public television program, unaware that the repercussions would bring him great emotional and physical strain. Derek endured ongoing verbal and physical assaults simply because he was gay. School officials thought it best to remove him as the problem, and he was transferred to three different high schools. The hostility at each site was just as severe as the site before. At Galena High School, some boys lassoed Derek and threatened to drag him from a pickup truck. At Wooster High School, a student punched him in the face repeatedly, and school security did nothing though they witnessed the event firsthand. At Washoe High School, the principal told him to act more masculine and quit "acting like a fag" (Lambda 2001, website). School officials never came to his aid. Derek ultimately left the system with a GED from the local community college. He stated, "It was a nightmare to be bounced from school to school while other students tortured me and administrators made me feel it was my fault. . . . Even after I repeatedly asked for help, none of the adults cared enough to try to stop the violence and daily taunts and threats" (Lambda, website).

Derek's case, *Henkel v. Ross Gregory, et al.,* will pursue punitive damages against the school under Title IX, state tort laws (for the emotional trauma), and First Amendment violation because he was forced to hide his sexual orientation.

The federal Equal Access Act is mentioned frequently throughout the literature on gay, lesbian, bisexual, and transgender youth. The

Equal Access Act makes it unlawful for schools to deny these youth from forming gay-related clubs, and youth can refer to the act when they believe they have been treated differently than other groups of students. The law was passed in 1984 to protect student groups that organize themselves with a purpose and a set of goals to accomplish during noninstructional time. The act was most notorious for making it possible for groups of youth to organize and maintain Bible clubs without crossing the line of separation of church and state. Schools that violate the act risk losing federal funding.

Schools generally offer two types of clubs: those that are directly related to the curriculum and those that are not. Clubs that have a curricular nature such as the student council, the Spanish club, and the school band are considered directly related to the curriculum and are officially endorsed by the school. School clubs such as the chess club, Future Teachers of America, and the bowling club are considered noncurricular clubs and consequently do not have a school's endorsement. When a school offers a group of students the opportunity to organize even one noncurricular club, they are legally obligated to afford all students an equal opportunity to start a club (Lambda 1998). Herein lies the significance for the youth at hand. Schools cannot bar a group of students from forming a gay-related club, such as Gay-Straight Alliance, when other clubs are in effect. Thus, gay-related clubs are entitled to the same privileges afforded to other clubs. Should a school be in violation of the act, attorneys will investigate the nature of the other clubs.

Two groups of youth, one in Orange County, California, and another in Salt Lake City, Utah, perceived themselves to be unjustly treated by their schools when they were denied the opportunity to start a gay-related club. The youth in Orange County had wanted to start a Gay-Straight Alliance, but the school district's long delay in approving the club caused the students to miss their meetings for a semester. Although the school district's policy included no tolerance for discrimination of any kind, school officials did not permit the students to meet all semester, set up a table at a school recognition event, or post their banner (Lambda 1999). Instead, the students were subjected to a final approval from a board vote that was postponed on more than one occasion. When the students were finally given the opportunity to defend themselves at a public forum, they encountered much hostility and censure. Despite the board's procrastination and the community's disapproval, the attorneys eventually negotiated a settlement that allowed the youth to organize themselves into a Gay-Straight Alliance (Lambda 2000).

Youth at East High School in Utah encountered a similar situation when they petitioned to organize a Gay-Straight Alliance. To avoid compliance with the Equal Access Act, the school board essentially banned all noncurricular clubs so that youth could not demand an equal opportunity to form their Gay-Straight Alliance. Because schools are not accountable to the act so long as no other noncurricular clubs exist on campus, the school district reclassified some of the clubs as curricular to allow the respective students to meet. (Some clubs were not reclassified at all and were still permitted to meet.) The message was clear, the school district did not want the Gay-Straight Alliance on their school's grounds. The students then petitioned to have a curricular-based club called PRISM (People Respecting Important Social Movements), but they were barred once again. After a two-year legal battle, the Salt Lake City School District lifted the ban on the gay-related clubs. A Lambda supervising attorney stated, "The school board cannot censure student speech and stop students—including lesbian and gay students and their friends—from organizing clubs just because officials disapprove of those clubs" (Lamba 1999, website).

In *Stopping Anti-Gay Abuse of Students in Public Schools: A Legal Perspective,* Buckel (1998) emphasizes that it is in the best interest of gay, lesbian, bisexual, and transgender youth who experience harassment to take the following actions.

Report All Forms of Abuse to School Officials

School officials cannot respond to antigay harassment if they do not know that it is occurring. When a youth files a complaint of harassment, administrators and/or teachers must take a course of action upon receiving the information. In some states, such as Alaska and Florida, teachers risk losing their teaching credentials if they fail to address an incident of sexual orientation discrimination. Teachers and counselors can verbally inform their principal of the incident, however it is critical that the principal receive a written complaint. Verbal complaints are not as effective as written ones that include details of the abuse, when and where it took place, by whom, and the names of witnesses.

Get Safe

Youth who have encountered the harassment should consider receiving support from counselors and teachers or those they can trust such as family members and friends. These youth should also consider the support provided from the local chapters of Gay, Lesbian, and Straight Educators Network (GLSEN) or Parents, Families, and Friends of Lesbians, and Gays (PFLAG).

Move Up the Hierarchy

Some principals trivialize or do not respond to antigay abuse. Should a principal fail to address the complaint, only lightly admonish the tormentor(s), or blame the victim, the victim is wise to follow up with the principal's superiors, usually the superintendent of schools. Principals, at the very least, should hold conferences with parents of both parties, suspend the abuser(s), or keep the abuser(s) in detention. For more severe complaints, the abuser(s) should be expelled and the students' class schedules should be readjusted.

Document Accurately

Youth who experience antigay abuse should maintain written records of their ordeal with the abusers and the school. Documentation of unfair treatment toward nonheterosexual youth is critical.

Have Solutions Available

Many principals know very little about gay, lesbian, bisexual, and transgender issues. Consequently, they may not know how to best handle a gay-related harassment. They may need some direction and guidance. Youth should have a plan in mind, or resources that can educate the principal, faculty, and student body.

In all, legal recourse is available for gay, lesbian, bisexual, and transgender youth who have been treated unfairly, encountered antigay abuse or harassment, or whose administrators have failed to respect them. Legal precedent has been established, and students can file suit for punitive damages. School administrators should therefore take a proactive approach and create a school spirit that embraces diversity, instead of taking a defensive one by resorting to litigation.

Demography: Who Are Gay, Lesbian, Bisexual, and Transgender Youth? What Do They Endure?

The size of this population of youth cannot be ignored. Ginsberg (1999) estimated that about 2,610,000 gay, lesbian, bisexual, and transgender youth exist in the United States. Parents, Families, and Friends of Lesbians and Gays (PFLAG 1995) suggest that of all youth enrolled in public schools, one in twenty is likely to be gay or lesbian. Bochenek (2001) of the Human Rights Watch found that two million gay youth are subjected to teacher and administrator indifference and subjected to abuse and assault. To better understand this population of youth, a discourse follows in two rubrics: who they are and what they endure.

Who They Are

Gay, lesbian, bisexual, and transgender youth come in all shapes, forms, and sizes. They live in urban, suburban, and in rural communities. They are white, black, Latino, and Asian, and they come from rich, poor, and middle-class homes. Some of their families are religious, and others are not. They are represented in every subculture imaginable. They are the same in many ways, and so different in others. Some are courageously visible and display pride in their sexual orientation; others, most in fact, are often invisible and impossible to distinguish from their heterosexual peers (Ryan and Futterman 1998).

A 1996 Safe Schools Coalition Anti-Violence Report (cited in *Oasis* 1996) found that 9 percent of high school students consider themselves nonheterosexual. Savin-Williams and Rodriguez (cited in Person Project 2000) found that although 1 percent of junior and senior high school students reported being gay, lesbian, or bisexual, 6 percent of the same population had homosexual attractions and/or behaviors. Another study of seventh through twelfth grade youth found that 1 percent considered themselves homosexual (Remafedi 1992), and another study revealed that 5 percent of youth between the ages of thirteen and fifteen had had sex with members of the same sex (American Academy of Child and Adolescent Psychiatry 2000). This type of variance is expected considering that it is nearly impossible to ascertain exactly how many youth are gay, lesbian, bisexual, or transgender. This stems from the fact that most of these youth do not self-identify their sexual orientation until after they have graduated from high school. Many, in fact, wait to come out to avoid the social stigma attached to homosexuality. Others may be confused about their sexual identity or uncertain about their sexual orientation. At any rate, most homosexuals come out when they are young adults (Haffner 1998).

The size of this population is also difficult to determine because sex with the same gender is common in youth (American Academy of Child and Adolescent Psychiatry 2000). In fact, research has found that although youth may engage in same-sex behavior, they are unlikely to identify themselves as gay or lesbian (Ryan and Futterman 1998). The exact number of nonheterosexual youth is not known, but this uncertainty doesn't overshadow the fact there are potentially thousands of youth who could be considered nonheterosexual and several thousand more who have a family member who could be identified as gay, lesbian, bisexual, or transgender. Youth Pride, Inc. (2001) has determined that one to three of every ten students is gay, lesbian, bisexual, or transgender or has a family member who is. A conservative estimate of 2 percent of the 24.6 million youth (between the ages of thirteen and nineteen) living in the United States (1990 census figure) would mean that there are nearly 492,000 gay, lesbian, bisexual, or transgender youth who find themselves challenged with their sexual orientation.

Most of these youth first become aware that their sexual orientation is different from their peers at the age of ten (D'Augelli and Hershberger 1993); some research has suggested 9.7 years (Herdt and Boxer 1996) and 12.2 years (National Coalition for Gay, Lesbian, Bisexual, and Transgender Youth 2000). Although most youth become aware that they are nonheterosexual at a young age, most who choose to disclose their sexuality during adolescence wait until the age of sixteen to come out to their family and friends (National Coalition for Gay, Lesbian, Bisexual, and Transgender Youth 2000). A new generation of youth is finding it easier to come out of the closet (Savin-Williams and Rodriguez 1999 cited in Person Project 2000). Youth of today are coming out at younger ages than ever before (National Gay and Lesbian Task Force 2001), and they are rebelling against the stigma attached to homosexuals and homosexual behavior.

What They Endure

This heterogeneous population comes from diverse family structures. They come from large and small families, families with two parents and families with a single parent. Many youth who come out to their families often risk rejection. One youth recalled his experience: "I left home when I was fifteen years old. My family did not accept my way of life. Everybody found out in school . . . I didn't know where to go" (Rhode Island Task Force on Gay, Lesbian, Bisexual, and Transgendered Youth 2001, website). Hershberger and D'Augelli (1995) found that 12 percent of mothers and 18 percent of fathers rejected their children because of their sexual orientation. Some youth are physically assaulted and others are thrown out of their homes. One Philadelphia study found that nearly one-third of gay men and lesbian women reported that their family members abused them simply because they were gay or lesbian (Philadelphia Lesbian and Gay Task Force 1996). In New York City, one agency found that nearly 60 percent of gay and lesbian youth experienced gay-related violence in their homes (Hunter 1992 cited in Ryan and Futterman 1998). In San Francisco, gay and lesbian youth encounter more verbal and physical violence than their heterosexual peers do (National Gay and Lesbian Task Force 2001). Not surprisingly, many youth run away from home because of hostility they endure there. About 26 percent of these youth leave home because of conflicts with their families over their sexual orientation (Person Project 2000). Telljohann, Price, Poureslami, and Easton (1995) found that 48 percent run away from home. Kruks (1991), moreover, found an overwhelming 80 percent of the Los Angeles street youth reported they left home because of the homophobic treatment they endured in their homes.

Research has found that a large percentage of the runaway population is gay, lesbian, bisexual, or transgender. Although the exact percentage is difficult to determine, the U.S. Department of Health and Human Services (1989 cited in The PERSON Project 2000) estimated that as many as 25 percent of all runaways in the United States are gay, lesbian, bisexual, or transgender, and others have found that 42 percent of street youth identify themselves as gay or lesbian (Victim Services/Traveler's Aid 1991 cited in Gay, Lesbian, Straight Educators Network 2000). More than 40 percent of the street youth in Seattle and 25 to 35 percent in Los Angeles are gay, lesbian, bisexual, or transgender (Kruks 1991). In Minneapolis-St. Paul, the number of gay and lesbian street youth ranges from 80 to 120 on a given night (Beckstrom 1997 cited in Lipkin 1999). Unfortunately, some of these youth find themselves in precarious situations. With no high school diploma, an unstable living situation, and no work skills, many are left to sell themselves sexually to sustain themselves financially. Nearly half will engage in prostitution in order to support themselves (Hunter 1992). This puts them at great risk for HIV infection and AIDS. Farrow et al. (1992; cited in Ryan and Futterman 1998) found that as many as one in twelve street youth in New York City and one in eight in San Francisco are infected with HIV. In a sample of sixty street youth in Los Angeles, Sullivan (1996) found that 53 percent did not use a condom during intercourse, 29 percent had anal and vaginal intercourse five to six times a week without a condom, 7 percent practiced celibacy, and only 20 percent consistently used a condom. Despite the fact that many of these youth failed to practice safe sex, 63 percent had not been tested for the virus that causes AIDS.

Not only do these youth risk rejection from their family, they also risk rejection from friends. One study revealed that 41 percent of a sample of youth who disclosed their sexual orientation to their friends found that their friends reacted negatively to the news (Hershberger and D'Augelli 1995). Other studies of gay and lesbian youth have shown that nearly half lose friends because of their sexual orientation (Remafedi 1987; D'Augelli and Hershberger 1993). In a national survey of 1,459 fifteen- to nineteen-year-old males, Marsiglio (1993) underscored that only 12 percent felt comfortable enough to befriend a gay person. Fear of rejection, ostracism, and reprisal may very well explain why many gay, lesbian, and bisexual youth keep quiet about their sexual orientation. The National Coalition for Gay, Lesbian, Bisexual, and Transgender Youth (2000) survey found that most of the sample that had not come out explained they feared their parents' and friends' reactions (Savin-Williams 1994 cited in Person Project 2000).

Many gay, lesbian, and bisexual youth often feel socially, emotionally, and cognitively isolated (Hetrick and Martin 1987). Research has found that 80 percent of these youth report severe problems because they feel isolated (Remafedi 1987). They know that they are different early on, and at about the same time they learn that a severe stigma is attached to nonheterosexuals and their behaviors. Their parents, siblings, friends, classmates, and religion simultaneously reinforce that to be gay, lesbian, bisexual, or transgender is morally wrong and distasteful. They have heard the derogatory stereotypes. All the while, everywhere they look—magazines, media coverage, TV sitcoms, and everywhere they go—schools, church, parks, malls—they are reassured that a heterosexual lifestyle is the only normal lifestyle. They have no community to turn to, no peers to socialize and interact with, no family or friends to confide in, no role models to look up to, and no resources to learn about their situation. They have no support network whatsoever. Ryan and Futterman (1998) have indicated:

> Shunned by the social institutions that routinely provide emotional support and positive reinforcement for children and adolescents . . . lesbian and gay adolescents must negotiate many important milestones without feedback or support. They must learn to identify, explore, and ultimately integrate a positive adult identity despite persistent negative stereotypes of lesbian and gay people. They must learn to accept themselves, to find intimacy and meaning through relationships, work, and connection with the broader community. (4)

One Providence, Rhode Island, youth described his isolation. "There was no one in my school for me to talk to about my issues. I felt completely alone and unsupported. I had nowhere to unload the burden I was feeling unless I ended it all" (Youth Pride, Inc. 2001). To complicate matters, some youth cannot even turn to their counselors. One study found that one out of five school counselors noted they were not competent enough to counsel gay adolescents and would not find personal gratification in working with this population (Price and Telljohann 1991). If that were not enough, oftentimes school officials isolate these youth as a means of resolving the youth's sexual harassment. Jamie Nabozny recalled his ordeal. "Instead of teaching the value of respect for others, the school taught that if you are different you are the problem, and you are the one that has to be separated out and hidden" (cited in Buckel 1998, 3).

Being gay, lesbian, bisexual, or transgender is a risk factor for suicide and substance abuse. Some experts have titled antigay violence in schools a "suicidal script" for these students (Buckel 1998). Many youth have ended their lives instead of enduring rejection by family and close, trusted friends; hostility, harassment, or derisive comments from their peers; and feelings of isolation. Suicide is the leading cause of death for this population. Although suicide statistics vary, the rates of attempt and completion are high. The most frequently cited source is Gibson's (1989) Report of the Secretary's Task Force on Youth Suicide that revealed that half of gay and lesbian youth have had suicidal thoughts, and of all youth suicides in the United States each year, 30 percent were gay, lesbian, bisexual, or transgender youth. These youth are two to four times more likely to attempt suicide than their heterosexual peers (Safe Schools Coalition Anti-Violence Project 1996 cited in ReligiousTolerance.org 2001; National Gay and Lesbian Task Force 2001; Massachusetts Department of Education 1997 cited in PFLAG 2001). The American Journal of Public Health (1998 cited in Jones 1999) revealed that gay and bisexual boys are seven times more likely to attempt suicide than their peers are. Rotheram-Borus et al. (1994) found that 39 percent of gay and lesbian adolescents that utilized the services of a New York City social agency had attempted suicide, and the National Coalition for Gay, Lesbian, Bisexual, and Transgender Youth (2000) survey found that 23 percent had tried to commit suicide. One lesbian youth explained the events that led to her suicide attempt:

> Due to societal fear and ignorance, my teachers and counselors labeled my confusion as rebellion, and placed me in the category of a troubled discipline problem. But still I had nothing to identify with and no role models to guide me, to help me sort out this confusion, and I began to believe that I was simply alone. A few weeks into my sophomore year, I woke up in a psych hospital after taking my father's camping knife violently to my wrists and hoping for success. (Gay, Lesbian, Straight Education Network 2000, website)

Because of the problems that surround these youth, alcohol and drugs become a refuge for some. For instance, in Seattle, 35.8 percent of gay, lesbian, and bisexual youth engage in heavy drug use as compared to 22.5 percent of their heterosexual peers (Safe School Coalition of Washington 1999 cited in GLSEN 2000). In Vermont, 32 percent of youth who had had homosexual sex used cocaine compared to 6 percent of youth who had had heterosexual sex (National Gay and Lesbian Task Force 2001). The Commonwealth of Massachusetts Department of Education (1995, 1997) found that homosexual youth were up to three times more likely to have used alcohol, marijuana, and cocaine, and two times more likely to have smoked cigarettes than their heterosexual peers. In another population of gay and lesbian youth, 68 percent of the gay males reported using alcohol and 44 percent reported using illicit drugs; 83 percent of the lesbian youth had used alcohol and 67 percent had used drugs (Rosario, Hunter, and Rotheram-Borus 1992). These youth apparently use drugs and alcohol as a means to cope with their internal and external struggles. Unfortunately for them, however, many will become dependent on them as adults (alcoholism is 20 to 33 percent more prevalent in the gay community (Herbert, Hunt, and Dell 1994), and drug and alcohol abusing youth are prone to risky sexual conduct that leads to HIV infection.

The severe stigma that youth maintain against homosexuality is why gay, lesbian, bisexual, and transgender youth are harassed, assaulted, and taunted. Among youth, to be other than heterosexual is considered abnormal. In fact, up to 48 percent of high school youth have reported their prejudice toward homosexuals (National Gay and Lesbian Task Force 2001). Youth do not want to be gay or be perceived as gay. This seems to hold especially true of boys. *Real Boys' Voices* author Pollack (2000) called homophobia "the cruelest form of the Boy Code prejudice" (p. 286). Most boys, at least in the sample included in Pollack's book, seem tolerant and to a point sympathetic of gay men. Suffice it to say, however, they make bold statements expressing their heterosexuality. Pollack reflects, "Despite how much they want it to be acceptable to become close with one another, and as mindful as they are about not wanting to mistreat or discriminate against gay people, they are still afraid they could be seen as gay—when perhaps, in fact, they are not" (286). The American Association of University Women (AAUW 2001) study on sexual harassment found that youth become upset and disturbed if they are described as homosexual. The boys in the AAUW (1993) study were more likely to become disturbed if they were called *gay* than if they were physically assaulted. Boys evidently know the impact this can have because 58 percent of the boys mentioned they had called someone else *gay.* The Shakeshaft et al. (1997) study on sexual harassment found that boys feared being labeled homosexual. Boys did everything they could to conform to the "boy code." Those who did not were subject to the most common verbal assault from one boy to another—being called *gay* or something that identified him as effeminate. Any boy who was perceived as weak or odd or failed to conform to the "boy code" in other ways was labeled a homosexual.

A 1999 Gay, Lesbian and Straight Network (cited in ReligiousTolerance.org 2001) survey found that 91 percent of their sample heard other youth make antigay comments such as *faggot* and *dyke*, either sometimes or frequently, in school. A Massachusetts 1993 study found that 97 percent of high school youth hear homophobic comments on a regular basis (cited in Youth Pride, Inc. 2001). When the homophobic remarks are made, reported 39 percent of gay, lesbian, bisexual, and transgender youth, rarely does anyone intervene (GLSEN 2000). In fact, 53 percent of youth in the Massachusetts study mentioned they heard school staff make the homophobic comments. Although verbal assaults seemingly lack the severity of the physical ones, verbal assaults all too often contribute to a hostile environment that is conducive to antigay physical assaults. One gay boy noted, "the smart remarks, passing through the hallways . . . 'queer, queen, fag, gay' . . . , etc. They get to be amusing after a while" (cited in Jones 1999). But another gay boy recalled, "At first, it just started with name-calling and people talking. . . . But then it was the physical stuff" (cited in ReligiousTolerance.org 2001). The physical assaults can get severe, as in another gay boy's account of his ordeal: "I just began hating myself more and more, as each year the hatred toward me grew and escalated from just simple name-calling in elementary school to having persons in high school threaten to beat me up, being pushed and dragged around the ground, having hands slammed in lockers, and a number of other daily tortures" (GLSEN 2000).

These youth are at greater risk for bullying than any other group of high school youth (Bochenek 2001). Nearly 41.7 percent do not feel safe in their schools (GLSEN 2000). How could they feel safe in an environment where research has found that one third to one half of these youth experience some form of harassment (Pilkington and D'Augelli 1995). The Safe Schools Coalition (1995 cited in National Gay and Lesbian Task Force 2001) indicated that gay, lesbian, bisexual, and transgender youth are more than five times more likely to have been targets of violence than their heterosexual peers. These youth struggle on a daily basis just to avoid a confrontation. They spend time worrying about how to elude waiting offenders on their way to and from school and in transition time between classes. Many of them are violently assaulted simply because of who they are. One study found that up to 70 percent of gay, lesbian, bisexual, and transgender youth encountered verbal and physical assaults (GLSEN 2000). Another study found that nearly 62 percent of gay, lesbian, bisexual, and transgender youth reported they witnessed antigay harassment that largely went ignored; 64 percent of the sample were verbally assaulted, 28 percent were threatened, and 14 percent were physically assaulted (National Coalition for Gay, Lesbian, Bisexual, and Transgender Youth 2001). Hershberger and D'Augelli (1995) and Hunter (1992) both found that 40 percent of their sample experienced physical violence. The GLSEN study found that 61 percent were verbally harassed, 47 percent were sexually harassed, and 28 percent were physically assaulted.

SCHOOLS FOR GAY, LESBIAN, BISEXUAL, OR TRANSGENDER YOUTH

In an ideal world, there would be no need for self-contained schools for gay, lesbian, bisexual, and transgender youth. But this is not an ideal world, and some of these youth really need a haven to call their own. They need safe learning environments where they can nurture their wounded spirits and strengthen their self-esteem and confidence. The testimony of one youth illustrates how his school empowered him:

> Harvey Milk (High School) was a true learning experience for me. I got support from my teachers. The fact that I was different was no longer a challenge for me. . . . I realized that I was many other things in addition to being gay. I was friendly and outgoing, and to my surprise I actually liked to be around people. . . . I actually grew to love school. . . . I learned that being gay was no barrier to my success. (Miranda 1993 cited in Owens 1998, 148)

Despite the fact that some believe that such schools are a bad idea because they either recruit youth and make them gay or further isolate them from their peers, two public and one private high school are currently available for gay, lesbian, bisexual, and transgender youth. The schools, Harvey Milk High School, Walt Whitman Community School, and EAGLES Center are refuges in which these youth can earn their education.

Harvey Milk High School, New York City

This school was founded in 1984 by the Hetrick-Martin Institute and the New York City Board of Education. The school was named after slain politician and gay rights activist Harvey Milk. Milk was the first openly gay elected city official in a major city, San Francisco, and considered a pioneer and martyr of the gay rights movement (Hogan and Hudson 1998). Dan White, a San Francisco politician who fought to maintain "traditional family values and conservative moral politics" (D'Emilio and Freedman 1997, 347) shot and killed Milk and then mayor of San Francisco George Moscone after a political dispute. Considering that Milk had been instrumental in passing antidiscrimination measures for gays and lesbians, the school was appropriately named.

The school was the first secondary school for gay, lesbian, bisexual, and transgender youth. Although the school is now physically located in an attractive loft-style building in Greenwich Village, the school had a challenging beginning in a modest facility. The Hetrick-Martin Institute, a social agency serving these youth along with youth questioning their sexuality, collaborates with the New York City Board of Education to administer the academic programs. (The board administers the school through its Alternative High School and Programs division. About thirty-six alternative schools are available for New York City youth who cannot function or benefit from the larger public school system.) The idea of the school was conceived in the early eighties when the staff at Hetrick-Martin noticed that a number of their clients were skipping school to avoid the verbal and physical assaults they endured because of their sexuality. The pattern was consistent; the youth avoided school to their detriment. Hetrick-Martin took advantage (with threats of a lawsuit) of a school board policy that makes it possible, if twenty-two truant youth can be identified, for a teacher to start a school for them (Owens 1998). On April 15, 1985, for the first time in world, U.S., and educational history, twenty-two openly gay youth gathered in donated church space in front of their openly gay teacher to start school. Fred Goldhaber was the school's first and only teacher for two years.

The school now has two teachers, two paraprofessionals, dedicated volunteers, and technical support from the Hetrick-Martin staff. Over the years, the graduation rate has been good (Woog 1995), despite the fact that many youth return to their home schools. Those that matriculate through the academic program earn the same number of credits as all other New York City public school graduates and are required to take the Regents competency exam (Owens 1998). The only difference for the Harvey Milk High School graduates is that they learn the content from teachers who sincerely care about them because they too are gay and understand their emotional plight. They learn about gays and lesbians in history and witness contemporary gay and lesbian role models. The supportive environment nonetheless affords them the opportunity to openly express themselves without fear of censure or ridicule. One of the teachers commented, "They come in angry, frightened, and incredibly hostile; even when we're gentle to them, they're suspicious. We give a lot of respect to the kids; we work very hard to make them feel good about themselves. . . . Gradually the hostility subsides, and we build their self-confidence . . . they learn to care about themselves, and about each other" (Woog, 40).

EAGLES Academy and OASIS, Los Angeles

The vast Los Angeles Unified School District offers two academic programs that serve gay, lesbian, bisexual, and transgender youth. EAGLES, an acronym for *Emphasizing Adolescent Gay and Lesbian Education Services,* and OASIS, for *Out Adolescents Staying In School,* operate within Central High School. Central High School is not a typical high school. It is known as a transitional high school (other districts would refer to the school as an alternative school) created to meet the needs of nontraditional youth—students who may not be able to succeed in their home school. There is no traditional physical campus per se. The seventy-five teachers who teach at this school teach at various locations throughout the Los Angeles area; five teachers compose the faculty in the two programs.

Five programs serve the total student body, and the two programs designated for gay, lesbian, bisexual, and transgender youth originated in 1992. EAGLES was created after a Los Angeles AIDS Blue Ribbon Task Force meeting recognized that some local youth were experiencing problems because of their sexual orientation. Prior to EAGLES these youth had very few options. Some of them simply stopped going to their local school because they were afraid of the harassment they encountered there. EAGLES started with one teacher, but the faculty had grown to three by 1995. By 1997, OASIS was created. Because many of the youth of the Central High School programs tend to identify themselves with their location, OASIS became a moniker of choice for a group of gay, lesbian, bisexual, and transgender youth. The two programs are essentially one in the same with no apparent philosophical or methodological differences, and both programs serve the same population of youth. The students attend the program that is most convenient for them.

The Los Angeles Unified School District is steadfast in the conviction that all their schools foremost should be safe for all youth. Yet, the district remains supportive of the two programs because some youth (for reasons of peer intolerance and safety issues) cannot succeed academically and/or socially in their home school. Unsurprisingly then, the basis of the EAGLES and OASIS mission statement is one that emphasizes a safe place for youth to receive their education. If that place is found in one of the two programs, the student is undoubtedly accepted. Faculty and school officials, however, would remain hopeful that the student would one day return to the home school to experience an education like everyone else.

The Walt Whitman Community School, Dallas

Known as the youngest of the three schools, this private high school opened its doors to gay, lesbian, bisexual, and transgender youth and youth of same-sex parents in September 1997. The school secured its name after American poet Walt Whitman, who was strongly believed to be homosexual. Whitman, best known for his short story "Death in the Schoolroom" and his book of poetry entitled *Leaves of Grass,* began his career as a teacher and later turned to newspaper editing. His contemporaries believed him homosexual when one of the *Leaves of Grass* editions implied a semblance of homoeroticism (Hogan and Hudson 1998). Although some believed that the edition could be interpreted as support for male camaraderie, others found the poetry blatantly offensive. Thereafter, Whitman spent much of his life covering up the fact that he was homosexual, but literature scholars unveiled that he did have homosexual relationships throughout his lifetime. Whitman has been hailed as a great American artist and his work continues to inspire homosexual and heterosexual writers alike.

The idea for the Walt Whitman Community School (WWCS) was conceived by Pamala Stone and Becky Thompson in May 1997 when the two realized that some gay, lesbian, bisexual, and transgender youth could benefit from (and needed) a school devoted totally to their needs (WWCS website 2001). The founders of the school believed that these students could experience academic and social success as long as their environment was free of harassment, ridicule, and unfair treatment. The school mission and vision reads:

> Because sexual orientation issues in adolescence can adversely affect school success, social acceptance, and the development of a positive self-esteem, our mission at The Walt Whitman Community School is to create an atmosphere of tolerance, an acceptance of sexuality confusion, and opportunities for personal growth so that each individual student can become a fully functioning and healthy member of society. Our vision is to assist those youth who are not attending school with their peers, considering dropping out because of harassment, turning

to drugs and/or alcohol because of feelings of isolation, or attempting suicide because of severe isolation. (WWCS 2001, website)

An outline of the school's beliefs is included in Appendix B. The institution believes that so long as some of these youth continue to encounter intolerance and hostility in their own schools, they need the sanctuary provided by those who understand their needs the best and care about and support them the most. The pillars of the institution long for the day that the students will be integrated safely into their home school, but until that ideal comes to fruition, the Walt Whitman Community School will remain open to welcome them.

The school is completely private and relies on gifts from generous donors, fundraising events, and tuition to remain in operation. The school doors opened again for the fifth time this 2001–2002 academic school year. Although the school has remained small with a handful of faculty and a student body as small at times as seven and as large as twenty-eight, the school is growing. The small class size and the individualized attention may contribute to the fact that the parents remain extremely satisfied with the academic strides their children have made (WWCS website 2001).

SEX EDUCATION AND SEXUAL ORIENTATION

Very little research and few articles exist that deal exclusively with sexual orientation within sex education. In fact, most articles on gay, lesbian, bisexual, and transgender youth address the challenges that these youth confront and implications for school officials. This is understandable considering that addressing the needs of these youth cannot solely be accomplished in sex education. Sex education can certainly address diverse sexual topics, but issues of acceptance, respect, and tolerance for this population must permeate the entire school environment.

Most organizations that serve gay, lesbian, bisexual, and transgender youth rarely provide recommendations for sex education alone but instead recommend avenues to transform schools into safe, assault-free learning environments. The Rhode Island Task Force on Gay, Lesbian, Bisexual, and Transgendered Youth (2001) for instance, recommend:

- legislation and school policies protecting gay and lesbian students from harassment, violence, and discrimination
- training for teachers and other school personnel (on sexual orientation, identity, stereotypes, and so on)

➥ increased presence of and access to material pertaining to gay and lesbian issues in schools

➥ development of school support systems for gay and lesbian students

➥ further dialogue for students, educators, and parents to discuss issues related to homophobia and school safety (3)

The Massachusetts Governor's Commission on Gay and Lesbian Youth (1993a) had similar recommendations but added that teachers should be trained in crisis intervention and violence prevention. Parents, Families, and Friends of Lesbians and Gays (PFLAG 2001) is in consensus with the recommendations to create safer school environments. However, they added that teachers should have ongoing professional development, and that gay, lesbian, bisexual, and transgender issues be integrated into the curriculum. The Public Education Regarding Sexual Orientation Nationally Project (PERSON Project 2000) was more specific about their recommendations for the curricula. They asserted that sexual orientation be discussed fairly and accurately in the academic areas including sex education. They hold that youth should learn about the significant contributions made by gay, lesbian, bisexual, and transgender persons, the challenges some individuals have encountered in their fight for equality, and the Gay Rights Movement.

As mentioned in previous chapters, the Sex Information and Education Council of the United States (SIECUS) gathered a task force comprised of education, health, and medical experts from various reputable organizations such as the American Medical Association, American School Health Association, and the U.S. Centers for Disease Control to develop *Guidelines for Comprehensive Sexuality Education: Grades K through 12*. The guidelines essentially serve as a framework for further development of sound sex education programs or to enhance existing ones (see chapter 1). Sexual orientation is included in the guidelines. SIECUS is very clear about its stand on sexual orientation. Its position (2001) reads:

> Sexual orientation is an essential human quality. Individuals have the right to accept, acknowledge, and live in accordance with the sexual orientation, be they bisexual, heterosexual, gay or lesbian. The legal system should guarantee the civil rights and protection of all people, regardless of sexual orientation. Prejudice and discrimination based on sexual orientation is unconscionable. (3)

The guidelines address notable inherent values, some of which formally address sexual orientation. They emphasize that there are diverse values and beliefs about sexuality in any given culture and that every individual is entitled to her or his beliefs and is worthy of respect and acceptance. The guidelines also outline a series of healthy life behaviors for youth. The behaviors that most closely correlate with sexual orientation can be found under the concepts of human development and society and culture (although a closer inspection finds that nearly all of the behaviors are linked to some aspect of sexual orientation). These behaviors include:

- ➡ affirmation of one's own sexual orientation and respect for the sexual orientation of others
- ➡ demonstration of respect for people with different sexual values
- ➡ avoidance of behaviors that exhibit prejudice and bigotry
- ➡ rejection of stereotypes about the sexuality of diverse populations (SIECUS 1996, 8)

Sexual identity and orientation, like all of the topics in the guidelines, are addressed in progressive levels. The first level is intended for the younger child in elementary school, and the fourth level is for the older adolescent. Level one starts with introductory statements that explain that people have different kinds of love. The youth learn about hetero- and homosexuality and how these groups of individuals differ. In level two, youth are introduced to the concept of sexual orientation and bisexuality. The youngsters learn that these individuals are as normal as everyone else, and consequently have meaningful relationships, fulfilled lives, and children of their own. At this point, youth learn that gay, lesbian, and bisexual individuals are often exposed to ridicule and mistreatment. By level three, youth are learning heartier material such as theories as to why some people are homosexual, social factors that influence beliefs about homosexuality, religions that oppose homosexuality, and that sexual orientation cannot be altered by therapy or medicine. All the while, the messages reinforce that gay, lesbian, and bisexual individuals can live happy, complete lives and enter lifelong committed relationships. The adolescents who graduate into level four learn about gender identity and the fact that sex with the same gender does not always lead to homosexuality. The youth are informed that they should approach a trusted and knowledgeable adult for support and that support systems and resources are available in their community. Sexual orientation is also addressed specifically under the umbrella of society and culture. Here, youth learn that society ultimately molds the notions about sexuality. Thus, norms, taboos, and beliefs about sexuality are defined by cultures within society. Youth need to understand this perspective in order to fully understand homophobia. Essentially, youth learn that diversity is beneficial in society and should be celebrated.

In all, youth who graduate from sex education programs that follow the SIECUS guidelines will inevitably discuss hundreds of developmental messages. Although the messages are not all clearly earmarked for sexual orientation such as the one found under dating, "Gay and lesbian youth, like heterosexual youth, may or may not date" (SIECUS 1996, 21), each message can be applied to some facet of sexual orientation. For instance, under the umbrella of relationships, youth learn that there are different kinds of families, that people can have different types of friends, and people can experience different types of love.

The Medical Institute for Sexual Health (MISH) has also published guidelines to facilitate the development of sex education programs. The guidelines, entitled *National Guidelines for Sexuality and Character Education,* are very similar to those published by SIECUS except the MISH guidelines are more conservative in nature and promote the development of abstinence-only programs. A task force composed of field experts from Focus on the Family, Project Reality, Educational Guidance Institute, and Teen-Aid, Inc. gathered to create the guidelines. The messages and values described in the MISH guidelines are as beneficial to youth as the SIECUS guidelines, but the MISH guidelines are grounded in conservative, Christian principles. Unfortunately, the guidelines make almost no explicit references to sexual orientation.

A bibliography of forty-five sex education curricula is available in the SIECUS (2001) database. Of these, only three explicitly address sexual orientation: *Choosing Health—High School: Sexuality and Relationships* (Hubbard 1997); *Filling the Gaps: Hard-to-Teach Topics in Sexuality Education* (SIECUS 1998); *Streetwise to Sex-Wise: Sexuality Education for High-Risk Youth* (Brown 1993). *Choosing Health* provides high school youth basic information on sexual orientation in addition to the skills that enable youth to act responsibly with regard to sex. *Filling the Gap* and *Streetwise to Sex-Wise* provide supplementary material on sexual identity and orientation to existing sex education programs. Once again, it is important to emphasize that there are many sex education programs available that facilitate the acquisition of a healthy attitude toward sex regardless of a youth's sexual orientation. Several curricula can be found that include social justice for all people, and respect, appreciation, and acceptance of themselves and others. These programs may not necessarily address sexual orientation, but youth learn to respect all persons with diverse sexual values. This is far more important than basic information on homosexuality per se.

Telljohann et al. (1995) are among the very few to have formally investigated sexual education and sexual orientation. The researchers studied whether secondary health education teachers taught about homosexuality, how much they taught about it, and how comfortable and competent they perceived themselves to be in teaching about homosexuality. The sample size included 208 health education teachers. In all, only 46 percent of the teachers said that they taught about homosexuality. Of these teachers, most of them taught about homosexuality in one to two class periods touching on topics such as definitions, prejudice, health issues, and myths. Only about one-third of the teachers responded that they felt very comfortable teaching about homosexuality, and only 20 percent believed they were very competent. About 35 percent of the teachers believed that their schools were not doing enough for their homosexual adolescents, and over half believed that a support group for gay and lesbian students would not be supported by the school administration. The researchers concluded with recommendations to better meet the needs of these youth: all preservice teachers should learn about homosexuality sometime during their professional preparation; teachers should have professional development on topics related to homosexuality; schools should make an effort to include homosexuality in health education and other content areas; schools should encourage the development of gay and lesbian support groups; schools should evaluate the attitudes held by administrators and school board members toward these youth since policies are generally made by these officials.

SUMMARY

Clearly, the latter part of the twentieth century has witnessed an uprising of the gay, lesbian, bisexual, and transgender community. As these people are becoming increasingly visible, society is becoming more accepting of them. Despite this progress and the fact that more and more youth are establishing gay-related clubs throughout the nation's schools, nonheterosexual youth today are at risk for severe censure from parents, family, peers, teachers, and school administrators. Many of these youth have had their spirits weakened by peers who have emotionally and physically assaulted them, and others have lost their lives simply because they did not fit in. The July 3, 2001, issue of *The Advocate* magazine ran a cover story on youth who torment others who are gay, lesbian, bisexual, and transgender. The following month, the editorial section found a reaction from a youth, a parent, and a teacher:

•• I am a sixteen-year-old gay boy living in a small Arkansas town. Junior high was the most horrible time in my life. There were days I wanted to skip school because I was so afraid. . . . We never went anywhere alone. . . . The names they called us were so horrible, we would go to the teacher's room and cry. When we entered high school, everything changed. When we decided to live openly, everyone thought that it was cool. . . . My friends said their parents taught them to hate gay people.

•• My twelve-year-old son is being bullied. I was bullied. I remember the pain. But the new angle for the bully, especially if the victim is a boy, is to call the victim *a fag, queer, or gay*. . . . My son lives in a no-win situation. He is the one forced to change routines and routes to stay safe. His grades are the ones that go down in every class in one semester. He is the one who skips lunch and won't use the rest rooms (he had his head shoved in a urinal this year).

•• As a fifth-grade teacher, I see bullying on a daily basis. The lack of action by our administration bothers me just as much as the bullying itself. I do not tolerate any kind of teasing in my classroom. . . . Unfortunately, I stand alone at my school. While most teachers at our school would intervene if one student made racial or ethnic slurs, these same teachers will laugh and encourage those who try to imitate gay stereotypes. (*The Advocate*, Reader Forum, August 28, 2001, 4)

Very few sex education curricula formally address sexual orientation. However, even if more curricula did approach the subject, a single class or two that might include references to homosexuality cannot change a school's attitude toward gay, lesbian, bisexual, or transgender youth. In order for there to be respect, acceptance, tolerance, and celebration of sexual diversity in a school, students and faculty alike must become better educated about sexual orientation and strive to ensure safe learning environments free of hostility for all students. President George W. Bush coined the phrase "Let's leave no child behind" during his political campaign. This should be taken to heart. Schools should meet the needs of all children, regardless of their sexual orientation.

REFERENCES

Adams, Bob. 2001. "Gay Sex on the Rise." *The Advocate*, 24 April, 17.

The Advocate Report. 2001. "Survey: Hate-Crime Surge." *The Advocate*, 22 May, 17.

American Academy of Child and Adolescent Psychiatry. 2000. *Your Adolescent: Emotional, Behavioral and Cognitive Development from Early Childhood through the Teen Years*. New York: Harper Collins Publishers.

American Association of University Women. (1993). *Hostile Hallways: The AAUW Survey on Sexual Harassment in America's Schools. Bullying, Teasing, and Sexual Harassment in School*. Washington, DC: American Association of University Women.

———. (2001). *Hostile Hallways: Bullying, Teasing, and Sexual Harassment in School*. Washington, DC: American Association of University Women.

American Counseling Association. 1999. *Just the Facts about Sexual Orientation and Youth: A Primer for Principals, Educators, and School Personnel*. Alexandria, VA: American Counseling Association.

American Psychological Association. 1995. *Publication Manual of the American Psychological Association*. Washington, DC: American Psychological Association.

Bochenek, Michael. 2001. *Hatred in the Hallways: Violence and Discrimination against Gay, Lesbian, Bisexual, and Transgender Students in U.S. Schools*. New York: Human Rights Watch.

Brown, Steve. 1993. *Streetwise to Sex-Wise: Sexuality Education for High-Risk Youth*. Morristown, NJ: Planned Parenthood for Greater Northern New Jersey.

Buckel, David S. 1998. *Stopping Anti-Gay Abuse of Students in Public Schools: A Legal Perspective*. New York: Lambda Legal Defense and Education Fund.

———. 2000. "Legal Perspectives on Ensuring a Safe and Nondiscriminatory School Environment for Lesbian, Gay, Bisexual, and Transgendered Students." *Education and Urban Society* 32: 390–398.

Child Study Association of America. 1943. *When Children Ask about Sex*. New York: Child Association of America, Inc.

Clendinen, Dudley, and Adam Nagourney. 1999. *Out for Good: The Struggle to Build a Gay Rights Movement in America*. New York: Simon and Schuster.

CNN.com, "Surgeon General Issues 'Call to Action' on Sexual Health," *http://cnn.health* (cited June 30, 2001).

Collins, Joseph. 1926. *The Doctor Looks at Love and Life*. New York: George Doran Company.

Commonwealth of Massachusetts, Department of Education. *Youth Risk Behavior Survey Results, 1995, 1997*. Boston: Commonwealth of Massachusetts, Department of Education.

D'Augelli, Anthony R., and Scott L. Hershberger. 1993. "Lesbian, Gay, and Bisexual Youth in Community Settings: Personal Challenges and Mental Health Problems." *American Journal of Community Psychology* 21(4): 313–318.

D'Emilio, John, and Estelle B. Freedman. 1997. *Intimate Matters: A History of Sexuality in America*. Chicago: University of Chicago Press.

Farrow, James A., Robert W. Deisher, Richard Brown, John W. Kulig, and Michele D. Kipke. 1992. "Health and Health Needs of Homeless and Runaway Youth. A Position Paper of the Society for Adolescent Medicine." *Journal of Adolescent Health* 13: 717–726.

Fone, Byrne. 2000. *Homophobia: A History.* New York: Henry Holt and Company.

Gallichan, Walter M. 1921. *A Textbook of Sex Education.* Boston: Small, Maynard & Company.

Gay, Lesbian and Straight Education Network. "Just the Facts: A Fact Sheet That Summarizes Important Statistics about the Impact of Homophobia on Gay and Lesbian Youth," *http://glsen.org/pages/sections/library/references/015.article* (cited August 11, 2000).

———. 2001a "Fred C. Martinez Jr.: Statement for Press," *http://www.glsen.org/templates/news/record.html?section=12&record=895* (cited July 20, 2001).

———. 2001b "Gay-Straight Alliances," *http://www.glsen.org/templates/issues/index.html?subject=3* (cited July, 20, 2001).

Gibson, Paul. 1989. Gay Male and Lesbian Youth Suicide. In *Alcohol, Drug Abuse and Mental Health Administration: Report of the Secretary's Task Force on Youth Suicide. Vol. 3: Prevention and Interventions in Youth Suicide.* Washington, DC: Government Printing Office.

Ginsberg, Roberta W. 1999. "In the Triangle/Out of the Circle: Gay and Lesbian Students Facing the Heterosexual Paradigm." *Educational Forum* 64(1): 46–56.

Groves, Ernest R., and Gladys Hoagland Groves. 1933. *Sex in Childhood.* New York: The Macaulay Company.

Guerrero, Lucio, and Annie Sweeney. 2001. "Out of the Closet, Into the Census." *Chicago Sun-Times,* 20 June.

Haffner, Debra W. 1998. "Sexual Health for American Adolescents." *Journal of Adolescent Health* 22: 453–459.

Herbert, James, Brandon Hunt, and Gina Dell. 1994. "Counseling Gay Men and Lesbians with Alcohol Problems." *Journal of Rehabilitation* 60(2): 52–57.

Herdt, Gilbert, and A. Boxer. 1996. *Children of Horizons: How Gay and Lesbian Teens are Leading a New Way Out of the Closet.* Boston: Beacon Press.

Hershberger, Scott L., and Anthony R. D'Augelli. 1995. "The Impact of Victimization on the Mental Health and Suicidality of Lesbian, Gay Male and Bisexual Youths." *Developmental Psychology* 31(1): 65–74.

Hetrick, E. S., and A. D. Martin. 1987. "Developmental Issues and Their Resolution for Gay and Lesbian Adolescents." *Journal of Homosexuality* 14: 25–43.

Hetrick-Martin Institute, "Education and Recreation Services," *http://hmi.org/education.html* (cited August 23, 2001).

Hirsh, E. D., Joseph F. Kett, and James Trefil. 1993. *The Dictionary of Cultural Literacy: What Every American Needs to Know.* Boston: Houghton Mifflin Company.

Hogan, Steve, and Lee Hudson. 1998. *Completely Queer: The Gay and Lesbian Encyclopedia*. New York: Henry Holt and Company.

Hoyman, Howard S. 1953. "Basic Issues in School Sex Education." *Journal of School Health* 43: 14–22.

Hubbard, Betty M. 1997. *Choosing—High School: Sexuality and Relationships*. Santa Cruz, CA: ETR Associates.

Hunter, J. 1992. Violence against Lesbians and Gay Male Youths. In *Hate Crimes: Confronting Violence Against Lesbians and Gay Men*, edited by G. M. Herek and K. T. Berrill. Newbury Park, CA: Sage Publications.

Jones, Rebecca. 1999. "'I Don't Feel Safe Here Anymore': Your Legal Duty to Protect Gay Kids from Harassment." *American School Board Journal* 186: 26–31.

Keesing, Alice. 2000. "Gay Student Rule Passes: School Board Votes 8–3, with 2 Members Abstaining." *The Honolulu Advertiser*, 3 November.

Kinsey, Alfred, et al. 1948. *Sexual Behavior in the Human Male*. Philadelphia: W. B. Saunders.

Kruks, Gabe. 1991. "Gay and Lesbian Homeless/Street Youth." *Journal of Adolescent Health* 12(7): 515–518.

Lambda Legal Defense and Education Fund. "Defending Gay/Straight Alliances and Other Gay-Related Groups in Public Schools Under the Equal Access Act," *http://www.lambdalegal.org* (cited March 16, 1998).

———. "High School Students Sue Salt Lake City School Board," *http://www.lambdalegal.org* (cited March 19, 1998).

———. "Gay/Straight Alliance Students Sue Orange County High School," *http://www.lambdalegal.org* (cited November 24, 1999).

———. "Lambda to Sue Reno School Officials for Failing to Protect Gay Student," *http://www.lambdalegal.org* (cited January 27, 2000).

———. "Judge Rules El Modena High Gay-Straight Alliance Must Be Allowed to Meet," *http://www.lambdalegal.org* (cited February 4, 2000).

———. "*Henkel v Gregory:* Preliminary Victory!" *http://www.lambdalegal.org* (cited July 5, 2001).

Lipkin, Arthur. 1999. *Understanding Homosexuality: Changing Schools*. Boulder, CO: Westview Press.

Marsiglio, William. 1993. "Attitudes Toward Homosexual Activity and Gays as Friends: A National Survey of Heterosexual 15- to 19-Year-Old Males." *Journal of Sex Research* 30(1): 12–17.

Massachusetts Governor's Commission on Gay and Lesbian Youth. 1993a. *Making Schools Safe for Gay and Lesbian Youth: Breaking the Silence in Schools and in Families: Education Report*. Boston: Massachusetts Governor's Commission on Gay and Lesbian Youth.

———. Massachusetts Governor's Commission on Gay and Lesbian Youth. 1993b. *Making Schools Safe for Gay and Lesbian Youth: Report of Massa-*

chusetts Governor's Commission on Gay and Lesbian Youth. Boston: Massachusetts Governor's Commission on Gay and Lesbian Youth.

McIntosh, Sabrina. 2001. The New Gay Youth Revolution. *The Advocate*, 10 April, 34–43.

Melody, M. E., and Linda M. Peterson. 1999. *Teaching America about Sex*. New York: New York University Press.

Miranda, D. 1993. This School Is Out. *The Advocate:* 7 September, 5.

National Coalition for Gay, Lesbian, Bisexual, and Transgender Youth, "Out-Proud/Oasis Internet Survey of Queer and Questioning Youth," *http://outproud.org* (cited October 11, 2000).

National Gay and Lesbian Task Force, "Information About Gay, Lesbian, Bisexual, Transgendered and Questioning Youth," *http://www.ngltf.org/issues/youthinfo.htm* (cited July 20, 2001).

Oasis Magazine, "News and Events: Anti-Gay Harassment in Schools Documented," *http://www.oasismag.com* (cited July 7, 2001).

Owens, Robert E. 1998. *Queer Kids: The Challenges and Promise for Lesbian, Gay, and Bisexual Youth*. New York: Harrington Park Press.

Parents, Families and Friends of Lesbians and Gays. 1995. *Act Out '95*. Austin, TX: PFLAG Youth Summit.

———. "Families and Educators Partnering for Safe Schools: A Brochure for Educators," *http://www.pflag.org/schools/educators.htm* (cited July 20, 2001).

———. "Just the Facts," *http://www.glsen.org/pages/sections/library/reference/015.article* (cited July 20, 2001).

The P.E.R.S.O.N. Project, "Fact Sheet on LGBT Youth Health Education Needs," http://www.youth.org/loco/PERSONProject.html (cited October 18, 2000).

The P.E.R.S.O.N. Project, "The PERSON Project Brochure," *http://www.youth.org/loco/PERSONProject/Resources/brochure.html* (cited July 20, 2001).

Philadelphia Lesbian and Gay Task Force. 1996. *Discrimination and Violence Toward Lesbian Women and Gay Men in Philadelphia and Commonwealth of Pennsylvania*. Philadelphia, PA: Philadelphia Lesbian and Gay Task Force.

Pilkington, N. W., and A. D'Augelli. 1995. "Victimization of Lesbian, Gay and Bisexual Youth in Community Settings." *Journal of Community Psychology* 23:34.

Pollack, William S. 2000. *Real Boys' Voices: Boys Speak Out about Drugs, Sex, Violence, Bullying, Sports, School, Parents, and So Much More*. New York: Random House.

Potter, La Forest. 1933. *Strange Loves: A Study in Sexual Abnormalities*. New York: Padell.

Price, James H., and Susan K. Telljohann. 1991. "School Counselors' Perceptions of Adolescent Homosexuals." *Journal of School Health* 61(10); 433–438.

ReligiousTolerance.org, "Protection of Les/Gay Students," *http://www.religioustolerance.org/hom_stud.htm* (cited July 20, 2001).

Remafedi, Gary. 1987. "Male Homosexuality: The Adolescent's Perspective." *Pediatrics* 79: 326–330.

———. 1992. "Demography of Sexual Orientation in Adolescents." *Pediatrics* 89, 714–721.

Reuben, David. 1969. *Everything You Always Wanted to Know about Sex, but Were Afraid to Ask.* New York: David McKay.

Reynolds, David S. 1995. *Walt Whitman: A Cultural Biography.* New York: Knopf.

Rhode Island Task Force on Gay, Lesbian, Bisexual and Transgendered Youth, "School Shouldn't Hurt: Lifting the Burden from Gay, Lesbian, Bisexual and Transgendered Youth," *http://members.tripod.com/~twood/safeschools.html* (cited July 20, 2001).

Richmond, Winifred V. 1934. *An Introduction to Sex Education.* New York: Farrar and Rinehart.

Rosario, M., J. Hunter, and M. J. Rotheram-Borus. 1992. *Unpublished Data on Lesbian Adolescents.* New York: HIV Center for Clinical and Behavioral Studies, New York State Psychiatric Institute.

Rotheram-Borus, M. J., J. Hunter, and M. Rosario. 1994. "Suicidal Behavior and Gay-Related Stress among Gay and Bisexual Male Adolescents." *Journal of Adolescent Research* 9(4); 498–508.

Ryan, Caitlin, and Donna Futterman. 1998. *Lesbian and Gay Youth: Care and Counseling.* New York: Columbia University Press.

Sex Information and Education Council of the United States. 1996. *Guidelines for Comprehensive Sexuality Education: Kindergarten–12th Grade.* New York: SIECUS.

———. 1998. *Filling the Gaps: Hard-to-Teach Topics in Sexuality Education.* New York: SIECUS.

———. "About SIECUS: SIECUS Believes," *http://www.siecus.org/about/abou0001.html* (cited August 21, 2001).

———. "Annotated Bibliographies: Sexuality Education Curricula," *http://www.siecus.org/pubs/biblio/bibs0010.html* (cited August 21, 2001).

Shakeshaft, Charol, Laurie Mandel, Yolanda M. Johnson, Janice Sawyer, Mary Ann Hergenrother, and Ellen Barber. (1997). "Boys Call Me Cow." *Educational Leadership* 55(2): 22–25.

Sullivan, Richard, T. 1996. "The Challenge of HIV Prevention among High-Risk Adolescents." *Health and Social Work* 21(1): 58–65.

Svetkey, Benjamin. 2000. "Is Your TV Set Gay? From Ellen to Will & Grace, How Television Led a Cultural Revolution." *Entertainment Weekly:* 6 October, 24–28.

Telljohann, Susan K., James H. Price, Mohammed Poureslami, and Alyssa Easton. 1995. "Teaching about Sexual Orientation by Secondary Health Teachers." *Journal of School Health* 65(1): 18–22.

Walt Whitman Community School. "Philosophy," *http://www.waltwhitman-school.org/about.htm* (cited August 23, 2001).

Weistheimer, Ruth K. 2000. *Encyclopedia of Sex.* New York: Continuum.

Woog, Dan. 1995. *School's Out: The Impact of Gay and Lesbian Issues on America's Schools.* Los Angeles: Alyson Books.

Youth Pride, Inc. "Creating Safe Schools for Lesbian and Gay Students: A Resource Guide for School Staff," *http://members.tripod.com/~twood/guide.html* (cited July 20, 2001).

Chapter Six

❧ Sex Education and Youth with Disabilities

Sexuality is a natural part of human life. All people, regardless of their mental or physical capacity, must contend with the mental, emotional, physical, and social aspects of sexuality. In terms of sexuality, youth with disabilities are no different from youth without disabilities. Despite the fact that some adults believe that these youth are incapable of love or sex, youth with disabilities must also confront the issues that revolve around acquiring and maintaining relationships—love, affection, physical pleasure, and desire. By the very definition of their disability, some of these youth often have a hard time learning or understanding abstract concepts, and learning about sexuality is further complicated by the fact that they are often sheltered from the outside world (Council for Exceptional Children 2001). This makes some of them vulnerable to a host of problems if they do not learn about sex. Some researchers have found that some youth, especially those with mental retardation, are at risk for sexual exploitation and/or learning inappropriate sexual behaviors when they are not taught sex education (McClennen 1988).

Special education is a mammoth entity within the nation's educational framework and has experienced overwhelming growth since the 1960s. Moreover, youth with disabilities are a heterogeneous group within special education, and individuals' abilities vary widely within types of disabilities. Unfortunately, many youth with special needs do not receive sex education (Council for Exceptional Children 2001) or receive very little sex education in special education (Lero 1994). In fact, research literature seems to support that youth with disabilities often lack vital sexual knowledge. Erickson and Erickson (1992), for instance, found that among a sample of adolescents with spina bifida, many of the youth were uninformed about the role of sex in their lives. Another study of adolescents with spina bifida also found that they knew less about sex than their counterparts without disabilities even though most of them desired marriage and children (Cromer et al. 1990). Only 20 percent of the adolescents with disabilities had information about human sexuality or human reproduction. In their sample of youth with cerebral palsy, spina bifida, muscular dystrophy, and other physical disabilities, Berman et al. (1999) found that the youth were either uninformed or misinformed about sex and/or had misconceptions about sex. The literature on youth with special needs and sex education is sparse. Most of the available literature is focused on youth with mental retardation, but few studies have been published that address sexuality among youth with learning disabilities, behavior disorders, physical disorders, and so forth (Berman et al. 1999).

Special education is based largely on the philosophy of normalization. Wolfsenberger (1972) defined normalization as "means which are as culturally normative as possible, in order to establish and/or maintain personal behaviors and characteristics which are as culturally normative as possible" (28). Translated, this simply means that youth with disabilities should be able to attend school with other children and be taught and treated in a fashion that is as normal as possible. If and when this happens, the youth will inevitably acquire certain knowledge and skills and learn behaviors necessary to live a normal, productive, and fruitful life. Given that love, affection, and sexual desire are basic functions of life, sexual knowledge is crucial if youth with disabilities are expected to live normal lives.

Most professionals agree that youth with disabilities deserve sexual knowledge (American Academy of Pediatrics 1996). Through sex education, these youth can learn about human sexuality and how to contend with their sexual needs and feelings, express love and affection, develop meaningful and lasting human relationships, behave appropriately in social circumstances, protect themselves from maltreatment and diseases, make informed decisions, and respect the rights of others. The scope of this chapter is to present the issues that revolve around the sex education of youth with disabilities. The contents of this chapter are divided into the following: Background on Special Education and Sex Education and Special Education.

BACKGROUND ON SPECIAL EDUCATION

Before discussing the dynamics of sex education in special education, it is important to understand the youth that are served. The information discussed in this section of the chapter is presented in Terms that Describe the Population at Hand, A Historical Perspective, and Special Education Today.

Terms That Describe the Population at Hand

Teachers, parents, and school officials use the following terms in the field of special education. Many people outside the field believe that these words are synonyms, and mainstream media often use these words interchangeably. However, these terms have different meanings.

- **Disorder**—"a general malfunction of mental, physical, or psychological processes . . . a disturbance in normal functioning" (Hardman, Drew, and Egan 1999, 3)
- **Disability**—"reduced function or loss of a particular body part or organ . . . it is often used interchangeably with the term impairment" (Heward 1996, 8)
- **Handicap**—the word literally refers to the time when persons with disabilities used to beg with a cap in their hand. Now the term has come to mean an environmental imposition that limits a person's ability
- **Exceptional**—"refers to individuals . . . whose behavior and/or features deviate from the norm, either above or below, to such an extent that special needs are present and certain services and/or supports may be warranted" (Patton, Blackbourn, and Fad 1996, 4)

In addition, youth with disabilities should be addressed in "person-first" terminology. In other words, the person precedes the disability. Instead of referring to the "learning disabled student," the youth is referred to as the "student with learning disabilities." The emphasis is on the person and not the condition.

A Historical Perspective

Special education has had an interesting history. Persons with disabilities have always had a presence in society. Martin Luther (1483–1546), for instance, believed that people with mental retardation were possessed by the devil, and Danish astronomer Tycho Brahe (1546–1601) regarded his companion, whom he called "imbecile," as having divine connections (Patton, Blackbourn, and Fad 1996). In some instances, people with disabilities were treated horribly. One Massachusetts community in 1699 compensated a citizen for keeping his sister, who evidently had a mental illness, in a kennel-like structure (Schmid 1981). In other civilizations, such persons were considered children of God and were granted certain social privileges (Patton, Blackbourn, and Fad).

Throughout history, however, most people with disabilities have been treated as subhuman and subjected to incarceration, whippings, and execution. Some were cared for, others were institutionalized, but few were educated. The education that did occur was often reserved for youth who were deaf and/or blind. Some of the early special education teachers included:

- ➥ Jean Marc Gaspard Itard (1775–1838). Itard was a leading French physician employed by the National Institute for Deaf-Mutes in Paris. He initially worked with persons who were deaf and later worked with persons considered unteachable. He ultimately believed that physiological stimulation would contribute to a learner's potential (Hardman, Drew, and Egan 1999). His most famous student was Victor, the "wild boy of Aveyron," who was found in a French forest at the age of twelve. Itard devoted five years of intensive attention, education, and stimulation to Victor, and despite the fact that the boy learned some words and became somewhat socialized, Itard considered his work futile. Itard is often considered the father of special education (Smith 2001, 12).
- ➥ Philippe Pinel (1745–1826). Pinel was a French physician and advocate for persons considered insane or "idiots." He believed that these persons needed to be treated humanely, and his teachings incorporated special diets, massages, exercise, and music therapy (Bullock 1992). He believed that these persons were incurable but nonetheless should be treated with dignity.
- ➥ Edouard Seguin (1812–1880). Seguin was a physician educated in the United States who believed in and advocated for the moral treatment of so-called idiots. He used many of the teaching methods he learned from his mentor, Itard.
- ➥ Maria Montessori (1870–1952). Montessori is best known for her teaching methods in early childhood education. The Italian physician initially worked with youth who had mental retardation and later expanded her work to fit the needs of young children.
- ➥ Louis Braille (1809–1852). In 1829, Braille introduced his system of communication for those who were blind. People who are blind continue to read and write through his system of raised dots (called cells) that represent letters, numbers, and words.
- ➥ Thomas H. Gallaudet (1787–1851). Gallaudet is best known

for his association with the university in Washington, D.C., for people who are deaf or hard of hearing. However, it is little known that Gallaudet, the educator and minister, founded the first residential school for the deaf, the American Asylum for the Deaf and Dumb.

•• Samuel Gridley Howe (1801–1876). Howe was a physician who initially worked with youth who were blind but later worked with youth who were labeled *idiotic* and *feeble* (Patton, Blackbourn, and Fad). He founded the Perkins School for the Blind.

•• Dorothea Dix (1802–1887). Dix was a teacher who advocated the humane treatment of people who were mentally ill. She opposed their imprisonment and led reforms to improve the conditions of mental hospitals (Hirsh, Kett, and Trefil 1993).

Special education could not have advanced as it did without the crusading efforts of these advocates and others who are far too numerous to mention.

The formal special education system as it operates today was not built over night. Throughout the twentieth century, the work of psychologists, physicians, sociologists, and teachers contributed to the development of the field as a profession. Despite their contributions, however, youth with disabilities were largely excluded from general education classrooms for nearly three-quarters of the century. Many are surprised to learn that prior to the 1970s, school districts could legally deny education services and enrollment to youth with disabilities (Heward 1996). One youth with a physical disability (and no apparent mental disability) in 1919, for instance, was denied the opportunity to study in his community school because officials believed he "produces a depressing and nauseating effect upon the teachers and school children. . . . [H]e takes up an undue portion of the teacher's time and attention, distracts attention of other pupils, and interferes generally with the discipline and progress of the school" (Johnson 1986, cited in Heward 1996). Even in the 1960s, youth with mild disabilities such as learning disabilities or emotional disorders were educated in the general classroom with no special education services. They were often dismissed as "out of control," "disciplinary problems," "slow learners," "failures," or "ineducable" (Heward). Youth with more severe disabilities such as those who were deaf or blind, were educated in segregated placements. In addition, very little was available for those who were gifted and talented.

The civil rights movement of the 1950s and 1960s contributed to the growth of the field as the movement called for an end to the social discrimination of all minority groups. One of the landmark cases of the movement, *Brown v. Topeka, Kansas, Board of Education*, reaffirmed that all U.S. citizens must have an equal opportunity to an education. The Supreme Court ruled, "In these days, it is doubtful that any child may reasonably be expected to succeed in life if he is denied the opportunity of an education. Such an opportunity, where the state has undertaken to provide, is a right which must be made available to all on equal terms" (*Brown v. Topeka, Kansas, Board of Education*, 1954 as cited in Hardman, Drew, and Egan 1999, 20). For nearly twenty-one years, however, youth with disabilities continued to be denied their right to a public education.

In the 1960s, people with disabilities began to receive national attention. In 1962, for instance, President John F. Kennedy, whose sister Rosemary had a form of mental retardation, established a federal commission on mental retardation. In 1963, the Learning Disabilities Association of America (formerly Association for Children with Learning Disabilities) was formed. In 1965, President Lyndon B. Johnson's War on Poverty initiated the early intervention project, Head Start. That same year, the passage of the Elementary and Secondary Education Act granted education services to youth with disabilities. In addition, a 1966 amendment created the Bureau of Education for the Handicapped (now known as the Office of Special Education and Rehabilitative Services).

In the 1970s, major litigation collectively paved the way for a landmark law that would officially establish special education, PL 94–142, Education for All Handicapped Children Act. The court cases are found in and described further in figure 6.1. These rulings confirmed that all youth with disabilities have a right to an appropriate education regardless of the severity of their disability. In 1975, President Gerald Ford enacted PL 94–142. The law dramatically changed the service delivery for youth ages five to twenty-one with disabilities and guaranteed their legal right to a free, appropriate public education. The provisions included:

- requirements that states develop statewide plans that (a) detailed the delivery of instructional services for youth with disabilities, and (b) outlined the procedures to locate and identify youth with disabilities
- certain rights for the child and parents/guardians; that parents would be notified of any assessments or adjustments to their child's label, placement, or instructional plan; that parents would have the right to an impartial due process hearing if they disagreed with the school's decision

Figure 6.1. Major Court Cases that Impacted Special Education

Year	Court Case	Outcome
1967	*Hobson v. Hansen*	Court ruled that school districts cannot use standardized test scores as a sole criterion for special education placement; ability tracking of students is unconstitutional.
1970	*Diana v. State Board of Education*	Court ruled that school districts cannot make an educational placement based on culturally biased measures; youth have to be tested in their native language.
1971	*Pennsylvania Association for Retarded Children (PARC) v. Commonwealth of Pennsylvania*	Court confirmed that children with mental retardation have a right to an education; parents have a right to access records and be notified of placement or service delivery adjustments; service delivery should be free; individual programs should be completed in order to receive an appropriate education.
1972	*Mills v. Board of Education*	Court confirmed that every youth has a right to an education; a lack of funds is no excuse for denial of or the provision of insufficient services.
1972	*Larry P. v. Riles*	Court ruled that IQ scores alone cannot be the criterion for special education placement.
1972	*Wyatt v. Stickney*	Court ruled that institutionalized persons had the right to appropriate treatment.

- nondiscriminatory and bias-free testing conducted in the youth's native language
- confidentiality of students' records
- creation of individualized education programs (IEP) for every student with a disability, with goals and objectives based on the student's present level of functioning
- requirement that every student with a disability be educated in the least restrictive environment composed of youth without disabilities whenever possible

Additional legislation has since been enacted that has further ensured the equal rights of youth with disabilities (some are found in fig-

Figure 6.2. Critical Federal Legislation in Special Education since 1975

Year	Legislation	Outcome
1986	PL 99-457, Education of Handicapped Act amendments	Mandated extension of services to preschoolers (three to five year olds). This population would be entitled to the same services and protections as older children with disabilities. States were given financial incentives to provide early intervention for infants and toddlers. An individualized family service plan would be developed to meet the unique needs of the youth and their families.
1990	PL 101-476, Individuals with Disabilities Education Act	The 1975 law was renamed to reflect person-first terminology. Autism and traumatic brain injury were recognized as new categories of disability. Schools had to offer transition services. Individual transition plans were to be developed for youth no later than age 16. Rehabilitation and social work were added to the definition of related services.
1990	PL 101-336, Americans with Disabilities Act	Considered the civil rights protection for people with disabilities. Such individuals were provided protection in public and private employment, public services, public accommodations, public transportation, and telecommunications.
1997	PL 105-17, amendments to the Individuals with Disabilities Education Act	Emphasis shift from right to education to achievement outcomes (Hardman, Drew, and Egan 1999). Functional behavioral assessment and behavioral intervention plans may be required for students with behavioral problems.

ure 6.2). Some special education professionals have coined the phrase "from the womb to the tomb" to underscore that persons with disabilities are protected for their lifetime. Indeed, federal legislation in the last forty years has made it possible for persons with disabilities today to live their lives as normally as possible. These people have become empowered as they have learned that they too are entitled to inalienable human rights.

Figure 6.3. Youth with Disabilities Served in Special Education, 1997–1998

Type of Disability	Number Served in Thousands	Percentage Distribution	Number Served as a Percent of Total Enrollment
High-Incidence Disabilities			
Specific Learning Disabilities	2,726	46.2	5.91
Speech or Language Impairments	1,059	17.9	2.30
Mental Retardation	589	10.0	1.28
Serious Emotional Disturbance	453	7.7	0.98
Low-Incidence Disabilities			
Hearing Impairment	69	1.2	0.15
Visual Impairment	25	0.4	0.05
Multiple Disabilities	106	1.8	0.23
Deaf-Blindness	1	<0.05	<0.05
Autism and Traumatic Brain Injury	54	0.9	0.12
Physical and Health Disabilities			
Orthopedic Impairments	67	1.1	0.15
Other Health Impairments	190	3.2	0.41
Early Intervention			
Developmental Delay	2	<0.05	<0.05
Preschoolers with Disabilities	564	9.6	1.22
Total	5,904	100	12.80

Source: Adapted from U.S. Department of Education, Office of Special Education and Rehabilitative Services, *Annual Report to Congress on the Implementation of the Individuals with Disabilities Education Act,* National Center for Education Statistics, Common Core of Data survey, 1999.

Special Education Today

Contemporary special education is not an isolated domain in the education system. Instead, special education is interdisciplinary, with psychologists, audiologists, social workers, physical therapists, occupational therapists, speech pathologists, and others collaborating to deliver instruction and related services to meet the needs of youth with disabilities, regardless of the severity. The most unique feature of special education is that every youth in special education (K–12) has an individualized education program (IEP) made up of goals and objectives written according to his or her ability. The services and instruction are free and, whenever possible, provided in the environment of youth without disabilities. According to the 1998 *Annual Report to Congress on*

the Implementation of the Individuals with Disabilities Education Act,
5,904,000 youth received special education services in the 1997–1998
school year. This figure represents 12.8 percent of the total population of
youth served by federal education programs (see figure 6.3).

All youth in special education should receive a nondiscriminatory and multidisciplinary assessment, and parents should be involved
in the referral process from the moment a professional suspects that a
disability is present. A team of professionals should gather to assess individual youth in their native language, use assessment tools that are
free of cultural bias, and several sources of information should be used
to make decisions about the service delivery. Parents should be notified
of the entire process, their written consent should be obtained prior to
any evaluation, and they should be invited to contribute to the process
whenever possible. Based on the evaluations, the team, inclusive of parents, should gather to write the IEP. The IEP is composed of written
statements that outline the delivery of instructional and related services. The IEP generally includes the following.

- information on the student's present level of ability and performance and how these affect academic and social progress
  in general education
- a statement of measurable, short- and long-term annual
  goals based on the student's level of performance
- a statement of the services or supplementary aids to be provided to the student
- a statement of parties responsible for providing instruction
  and related services
- the date of service delivery implementation: when services
  start, how often, and how long
- a statement addressing the continuous assessment of the student's progress toward the annual goals

The team has to determine the placement best suited for the student, and a concerted effort should be made to educate the student in
the least restrictive environment. Schools are required to offer a continuum of placement options that range from the least restrictive environment to the most restrictive. The least restrictive environment is the
general education classroom; the most restrictive is a homebound or
hospital program. As many as 95 percent of youth with disabilities receive special education services within a general education building (for
instance, in a general education classroom, resource classroom, or self-
contained classroom), and the remaining 5 percent are placed outside

the general education (in hospital programs, institutions, and so forth) (Hardman, Drew, and Egan 1999).

Finally, special education cannot be addressed without a discussion of inclusion. *Inclusion* became one of the buzzwords of the 1990s, and a mention of the concept is likely to cause a heated debate. Inclusion means that students with disabilities attend their home school and receive instructional and related services in general education classrooms with their peers of the same age and grade level. Instead of resource or self-contained classrooms, special education comes to the students, and there are never segregated special areas, schools, or institutions. The concept of inclusion evolved because some educators failed to see the success of dual education programs— one for the general population of youth and another for youth with disabilities. Some found the continuum of services to be divisive, ineffective, and costly (Kaplan 1996), and consequently, they advocated the inclusion of youth with disabilities in the general education classroom. Those that advocate inclusion believe that it works because teachers tend to use similar teaching strategies, and adaptations and modifications can be implemented in the general education classroom. Inclusion advocates argue that a separate special education system makes communication between teachers difficult and pullout programs (such as the resource classroom) are disruptive. Moreover, they believe that segregation gives all youth the impression that people with disabilities should be segregated. The full integration of students with disabilities not only dispels the assumption that those who are different should be segregated but inclusion also reinforces that persons with disabilities have a right to participate fully and can succeed in the community.

Professionals who are doubtful or skeptical of inclusion are generally those who have had students with disabilities in their classrooms and failed to receive the support to teach them. These professionals believe they have not received the teaching strategies that youth with disabilities require, and simple adaptations and modifications alone cannot satisfy their unique needs (Kaplan 1996). Many of them have not acquired the training to adapt or modify their instruction for youth who have visual or hearing impairments, for instance, and many do not want to. They favor the continuum of options because they believe that parents, professionals, and youth should have choices when considering a placement. No one placement, they assert, satisfies the needs of all students with disabilities. Based on their experiences, these professionals further assert that teaching students with disabilities in the general education classroom is not plausible given that they already teach a classroom full of students who have diverse abilities and needs. Inclusion will be debated for a long time, and until parents, teachers, school officials, and special education service providers can reach a consensus on inclusion, youth will continue to receive special education services in the least restrictive environment.

SEX EDUCATION AND SPECIAL EDUCATION

Youth with disabilities have a right to sex education (Colson and Carlson 1993); nothing should preclude their opportunity to learn about human sexual development. As the American Academy of Pediatrics (1996) asserted, they have "similar curiosities, drives, and interests in their own bodies and in the bodies of others" (1). Historically, however, these persons have been denied their right to sexual expression and freedom (Kaplan 1996). Society has generally frowned upon the sexuality of persons with disabilities, especially those with mental retardation. Persons with disabilities were often subject to sterilization, and the idea of sex or marriage was quashed. President John F. Kennedy's sister, who was mentally retarded, is a disastrous case in point. In 1941, her father, Ambassador Joseph P. Kennedy, had her lobotomized to curtail her developing interest in sexuality. Tragically, the lobotomy failed and left her more severely disabled. Since then, she has lived her life in a Wisconsin institution.

Youth with disabilities have been sheltered from sex education. For decades, many professionals and parents have sought to protect them from sex education for fear that it would disrupt them and cause them to act out sexually. These youth were taught to repress sexual feelings, and those who did not were censured and made to feel deviant (Walker-Hirsh and Champagne 1988 cited in Colson and Carlson). In the sixties, institutionalized persons with disabilities who were caught masturbating were given medication to curtail what was seen as a serious problem (Woodhill 1992 cited in SafePlace 2001). Some parents and professionals have denied their children sex education because they wanted to protect and preserve their naïve, childlike character (SafePlace 2001). Others have mistakenly assumed that youth with disabilities are uninterested in or incapable of establishing and maintaining romantic relationships. Some parents become far more consumed with the disability itself, and sexuality is one of the aspects of their child's life that is ignored. The American Academy of Pediatrics (1996) emphasized that many parents are reluctant to discuss sex with their children because they cannot find sexually healthy role models with disabilities.

In schools, very few youth with disabilities receive formal sex education (Zetlin and Turner 1985). When sex education programs are available, they are often fear-based with little or no discussion on relationships, intimacy issues, contraceptives, STDs, and the like (Berman et al. 1999). One study found that half of youth with physical disabilities did not receive sex education (Blum et al. 1991 cited in Berman et al. 1999); ironically, those students who did receive sex education did not learn specific information on sex in the context of their disability. Another study found that nearly 80 percent of youth with disabilities had some knowledge of sex; however, less than 20 percent had learned about sex from a school-based program (Blackburn 1995). Those who learned about sex from the programs found the information inadequate and irrelevant. Other studies have produced similar findings. Brantlinger (1992), for instance, found that only one-third of students with mild disabilities (for example, learning disabilities or emotional disturbances) received sex education. Another investigation found that individualized education programs rarely mention sex education as part of a student's short- or long-term IEP goals (Frith, Mitchell, and Lindsey 1981 cited in May and Kundert 1996).

Explanations vary as to why youth with disabilities are not provided with adequate sex education. No research was found to validate the following hypothesis; but arguably, if youth in general receive a limited sex education and most youth with disabilities are educated in general education classrooms, then it can be reasonably assumed that youth with disabilities would also receive a limited sex education. Some believe, however, that these youth do not receive sex education because they are segregated from the general population of students who do receive sex education. Others assert that sex programs are provided during physical education (PE), thereby making it impossible for youth with certain physical disabilities and who have adaptive PE in separate settings to participate in the programs (Berman et al. 1999).

The university special education training could be a factor in the likelihood that sex education is not provided. Some investigators have found that special education teachers, although willing to teach sex education, are not prepared to teach it (May and Kundert 1996). A study of 302 teachers, for instance, found that 41 percent of the special education teacher preparation programs across the nation offer no coursework on sex education (May and Kundert). Another study indicated that teachers of today are no more better prepared to teach sex education than special education teachers of previous generations.

Finally, despite the fact we live in the twenty-first century, some professionals continue to maintain that youth with disabilities are asexual beings and consequently do not need sex education. Some believe that these youth will never need sex education because they will never marry and have sex. Moreover, some still believe that youth with physical disabilities are uninterested or incapable of having sex (Garell 1994). This could not be farther from the truth.

Sexual Needs of Youth with Disabilities

Youth with disabilities are undoubtedly interested in and capable of intimate relationships. The following youth explain their experiences with dating, sexuality, and marriage.

- ❖ Joshua, 17 years old, has spina bifida.
  I have a very hard time dating. . . . A lot of girls I ask out get an impatient look in their eyes, or they look around because they're embarrassed to be seen with me. I wish they'd forget other people and get to know me. . . . I know whoever I end up marrying will have to have a lot of understanding and patience. I just haven't found my girl yet, that's all (Garell 1994, 66).
- ❖ John, 16 years old, has cerebral palsy, a speech impairment, and a hearing disability. He uses crutches or an electric wheelchair for mobility.
  I haven't even had a date yet. Sometimes I fantasize about marriage, but I haven't really thought about it much. Sex education at school last year gave me the general information. My parents have tried to talk to me about it, but we haven't had a real discussion yet (Kriegsman, Zaslow, D'Zmura-Rechsteiner 1992, 25).
- ❖ June, 17 years old, has cerebral palsy.
  I've been invited on dates for dinner and movies. Usually I find I don't have to be concerned about dates because I find myself with people who are understanding. I've thought about marriage and always wonder if there is something I could not do, with body posturing maybe. I would rather marry an able-bodied person, I think. But whoever I'm with will be understanding. I would like to have children, but I would worry about raising them. Younger children can be cruel, and I wouldn't want them to be teased about me (Kriegsman, Zaslow, D'Zmura-Rechsteiner 1992, 26).
- ❖ Tina, 12 years old, has muscular dystrophy and uses an electric wheelchair.

*I've had a boyfriend but no date; my mother says I can't
date until I'm sixteen. She has explained sex to me. I don't
think much about marriage, but I would like to have
children. I'd probably adopt at least one—maybe more, so
they wouldn't be lonely* (Kriegsman, Zaslow, D'Zmura-
Rechsteiner 1992, 27).

These testimonies convey that these youth have the same sexual
needs and desires as those without disabilities, and sex education could
address these issues. When sex education is not provided, these youth
grow up to be adults who are unsure of how to create and maintain relationships or are frightened of sex in general. The following adults with
disabilities share their experiences.

- Narelle is an adult with mental retardation.
  *Mum used to warn me against boys. She'd mention that boys
  can give you children, and say, don't get into trouble. I had only
  seen little boys running around without clothes and I didn't
  know they grew. When I had that experience I was
  frightened. . . . My periods started when I was eleven years old.
  Mum never told me that girls get periods. I started getting sick
  when I was at school and when I got home I had blood on my
  pants. Then Mum just told me that all girls get that* (Fegan,
  Rauch, and McCarthy 1995, 39).
- This 23-year-old man has a spinal cord injury.
  *My hormones are raging, but I have no outlet. I go out a
  lot with friends, but even friends who were potential lovers
  before are now certainly just friends. I can't seem to shake
  that "Wow, you are a great person" line. I know that in the
  long run I will end up with someone who is great, but I could
  really just go for a one-night stand or two! I'm a pretty good-
  looking guy so the prospects are there, but what do I do?*
  (Karp 1999, 330).
- David is an adult with mental retardation.
  *I didn't know anything about sex till I . . . was about twenty-
  eight or twenty-nine. I hit it off with one of the girls straight
  away and she invited me out and our relationship grew. She
  was very heavy on me sexually—she wanted to live with
  me. . . . Mum always hoped I would get married. I often wondered what would happen. I thought I would end up as an old
  bachelor* (Fegan, Rauch, McCarthy, 38).

Testimonies such as these affirm that youth with disabilities need sex education. In the last twenty-five years, the concept of normalization has been the impetus for federal legislation that has empowered people with disabilities. They now expect access to and participation in mainstream society (Smith 2001), and this has made them more visible in communities today than ever before. They are no longer institutionalized or segregated from society, and more youth with disabilities are educated in the general education environment. Given these relatively recent accomplishments, there are now greater opportunities for people with disabilities "to develop friendships and intimate relationships, . . . (that result) in marriage and having children" (Sundram and Stavis 1994, 255). For this reason alone, youth with disabilities need the skills that will enable them to have sexually healthy and fulfilled lives.

Youth with disabilities, especially those with mental retardation, need sex education so that they can learn to protect themselves from sexual abuse. The rate of sexual abuse among youth with disabilities is high. The National Center on Child Abuse and Neglect (1992) found that 36 of 1,000 youth with disabilities were sexually abused. This rate is 1.7 times higher than the rate for youth without disabilities. Youth with mental retardation are particularly vulnerable to sexual violence because they are often unaware that they are being abused. Without knowledge of sex and privacy issues, they are at risk for abuse or harassment (McClennen 1988). One young woman with mental retardation recalled her childhood experiences this way: "The boys at school touched me in the private area—touched me here. I didn't know what they were doing—and why they were calling me bad names—because I didn't know anything about sex. Even when I was in primary school the boys got me that way, when I was seven or eight years old" (Fegan, Rauch, and McCarthy 1995, 40).

Many parents are rightfully protective of their children with mental retardation because they feel that their children are vulnerable. However, living an overprotected life increases the likelihood that they will be abused. The Council for Exceptional Children 2001 stated, "This overprotection often heightens the risk of abuse. Lack of knowledge, habitual overcompliance, limited assertiveness, and undifferentiated trusting are frequent by-products of this 'protected' lifestyle" (1).

Sex education is particularly beneficial to youth with learning disabilities because some of them lack the cognitive ability, emotional maturity, and judgment skills that are needed in potentially risky sexual situations (Smith and Strick 1997). Some of these youth have reasoning problems and find it difficult to interpret social cues such as body language, facial expression, and human emotions. Research has well documented that youth with learning disabilities are often unpopular among their peers because they have "an inability to use language in social situations, an insensitivity to social cues, an inability to correctly perceive their own social status, and an inability to adapt to social situations" (Bender 1998, 110). These inabilities, compounded with the fact that most youth will do whatever it takes to fit in or become popular, make them vulnerable to being manipulated into a sexual situation. One girl with a learning disability was reported to have unprotected sex with boys because she craved their attention and her standards were easily compromised (Osman 1982). Another 16-year-old girl completely misjudged a boy's intention when she believed she was going out on a date. Instead, she found herself humiliated at a parking lot where she was told how to perform oral sex; she was the victim of a cruel joke. She was heartbroken because she had believed the boy was romantically interested in her (Smith and Strick 1997). This girl and other youth like her need sex education because they often do not have friends with whom to share important milestones (first date, first kiss, crushes, and so forth). They ultimately fail to learn the dating and intimacy standard if they have no peer support from which to draw feedback.

Professional Recommendations for Sex Education

Associations and professionals alike offer recommendations for sex education programs for persons with disabilities. Some of the recommendations stress the importance of validating the right to a sexually healthy lifestyle. The Association of Retarded Citizens (2001), for instance, outlined the inherent sexual rights for persons with mental retardation and related developmental disabilities. They believe that these persons are rightfully entitled to

- privacy
- shared love
- friendships and emotional relationships
- information on all aspects of sexuality
- marriage and children (as an informed decision)
- sexual expression that is respective of social and cultural norms

Others offer recommendations to the sex education content. The Council for Exceptional Children (CEC), for example, believes that youth with mental retardation can benefit from content and materials that are

- simple but appropriate for the student's intellectual ability
- concrete and that reinforce the presented concepts or skills
- closely related to real life

The CEC further asserts that these youth should have ample opportunities to interact with youth without disabilities to learn some appropriate social behaviors from those they may regard as role models.

Romaneck and Kuehl (1992) stated similar recommendations for youth with learning disabilities, mild mental retardation, and moderate emotional disturbances. They believe that these youth should be exposed to material that is chronologically appropriate for their age and modified to meet the needs of the students. They stress that teachers should be mindful of their own values and avoid judgment calls. Instead, teachers need to listen to their students and validate the values that they may have. The American Academy of Pediatrics (1996) recommended that sex education for youth with developmental disabilities have core objectives. The objectives are focused on acceptable displays of affection and self-protective skills. Sex education should teach these youth

- age-appropriate forms of affection
- societal expectations for privacy and modesty
- acceptable private and public behaviors
- the difference between pleasure and affection
- their right to refuse being touched and to notify someone when they have been violated

McClennen (1988) had similar recommendations. She added, however, that these youth need to learn about the mechanics of their physical bodies, the act of and consequences of sexual intercourse, and how to contend with genital sexual feelings (masturbation).

In addition, these youth need to have opportunities to share their thoughts in a safe learning environment. Some of these youth may be confused or ashamed of their sexual feelings, and they need to know that everyone has similar feelings. SafePlace (2001) offered recommendations that are more specific. In sex education, she added, youth with developmental disabilities should learn

- personal boundaries—appropriate touches at appropriate times and places
- professional terminology to describe sexual anatomy
- about basic emotions and feelings associated with various touches

⟶ how to resolve an uncomfortable situation
⟶ that they are entitled to choices or preferences and to recognize differences (some may choose to abstain, others may be homosexual)

Colson and Carlson (1993) provided an elaborate AIDS/sex education program for youth with disabilities. Their program was composed of eight skill areas, each divided into four levels (readiness, beginning, intermediate, and advanced). The skills and goals are included in figure 6.4. The students learn about each skill at the level that best meets their intellectual ability and progress upward (as much as possible) to *advanced*. If students have moderate mental retardation, for example, they start at *readiness* and work toward *advanced*. They have different starting points within each skill so that the same group could begin at *readiness* for General Knowledge but at *intermediate* for Positive Self-Esteem. Another group of students with learning disabilities, for instance, may all be able to start developing a skill at the advanced level.

Other sex education curricula for youth with disabilities are commercially available. According to a SIECUS (2001) bibliography devoted to sexuality and disability, twenty programs can address various aspects of sexuality. Some of the programs serve certain youth with disabilities (for example, hearing impairment, mental retardation, and so on) and other programs are focused on particular topics such as sexual abuse or menarche. Some of the programs include

⟶ Being Sexual: An Illustrated Series on Sexuality and Relationships, Dave Hingsburg and Susan Ludwig
⟶ Changes in You: An Introduction to Sexuality Education through an Understanding of Puberty, Peggy C. Siege
⟶ Janet's Got Her Period, Judi Gray and Jitka Jilich
⟶ "No-Go-Tell," Elisabeth J. Krents and Shella A. Brenner
⟶ Signs for Sexuality: A Resource Manual for Deaf and Hard of Hearing Individuals, Their Families, and Professionals, Marlyn Minkin and Laurie Rosen-Ritt
⟶ Talking Sex! Practical Approaches and Strategies for Working with People Who Have Developmental Disabilities When the Topic is Sex, Lisa T. Maurer

The limited literature available is consistent: youth with disabilities would benefit substantially from sex education. Professionals have presented their arguments, and others can qualitatively attest to the fact that their programs work. However, no quantitative data was found to

Figure 6.4. Colson and Carlson (1992) Sex Education Model for Students with Disabilities

Skill Area	Students Learn:
1. General Knowledge	The AIDS basics, from identification to risk factors
2. Affective Development	The social and emotional impact of AIDS
3. Sexuality and Physical Growth	About the physical body and sexual feelings
4. Positive Self-esteem	About themselves and how esteem affects sexual behavior
5. Personal Relationships	Relationship dynamics, from peers to family
6. Sexual Abuse	Identification, prevention, and intervention skills regarding sexual abuse
7. Drug Abuse	Identification, prevention, and intervention skills regarding drug abuse
8. Sexual Responsibility and Safer Sex Practices	To exercise responsible sexual choices and behaviors

Source: Adapted from "HIV/AIDS Education for Students with Special Needs," by Steven E. Colson and Judith K. Carlson, 1993. In *Intervention in School and Clinic* 28(5): 262.

support whether sex education has increased the sexual knowledge or enhanced a positive sexual attitude of youth with disabilities (Whitehouse and McCabe 1997). By no means does this suggest that sex education should not be provided to these youth. However, this does call attention to the need to make a concerted effort to empirically measure the effectiveness of these programs. Until this is accomplished, these youth may not acquire the skills they need to succeed as an independent community member.

SUMMARY

Historically, persons with disabilities were believed to be incapable of and/or uninterested in love, marriage, sex, and childbearing. They were often sterilized, institutionalized, or overprotected to their detriment. If they exhibited any sexual behaviors, they were immediately reprimanded. Rarely did they receive a sex education that promoted a sexually healthy lifestyle. Times have definitely changed for people with disabilities living in the United States. In the last twenty-five years, several laws have been enacted that entitle them to access to and active participation in mainstream society. Institutions and asylums are becoming obsolete, and people with disabilities are contributing members of society living in the community and learning in the general education classroom. People with disabilities need sex education if society expects them to live healthy lives. Sex education validates that they have sexual needs and desires as does everyone else, and it teaches them how to develop and maintain intimate relationships. These youth need sex education for the very same reason that all youth need sex education—to become sexually healthy and have sexually fulfilled lives.

REFERENCES

American Academy of Pediatrics. 1996. "Sexuality Education of Children and Adolescents with Developmental Disabilities." *Journal of the American Academy of Pediatrics* 97(2): 275–278.

American Psychological Association. 1995. *Publication Manual of the American Psychological Association.* Washington, DC: American Psychological Association.

Association of Retarded Citizens, "Sexuality: Position Statement #9," *http://thearc.org/posits/sex.html* (cited October 6, 2001).

Bender, William L. 1998. *Learning Disabilities: Characteristics, Identification, and Teaching Strategies.* Boston: Allyn and Bacon.

Berman, Helene, Dorothy Harris, Rick Enright, Michelle Gilpin, Tamzin Cathers, and Gloria Bukovy. 1999. "Sexuality and the Adolescent with a Physical Disability: Understandings and Misunderstandings." *Issues in Comprehensive Pediatric Nursing* 22: 183–196.

Blackburn, M. 1995. "Sexuality, Disability and Abuse: Advice for Life . . . Not Just for Kids." *Child: Care, Health, and Development* 21(5): 351–361.

Blum, R. W., M. D. Resnick, R. Nelson, and A. St. Germaine. 1991. "Family and Peer Issues among Adolescents with Spina Bifida and Cerebral Palsy." *Pediatrics* 88: 280–285.

Brantlinger, E. 1992. "Sexuality Education in the Secondary Special Education Curriculum: Teachers' Perceptions and Concerns." *Teacher Education and Special Education* 15: 32–40.

Brown v. Topeka, Kansas, Board of Education. 1954. 347 U.S. 483.

Bullock, Lyndal M. 1992. *Exceptionalities in Children and Youth.* Boston: Allyn and Bacon.

Colson, Steven E., and Judith K. Carlson. 1993. "HIV/AIDS Education for Students with Special Needs." *Intervention in School and Clinic:* 262–274.

Council for Exceptional Children/ERIC Clearinghouse on Disabilities and Gifted Education, "Mental Retardation and Sex Education—FAQ," *http://www.cec.sped.org/ericec/faq/mr-sexed.html* (cited October 10, 2001).

Cromer, B. A., B. Enrile, K. McKoy, M. Gerhardstein, M. Fitzpatrick, and J. Judis. 1990. "Knowledge, Attitudes, and Behavior Related to Sexuality in Adolescents with Chronic Disability." *Developmental Medicine and Child Neurology* 32: 602–609.

Erickson, D., and L. Erickson. 1992. "Knowledge of Sexuality in Adolescents with Spina Bifida. *Canadian Journal of Human Sexuality* 1(4): 194–199.

Fegan, Lydia, Anne Rauch, and Wendy McCarthy. 1995. *Sexuality and People with Intellectual Disability.* Baltimore: Paul H. Brookes Publishing Company.

Frith, G., J. Mitchell, and J. Lindsey. 1981. "Sex Education: The Neglected Dimension on the Secondary Level Individualized Plans." *The Clearing House* 54: 197–199.

Garell, Dale C. 1994. *The Encyclopedia of Health: Medical Disorders and Their Treatment.* New York: Chelsea House Publishers.

Hardman, Michael L., Clifford J. Drew, and M. Winston Egan. 1999. *Human Exceptionality: Society, School, and Family.* Boston: Allyn and Bacon.

Heward, William, L. 1996. *Exceptional Children: An Introduction to Special Education.* Englewood Cliffs, NJ: Merrill Prentice Hall.

Hirsh, E. D., Joseph F. Kett, and James Trefil. 1993. *The Dictionary of Cultural Literacy: What Every American Needs to Know.* Boston: Houghton Mifflin Company.

Johnson, T. P. 1986. *The Principal's Guide to the Educational Rights of Handicapped Students.* Reston, VA: National Association of Secondary School Prinicipals.

Kaplan, Paul S. 1996. *Pathways for Exceptional Children: School, Home, and Culture.* St. Paul, MN: West Publishing Company.

Karp, Gary. 1999. *Life on Wheels: For the Active Wheelchair User.* Sebastopol, CA: O'Reilly and Associates, Inc.

Kriegsman, Kay H., Elinor L. Zaslow, Jennifer D'Zmura-Rechsteiner. 1992. *Taking Charge: Teenagers Talk about Life and Physical Disabilities.* Bethesda, MD: Woodbine House, Inc.

Lero, Marc. 1994. "Teaching Adolescents about AIDS." *Teaching Exceptional Children* 26(4): 49–51.

May, Deborah C., and Kundert, D. K. 1996. "Are Special Educators Prepared to Meet the Sex Education Needs of Their Students? A Progress Report." *The Journal of Special Education* 29(4): 433–441.

McClennen, Sandra. 1988. "Sexuality and Students with Mental Retardation." *Teaching Exceptional Children* 20(4): 59–61.

National Association of State Boards of Education. 1992. *Winners All: A Call for Inclusive Schools.* Alexandria, VA: National Association of State Boards of Education.

Osman, Betty B. 1982. *No One to Play With: The Social Side of Learning Disabilities.* New York: Random House.

Patton, James R., Joseph M. Blackbourn, and Kathleen S. Fad. 1996. *Exceptional Individuals in Focus.* Englewood Cliffs, NJ: Merrill Prentice Hall.

Romaneck, Greg M., and Robert Kuehl. 1992. "Sex Education for Students with High-Incidence Special Needs." *Teaching Exceptional Children* 25(1): 22–24.

SafePlace, "Providing Sexuality Education to People with Disabilities," *http://www.austin-safeplace.org/home.htm* (cited October 10, 2001).

Schmid, Rex. 1981. "Historical Development." In *Childhood Behavior Disorder: Applied Research and Educational Practice,* ed. R. A. Algozzine, R. Schmid, and Cecil D. Mercer. Austin, TX: PRO-ED.

Sex Information and Education Council of the United States, "Sexuality and Disability," *http://www.siecus.org/pubs/biblio/bibs0009/html* (cited October 6, 2001).

Smith, Corrine, and Lisa Strick. 1997. *Learning Disabilities: A to Z: A Parent's Complete Guide to Learning Disabilities from Pre-School to Adulthood.* New York: The Free Press.

Smith, Deborah Deutsch. 2001. *Introduction to Special Education: Teaching in an Age of Opportunity.* Boston: Allyn and Bacon.

Sundram, Clarence J., and Paul F. Stavis. 1994. "Sexuality and Mental Retardation: Unmet Challenges." *Mental Retardation* 32(4): 255–264.

Whitehouse, Michele A., and Marita P. McCabe. 1997. "Sex Education Programs for People with Intellectual Disability: How Effective Are They?" *Education and Training in Mental Retardation and Developmental Disabilities* 31: 229–240.

Wolfsenberger, W. 1972. *The Principle of Normalization in Human Services.* Toronto: National Institute on Mental Retardation.

Zetlin, A. G., and J. L. Turner. 1985. "Transition from Adolescent to Adulthood: Perspectives of Mentally Retarded Individuals and Their Families." *Teaching Exceptional Children* 26(4):49–51.

Chapter Seven

☙ Organizations, Associations, and Governmental Agencies

A vast number of organizations base their mission on some aspect of sex education. Many of these organizations were sources of information included in this text. The following organizations can provide additional information on sex education not contained herein. The organizations are divided according to the aspect with which they are most closely associated: General Sex Education; Sexual Abuse and Harassment; Sexual Orientation; and Youth with Disabilities.

GENERAL SEX EDUCATION

Professional Associations

American Academy of Pediatrics
Division of Child and Adolescent Health
141 Northwest Point Blvd.
Elk Grove Village, IL 60007-1098
Telephone: (847) 434-4000
http://www.aap.org

Dedicated to the emotional and physical health of children from birth to young adulthood, the association addresses an array of topics related to the well-being of this age group. Its home page provides information on topics such as back-to-school tips for parents and the presidential address on stem cell research. The site search button will locate articles and other resources on sex education.

American Association for Health Education
(An Association of the American Alliance for Health,
Physical Education, Recreation, and Dance)
1900 Association Drive
Reston, VA 20191

Telephone: (800) 213-7193
http://www.med.usf.edu/~kmbrown/AAHE.htm

The organization is comprised of more than 7,500 health education professionals and is the oldest organization dedicated to health education. The association has eleven special interest areas and a project devoted to HIV/AIDS prevention education. The association publishes the *Journal of School Health.*

American Association of Sex Educators, Counselors and Therapists
P.O. Box 5488
Richmond, VA 23220-0488
http://www.aasect.org

The association promotes sexual health through sexual therapy, counseling, and education and provides professional training and certification on sex education. To encourage active research and further develop sex education, the association publishes the *Journal of Sex Education and Therapy.*

American Foundation for AIDS Research
1515 Broadway, Suite 3601
New York, NY 10036
Telephone: (212) 719-0033
http://www.amfar.org/

Considered the leading organization on HIV/AIDS research and advocacy, the foundation remains loyal to all aspects of AIDS inclusive of treatment and education. The website finds current news related to HIV/AIDS, programs, grants, treatment centers, etc. The site search button will locate specific information related to HIV/AIDS.

American Medical Association
Child and Adolescent Health Program
515 North State Street
Chicago, IL 60610
Telephone: (312) 464-5000
http://www.ama-assn.org/

This organization of physicians is dedicated to the health and physical well-being of youth, adolescents, and adults alike. The AMA is an enormous organization with advocacy and research in all areas of health and medicine. The site search button will find information on most aspects of sex education.

American Public Health Association

800 I Street, NW
Washington, DC 20001-3710
Telephone: (202) 777-APHA
http://www.apha.org/

The APHA is one of the oldest organizations concerned with disease prevention and health promotion. Its website is extensive, complete with button links to programs, current legislation, continuing education, special interest groups, state public health associations, etc. The association has a publication catalog, and publishes the *American Journal of Public Health* and *The Nation's Health*. A button link will search databases for sex education information.

American School Health Association

7263 State Route 43
P.O. Box 708
Kent, Ohio 44240
Telephone: (330) 678-1601
http://www.ashaweb.org/

With its mission to "Promote the health of the nation's youth," ASHA is comprised of professionals from multiple disciplines who cater to the health of children. The association seeks to improve and maintain the physical and emotional well-being of school children through a comprehensive school health program. Its publications catalog offers material to enhance school health programs including sex education. A website link to www.HealthTeacher.com provides teachers with lesson plans related to health education. The association publishes *Journal of School Health*.

American Social Health Association

P.O. Box 13827
Research Triangle Park, NC 27709
Telephone: (800) 230-6039
HIV/AIDS Hotline: (800) 342-AIDS
STD Hotline: (800) 227-8922
Herpes Hotline: (919) 361-8488
http://www.ashastd.org/

The association is steadfast in its fight to curtail the spread of sexually transmitted diseases (STDs) and reduce the impact these can have on an individual, family, and community. Current news related to sexual health and behavior, such as condom breakage and responsible sexual behavior can be found on the home page. Facts about STDs, resource centers throughout the United States, the national STD action plan, and legislative advocacy are some of the button links.

Association for Reproductive Health Professionals
2401 Pennsylvania Avenue, NW, Suite 350
Washington, DC 20037-1718
Telephone: (202) 466-3825
http://www.arhp.org/

The members of this medical association represent various health and education fields that serve the public with accurate information on reproductive health, sexually transmitted diseases, HIV/AIDS, sexuality, etc. The bookstore button link will locate resources on teenage pregnancy and sexuality. Current news related to reproductive health can be found on the home page.

Society for Adolescent Medicine (SAM)
1916 N.W. Copper Oaks Circle
Blue Springs, Missouri 64015
Telephone: (816) 224-8010
http://www.adolescenthealth.org/

This society of professionals from multiple disciplines is committed to the physical and psychosocial health of adolescents. SAM pursues effective communication and collaboration, research, public awareness, access to health, and special training in adolescent health. Its website button links will locate additional information about sex education and about the organization. SAM publishes a host of resources including the *Journal of Adolescent Health.*

Society for Public Health Education
750 First St. NE, Suite 910
Washington, DC 20002-4242
Telephone: (202) 408-9804
http://www.sophe.org/

SOPHE is composed of health education professionals whose primary mission is to promote health for all people. Its members are actively involved in various areas of public health from asthma to unintentional injury. One of the nine special interest groups attends to children, adolescents, and school health. In addition to serving as an advocate of public health, SOPHE offers continuous professional development to its members, and publishes *Health Education and Behavior* and *Health Promotion Practices.*

Resources

The Alan Guttmacher Institute

120 Wall Street, 21st Floor
New York, NY 10005
Telephone: (212) 248-1111
http://www.agi-usa.org/

Considered one of the largest organizations dedicated to sexuality, the institute is a resource for information on aspects related to sexuality, such as abortion, pregnancy and birth, birth prevention and contraception, sexual behavior, and sexually transmitted diseases. The home page posts current news related to sexuality, and recent publications and studies are available in PDF format. A search button will find most topics related to sexuality including sex education. The Institute publishes *Family Planning Perspectives, The Guttmacher Report on Public Policy, and International Family Planning Perspectives.*

American Values 2001

1841 Broadway, Suite 211
New York, NY 10023
Telephone: (212) 246-3942
http://www.americanvalues.org/

Known as the Institute for American Values, this organization is committed to marriage and family in the United States and how these build and renew competence, character, and citizenship. To this end, the institute discourses the American culture through lively debates and publications such as *Fatherless America: Confronting Our Most Urgent Social Problem* and *Watch Out for Children: A Mothers' Statement to Advertisers.* A bookstore button link locates the institute's publications, and a button link will search for information on sex education.

Carnegie Council on Adolescent Development

437 Madison Avenue
New York, NY 10022
Telephone: (212) 371-3200
http://www.carnegie.org/sub/pubs/ccadpubs.htm

The Carnegie Foundation of New York conducts research and grant development in four primary areas: education, international peace, international development, and strengthening the nation's democracy. A series of books, reports, and working papers can be found on the promotion of health and health care, physical development, violence prevention, and risk taking.

Centers for Disease Control and Prevention
Division of Adolescent School Health
MS K-31
1600 Clifton Road
Atlanta, GA 30333
Telephone: (404) 488-5372
http://www.cdc.gov

As a service of the Department of Health and Human Services, the CDC strives to make the nation a safe and healthy one, free of diseases. The CDC provides a wealth of accurate, scientifically based information on diseases, prevention and control techniques, and environmental health. The CDC aims to educate the American public in ways that promote good health. Its mission reads, "To promote health and quality of life by preventing and controlling disease, injury, and disability." Resources can be located on the website through button links titled: *In the News; Health Topics A-Z; Publications;* and *Data and Statistics.* A search button will retrieve specific information related to most aspects of sexuality.

Children's Aid Society
Bernice and Milton Stern National Training Center for Adolescent Sexuality and Family Life
350 East 88th Street
New York, NY 10128
Telephone: (212) 976-9716
http://www.childrensaidsociety.org/welcome.html

As the organization's name indicates, the CAS provides children and their families health, education, and recreational services. Four button links are found on its home page: family, recreation, education, and health. The health button will display information about the CAS teen pregnancy prevention program.

Family Research Council
801 G Street, NW
Washington, DC 20001
Telephone: (202) 393-2100
http://www.frc.org/

A conservative organization that espouses to "Defend Family, Faith and Freedom," the council works to preserve and promote traditional family values and Judeo-Christian principles. The home page publishes current news related to the organization's mission and progress on legislative and public policies. The council addresses sexuality in a publication titled *Living It Out: A Teen's Guide to Today's Most Important Issues.* A search button is available to find resources on sex education.

Institute for Advanced Study of Human Sexuality
1523 Franklin Street
San Francisco, CA 94109-4522
Telephone: (415) 928-1133
http://www.iashs.edu/

This institute is a graduate school with a primary focus on training professionals in human sexuality. Five programs prepare students to work more effectively in the field. Certificate courses are available in Sex Education, Clinical Sexology, AIDS/STD Prevention, and Erotology. *The Electronic Journal of Human Sexuality* can be accessed through a button link.

International AIDS Society—USA
Presidio of San Francisco
1001 B O'Reilly Avenue
P.O. Box 29916
San Francisco, CA 94129-0916
Telephone: (415) 561-6720
http://www.iasusa.org/

The society sponsors continuing medical education for primary care physicians throughout the country. Through its education programs, the society provides primary care professionals accurate information about HIV/AIDS and trains them with the skills to work effectively with people living with HIV/AIDS. The electronic journal, *Topics in HIV Medicine,* is available online.

Kaiser Family Foundation
2400 San Hill Road
Menlo Park, CA 94025
Telephone: (800) 656-4533
http://www.kff.org/

The foundation is as extensive as the Alan Guttmacher Institute and SIECUS. The foundation disseminates the most recent information on sexuality and sex education, and it actively pursues research in these areas. As a national advocate of sex and health education, it is involved in federal legislation and public policy. The foundation's home page includes its multidisciplinary research efforts, current news, and links to a network of partners. A search button of the database is available.

Kinsey Institute for Research in Sex, Gender and Reproduction
Morrison 313
Indiana University, Bloomington
Bloomington, IN 47405
Telephone: (812) 855-7686
http://www.indiana.edu/~kinsey/

The institute promotes human sexuality with an overall mission to continue field growth through clinical and research training and teaching.
Graduate programs in sexuality are available through the institute. The
website consists of button links to research and publications on sexuality and sex education, access to a library of special collections, and a
search of the database.

Medical Institute for Sexual Health
P.O. Box 162306
Austin, Texas 78716-2306
Telephone: (512) 328-6268
http://www.medinstitute.org/

The institute provides information on sexually transmitted diseases and
nonmarital pregnancies to health professionals, teachers, families,
youth, and government agencies. The institute is grounded in the belief
that abstinence from sex until marriage is the only way to eliminate the
risk of disease or pregnancy. The home page includes links to the institute's publications and medical updates.

National Adolescent Health Resource Center
The University of Minnesota
Division of General Pediatrics and Adolescent Health
1313 Fifth Street, SE, Suite 205
Minneapolis, MN 55414
Telephone: (612) 627-4488
http://www.umn.edu/

The center is one of five sponsored by the Bureau of Maternal and Child
Health. These centers, located throughout the nation, specialize in
training health care providers in adolescent health issues and providing
information on youth and sexuality. Research on adolescent health is
available on the website.

National AIDS Clearinghouse
Centers for Disease Control and Prevention
1600 Clifton Rd.

Atlanta, GA 30333
Telephone: (800) 311-3435
http://www.cdcnpin.org/

Also known as the CDC National Prevention Information Network, this is a clearinghouse for information on HIV, AIDS, STDs, and TB. This website has a link button for each of these topics, and a button link will search the databases.

National Campaign to Prevent Teen Pregnancy
2100 M Street, NW, Suite 300
Washington, DC 20037
Telephone: (202) 857-8655
http://www.teenpregnancy.org/

The National Campaign's overall mission is to reduce the number of adolescent pregnancies by the year 2005. Its home page has many links on adolescent pregnancies and tips for parents, health care providers, and teachers to use in their conversations with adolescents. The website has button links to resources and fact sheets on adolescent sexuality.

National Coalition for Abstinence Education
P.O. Box 536
Colorado Springs, CO 80901-0536
Telephone: (719) 531-3492
http://www.sexrespect.com/FundInfo.html

The coalition was initially formed in 1997 to ensure that Title V abstinence programs comply with federal law. The coalition evaluates each funded program for their abstinence-only education principles and curriculum and program implementation and operations. The website listed above is for Sex Respect (an abstinence-only education program), and more information about the coalition can be found on the site's FAQ page.

National Family Planning and Reproductive Health Association
1627 K Street, NW, 12th Floor
Washington, DC 20006
Telephone: (202) 293-3114
http://www.nfprha.org/

The association advocates family planning and reproductive health care. Affiliations include health care clinics, health agencies, Planned Parenthood clinics, and other family planning clinics throughout the nation. Its home page has button links to information on sexual health, fact sheets, and action tool kits, and to locate local clinics.

National HIV/AIDS etc. Program
Bureau of Health Professions
5600 Fishers Lane, Room 9A39
Rockville, MD
Telephone: (301) 443-6364
http://www.aids-ed.org/welcome.html

This national umbrella of fourteen regional centers enhances primary care professionals' knowledge and skills of HIV/AIDS. Education and training is conducted at various national locations with the primary goal to help these professionals better understand and treat patients living with HIV/AIDS. The home page is composed of various links to HIV/AIDS material and sexuality in general. A button link will locate a regional service center.

**National Organization on Adolescent Pregnancy,
Parenting and Prevention**
2401 Pennsylvania Avenue, NW, Suite 350
Washington, DC 20037
Telephone: (202) 293-8370
http://www.noappp.org/

The organization exists to provide the most current information on adolescent pregnancy, parenting, and prevention, and strives to make all adolescents responsible decision makers with regard to their sexuality. This website includes a database to search for information on teen pregnancy, parenting, and prevention. A description of programs and services can be found through the home page button links.

San Francisco AIDS Foundation
995 Market Street #200
San Francisco, CA 94103
Telephone: (800) 367-AIDS
http://www.sfaf.org/

The foundation was created in 1982 in response to the AIDS epidemic in San Francisco. The foundation initially served as a center of information on AIDS for gay men living in the city but now educates the U.S. public about AIDS and provides services to those living with HIV/AIDS. The foundation's home page displays current news related to HIV/AIDS, and button links will lead to information on HIV/AIDS treatment, prevention, and policy. The foundation sponsors an HIV website called the www.AIDSHotline.org.

Sexuality Information and Education Council of the United States
130 West 42nd Street, Suite 350
New York, NY 10036-7802
Telephone: (212) 819-9770
http://www.siecus.org

SIECUS has been cited many times throughout the text; it appears to be the largest organization to disseminate information on sexuality, sexual health, and sex education. SIECUS is a firm believer in the benefits of comprehensive sex education and that sexuality is a natural and healthy part of human existence. In addition to button links on SIECUS, resources for parents and adolescents, religious institutions, and policy makers, a button link will search the SIECUS clearinghouse and databases for specific information relevant to sexuality.

Advocacy

Advocates for Youth
1025 Vermont Avenue, NW, Suite 200
Washington, DC 20005
Telephone: (202) 347-5700
http://www.advocatesforyouth.org/

As implied by its name, Advocates for Youth strives to inform the general public, policy makers, and other organizations that serve youth about sexual and reproductive health. The organization's overall vision is one that promotes the tenet that sexuality is a normal, positive, and beneficial aspect of human life. Members seek to instill this value and teach youth responsible decision-making skills. This website contains two clearinghouses: Peer Education Clearinghouse and National Center for Sexuality Educators. To enable adolescents to learn about sexual health, a button link is provided for them. Adolescents can retrieve information on peer education and local resources, and become involved in national sexual health issues. Another part of the website is devoted to gay, lesbian, bisexual, and transgender youth.

AIDS Alliance for Children, Youth, and Families
1600 K Street, NW, Suite 300
Washington, DC 20006
Telephone: (202) 785-3564
http://www.aidspolicycenter.org/

This national organization was created to serve children, youth, women, and families who suffer directly or indirectly from HIV/AIDS. This advocacy group works on public policy issues and educates the general public about the prevention of HIV/AIDS. The website has links to AIDS facts, current news, and testimonies. Various research projects and other publications are available through a button link.

Support Services

Emergency Contraception Connection (ECC)
Hotline: (877) EC-PILLS
http://www.ecconnection.org/

ECC is operated by Planned Parenthood of Georgia. Callers can get a medical assessment and prescription for birth control but only on an emergency basis. The website clearly states that the only contraceptive that keeps a person free of sexually transmitted diseases and HIV/AIDS is a condom.

Emergency Contraception Hotline
Hotline: (888) NOT-2-LATE
http://opr.princeton.edu/ec/

The website, served from the Office of Population Research at Princeton University, provides information about emergency contraception. The website describes emergency contraception and a page link is provided to answer frequently asked questions.

Familyeducation.com
http://www.familyeducation.com/home

This website is devoted to various issues and advice related to the family, parenting, and schools. Parents can learn about everything from ADHD to improving their child's reading skills. The site's search button can produce relevant pieces of information regarding sexual activity, behavior, or education.

HIV/AIDS Treatment Information Service
P.O. Box 6303
Rockville, MD 20849-6303
Telephone: (800) HIV-0440
http://www.hivatis.org

This federal project, sponsored by the U.S. Department of Health and Human Services, is considered a resource center for the federally approved HIV/AIDS treatment guidelines. The site's library contains information on the adolescent guidelines and links to two federal resources: *PubMed* and *Medline Plus Information*.

Iwannaknow.org

http://www.iwannaknow.org

The website is sponsored by the American Social Health Association and is devoted to adolescents who have questions about love and sex, pregnancy, sexually transmitted diseases, prevention, etc. A link button is available for gay teens. If teens cannot find their question in the FAQ page, they can ask an expert in the field and a response will be e-mailed to them.

James Bowman and Associates

614 Grand Avenue, Suite 400
Oakland, CA 94610-3523
Telephone: (501) 835-3700
http://www.jba-cht.com/index.html

James Bowman Associates provides health training through three regional Centers for Health Training: Southwest Region, Northwest Region, and Western Region. The centers provide the following services: research and evaluation, program development, and management systems. Their specialized services include training in HIV prevention and surviving sexual abuse. The centers' website offers a more complete description of their health services for local communities.

National AIDS Hotline

(800) 342-AIDS
http://www.ashastd.org/nah/

Cosponsored by the American Social Health Association and the Centers for Diseases Control, the hot line answers callers' questions related to HIV/AIDS. A million people a year call the hot line to have their questions answered, get a referral, or receive HIV/AIDS literature. Trained operators are standing by twenty-four hours a day, seven days a week. The website provides additional sources of information and links related to HIV/AIDS.

Planned Parenthood Federation of America, Inc.

810 Seventh Avenue
New York, NY 10019
Telephone: (212) 541-7800
http://www.plannedparenthood.org

Planned Parenthood is the oldest family planning organization. Its website includes current news related to sexuality, and a number of button links provide additional information on issues such as advocacy, research, and frequently asked questions. The site search button can retrieve information on sex education. A special link button is available for adolescents.

SEX EDUCATION AND SEXUAL ABUSE AND SEXUAL HARASSMENT

Professional Associations

American Association of University Women
Educational Foundation Research
Department RR.INT
1111 16th Street, NW
Washington, DC 20036
Telephone: (800) 326-AAUW
http://www.aauw.org

The AAUW is clearly an organization dedicated to advancing the educational and equity opportunities for women and girls. The AAUW has conducted research on justice issues related to women and girls, and more important, two seminal studies have brought sexual harassment in schools to American consciousness. The website has a button link that will search issues as they relate to sexual abuse, sexual harassment, and sexual violence among youth. Its home page consists of link buttons to current news, research, and issues related to women and girls in academic settings, the workplace, and the home.

American Bar Association
Center on Children and the Law
740 15th Street, NW
Washington, DC 20005-1009
Telephone: (202) 662-1030
http://www.abanet.org/child/home2.html

Widely known as the organization of attorneys, the ABA is extensive with well over 400,000 members. The ABA monitors the accreditation of law schools, provides legal assistance, and advocates improvement of the legal system. The website is for legal and justice matters that focus on improving the lives of children. The site has a search button to locate information on child sexual abuse and sexual harassment.

American Humane Association

63 Inverness Drive East
Englewood, CO 80112-5117
Telephone: (800) 227-4645
http://www.americanhumane.org/

Known largely for their work with household pets, the association is equally protective of other animals and of children. Its extensive network of professionals and volunteers collaborate to "prevent cruelty, abuse, neglect and exploitation of children." Its website contains current news on child and animal welfare, and a button link will find specific information on child sexual and physical abuse and family violence.

American Professional Society on the Abuse of Children

P.O. Box 260901
CHO 3B-3406
Oklahoma City, OK 73190
Telephone: (405) 271-8202
http://www.apsac.org/

This association is made up of professionals from multiple disciplines that serve children and anyone affected by the victimization of children. It is actively involved in responding to and educating the public about child maltreatment. It publishes *Child Maltreatment* and *APSAC*, and a host of other publications on child maltreatment are available through the website.

American Public Human Services Association

810 First Street, NE, Suite 500
Washington, DC 20002-4267
Telephone: (202) 682-0100
http://www.aphsa.org

The association seeks to improve the health and well-being of children, their families, and other adults by educating the U.S. public, state and federal legislatures, and the media about child and family welfare and health care reform. The association has extensive affiliations with other professional organizations that serve children and their families. The association's home page has numerous links to state contacts, testimonies, publications, policies, etc. Information specific to child sexual abuse can be located via a search button link.

Resources

Bureau for At-Risk Youth
135 Dupont Street
P.O. Box 760
Plainview, NY 11803-0760
Telephone: (800) 99-YOUTH
http://www.at-risk.com/

The bureau is a publisher and distributor of resources for youth considered at-risk or for professionals who serve them. Sexual abuse, teen pregnancy, and sexuality in general are among the resources available in this extensive catalog.

Center for the Prevention of Sexual and Domestic Violence
2400 North 45th, #10
Seattle, WA 98103
Telephone: (206) 634-1903
http://www.cpsdv.org/

Considered a resource center on abuse and religion, the center's main goal is to bring together religious leaders from all denominations to end sexual and domestic violence. The website is complete with button links to sexual abuse, sexual violence, domestic violence, healthy teen relationships, etc. An administrator will answer e-mail and locate information through the center's national clearinghouse on religion and abuse.

Family Research Laboratory
126 Horton Social Science Center
University of New Hampshire
Durham, NH 03824-3586
Telephone: (603) 862-1888
http://www.unh.edu/frl/

The laboratory addresses violence in the family by investigating all types of violence that could affect families, including sexual abuse of children, dating violence, rape, and pornography. Its website is home to the *Crimes Against Children Research Center,* which houses sexual abuse publications.

National Center for Victims of Crime
2000 M Street, NW, Suite 480
Washington, DC 20036
Telephone: (202) 467-8700
http://www.ncvc.org/

As an advocate for crime victims, the center's mission is to help anyone who has been harmed by a crime or affected by a crime in some way. It provides direct services and resources and offers training and technical assistance to organizations that serve victims of crime. The website has button links to a virtual library that offers information on child sexual abuse, cyber crime, hate crime, relationship violence, sexual assault, school crime, teen dating violence, and youth violence.

National Clearinghouse on Child Abuse and Neglect

U.S. Department of Health and Human Services
330 C Street SW
Washington, DC 20447
Telephone: (800) FYI-3366
http://www.calib.com/nccanc

The clearinghouse is sponsored by the U.S. Department of Health and Human Services and is a database of statistics, prevention efforts, state statutes, funding sources, publications, and catalog. The website has a button link to report suspected incidents of child abuse and a link to search the databases and retrieve specific information on child sexual abuse.

National Criminal Justice Reference Service (NCJRS)

P.O. Box 6000 Rockville, MD 20849-6000
Telephone: (800) 851-3420
http://www.ncjrs.org

The NCJRS is a service of the U.S. Department of Justice that houses information on corrections, courts, drugs and crime, juvenile justice, law enforcement, victims of crime, and statistics. Several reports are available through button links on its home page, and a button link will search the databases for specific information related to sexual abuse and harassment.

National Institute of Justice

U.S. Department of Justice, National Criminal Justice
    Reference Service
810 Seventh Street, NW
Washington, DC 20531
Telephone: (202) 307-2942
http://www.ojp.usdoj.gov/nij/

The NIJ is the research and development branch of the U.S. Department of Justice that serves to investigate crime control and criminal justice.

The website search button will locate articles, fact sheets, and other information on any aspect of sexual violence related to youth.

National Resource Center on Child Abuse and Neglect
63 Inverness Drive East
Englewood, CO 80112-5117
Telephone: (800) 227-5242
http://www.casanet.org/library/abuse/nrccan.htm

The center is funded by the National Center on Child Abuse and Neglect and operated in part by the American Humane Association. The center offers private and public health organizations technical assistance and consultation services, and its toll free number provides callers information on child abuse and neglect.

National Youth Violence Prevention Resource Center
Telephone: (866) SAFEYOUTH
http://www.safeyouth.org/topics/suicide.htm

The center is sponsored in part by the Centers for Disease Control and Prevention and is a clearinghouse of information on prevention and intervention programs on youth violence. Link buttons provide access to after school violence, school violence, youth at risk, youth suicide, etc. A search and a link button to resources on sexual harassment and abuse are available.

NOW Legal Defense and Education Fund
395 Hudson Street
New York, NY 10014
Telephone: (212) 925-6635
http://www.nowldef.org

The National Organization for Women (NOW) has celebrated and defended women's rights for nearly thirty-one years. It has furthered women's equality in many avenues, one of which has been educating the public about sexual harassment. The home page is extensive, with current news related to social justice for women and progress in developing and promoting sound public policy. The site has a search button that will retrieve information on sexual abuse and sexual harassment.

Pandora's Box: The Secrecy of Child Sexual Abuse
http://www.prevent-abuse-now.com/

Pandora's Box is operated independently from any formal organization or agency. However, this directory of resources related to child sexual abuse is extensive. Dr. Nancy Faulkner manages the website complete with over 270 pages of information on protecting youth from sexual abuse. The button links are divided into five categories: Information, Offenses, Prevention, Victims, and Miscellany.

Safer Society Foundation
P.O. Box 340
Brandon, VT 05733-0340
Telephone: (800) 247-3132
http://www.safersociety.org

The foundation is a nonprofit organization with its roots in the prevention and treatment of sexual abuse. The foundation sponsors research, delivers training and consulting services, and serves as a referral center. Its publications deal primarily with sexual abuse, sexual offenders, molestation, and so forth and are available through the Safer Press button link.

Wellesley Centers for Women
Wellesley College
106 Central Street
Wellesley, MA 02481
Telephone: (781) 283-2500
http://www.wcwonline.org/

The centers are composed of the Stone Center for Developmental Services and Studies and the Center for Research on Women and seek "to promote positive change for women." The centers are involved in research projects that address abuse, adolescence, education, health, sexual harassment and bullying, sexuality, violence, and youth development. These can be accessed through the Research, Education, and Action button link. A search button will locate a plethora of material on sexual harassment.

Advocacy

Child Welfare League of America, Inc.
440 First Street, NW, Suite 310
Washington, DC 20001-2085
Telephone: (202) 638-2952
http://www.cwla.org/

The league develops and promotes policies that protect American children and their families from harm. Each year the league serves over three million abused and neglected children and their families. Its publications on children's well-being and the protection thereof are available through a button link.

Children's Defense Fund
25 East Street, NW
Washington, DC 20001
Telephone: (202) 628-8787
http://www.childrensdefense.org/

As one of the largest advocates for children, this organization is best known for its mission to "Leave no child behind." The organization vows to work toward ensuring an equitable, safe, healthy, moral start for all children. The website contains button links that describe the organization's progress in these endeavors and its efforts in public policy. A search button will locate information on child sexual abuse, and a publication catalog can be accessed via a button link.

Equal Rights Advocates
1663 Mission Street, Suite 250
San Francisco, CA 94103
Telephone: (415) 621-0672
Advice and Counseling: (800) 839-4ERA
http://www.equalrights.org/sexhar/index.htm

This organization functions as a legal resource center for women and will represent them when their rights have been violated. Women can receive legal advice and solutions if they call the toll-free hot line. A button link will lead to information on sexual harassment in schools.

National Association for Counsel for Children
1825 Marion Street, Suite 340
Denver, CO 80218
Telephone: (888) 828-NACC
http://www.naccchildlaw.org/

As legal advocates, the association's mission reads, "to achieve the well-being of children by promoting multidisciplinary excellence in children's law, establishing the legal interests of children and enhancing children's legal remedies." Its home page offers a link to other organizations dedicated to children's welfare.

Prevent Child Abuse America
200 S. Michigan Avenue, 17th Floor
Chicago, IL 60604-2404
Telephone: (312) 663-3520
http://www.preventchildabuse.org/

The name of the organization is also its mission—simply to stop the abuse and neglect of children. With chapters in more than forty states, this organization advocates for the physical and emotional well-being of children. The website consists of various buttons that relate to the organization's prevention efforts: Take Action, Community Resource Materials, and One Percent to Prevent Campaign. The organization also has several publications on child sexual abuse.

Support Services

Childhelp USA National Headquarters
15757 N. 78th Street
Scottsdale, AZ 85260
Telephone: (480) 922-8212
National Child Abuse Hotline: (800) 4-A-CHILD®
http://www.childhelpusa.org/index.htm

Childhelp USA is diligent in its efforts to prevent the abuse and neglect of children. Its programs and services range from the operation of the national child abuse hot line to treatment facilities throughout the nation. Child abuse, including sexual abuse, information can be located through various button links. A section of the website, Kids Corner, is accessible for children to learn how to protect themselves and report child abuse.

Kempe Children's Center
1825 Marion Street
Denver, CO 80218
Telephone: (303) 864-5252
http://www.kempecenter.org/

The Kempe organization is composed of the Children's Center, Kempe Therapeutic Preschool, Kempe Child Protection Team, and Kempe Perpetration Prevention Program. All of the programs collaborate to prevent child abuse and neglect. The center is "committed to multidisciplinary approaches to improving the recognition, treatment, and prevention of all forms of abuse and neglect." The center's professionals will serve children who have a history of abuse.

National Center for Missing and Exploited Children
Charles B. Wang International Children's Center
699 Prince Street
Alexandria, VA 22314-3175
Telephone: (800) THE-LOST
http://www.missingkids.org/

Most notable for the center's founders, John and Rene Walsh, whose son Adam was abducted and killed in 1981, the center exists to keep children safe and assist those whose children are missing or exploited. The toll free hot line is available twenty-four hours a day, seven days a week. The website has advice for parents and their children and a resource library of material on child sexual abuse and exploitation.

Rape, Abuse, and Incest National Network (RAINN)
635-B Pennsylvania Ave., SE
Washington, DC 20003
Hotline: (800) 656-HOPE
http://www.rainn.org/

RAINN operates the National Sexual Assault Hotline for victims of sexual assault. Callers receive free and confidential counseling and support twenty-four hours a day, seven days a week and referrals to a network of 869 crisis centers throughout the nation. The website has button links that describe the process to report victimization. A search button and a button link to a directory of counseling centers are available.

Survivors of Incest Anonymous (SIA)
World Service Office
P.O. Box 190
Benson, MD 21018
Telephone: (410) 893-3322
http://www.siawso.org/

SIA is considered a support organization for persons who have experienced incestuous sexual abuse. Independent support groups throughout the nation practice a twleve-step, self-help recovery program. The website has a button link that describes the effects of child sexual abuse.

VOICES in Action, Inc.
P.O. Box 148309
Chicago, IL 60614
Telephone: (800) 7-VOICE-8 (786-4238)
http://www.voices-action.org/index.html

VOICES, which stands for *Victims of Incest Can Emerge Survivors,* is an organization dedicated to disseminating information about incest and providing a support network for victims of incest or child sexual abuse. Member benefits include a bimonthly newsletter, special interest groups, on-going conferences, and a survival kit to help victims in the recovery process. The home page consists of various button links to resources on child sexual abuse.

SEX EDUCATION AND SEXUAL ORIENTATION

Professional Associations

American Counseling Association
Association for Gay, Lesbian, and Bisexual Issues in Counseling
5999 Stevenson Avenue
Alexandria, VA 22304
Telephone: (800) 347-6657
http://www.counseling.org/

This division of the ACA serves to inform counselors of the unique needs of gay, lesbian, bisexual, and transgender (GLBT) persons. Division members believe that all people, regardless of their sexual orientation, should develop to their full potential. Moreover, the division believes that counselors should have the expertise to work with these individuals since many of them experience inequality and injustice because of their sexual orientation. The division's webpage has current news related to gay, lesbian, bisexual, and transgender issues and a button link to related resources.

American Psychological Association (APA)
Lesbian, Gay, and Bisexual Concerns Office
750 First Street, NE
Washington, DC 20002-4242
Telephone: (800) 374-2721
www.apa.org/pi/lgbc/

The members of this APA office collaborate to bring justice to those who are gay, lesbian, bisexual, and transgender. They advocate eliminating bias, prejudice, and discrimination toward these individuals through public policy, technical assistance, and education of the public. The office works through the Public Interest Directorate that works on similar human welfare issues such as AIDS, violence, etc. The home page offers current news on GLBT issues and button links to related publications and resources.

National Education Association (NEA)
Gay and Lesbian Caucus
1201 16th Street, NW
Washington, DC 20036-3290
Telephone: (202) 833-4000
http://www.nea-glc.org/

The NEA is renowned for its advocacy of public education and is made up of members whose primary mission is to see all youth succeed academically and socially. The organization has six caucuses, one of which is devoted to gay and lesbian youth and the impact sexual orientation has in the classroom. The website has a button link to other organizations that serve this population, and a button link will display the caucuses' recent accomplishments. A search button is available through the NEA website.

Society for Adolescent Medicine
Gay and Lesbian Special Interest Group
1916 NW Copper Oaks Circle
Blue Springs, MO 64015
Telephone: (816) 224-8010
http://www.adolescenthealth.org/html/l_g_b_sig.html

As its name indicates, this group of SAM members is primarily concerned with the health care issues that gay, lesbian, bisexual, and transgender youth confront. This group engages in ongoing dialogue and research related to this population of youth. Its website has a list of professionals who will conduct lectures and workshops on the health care of these youth.

Resources

Evelyn Hooker Center for Gay and Lesbian Mental Health
Department of Psychiatry
The University of Chicago
5841 South Maryland Avenue
Chicago, IL 60637-1470
Telephone: (773) 702-9725

The Evelyn Hooker Center, located at the University of Chicago, remains dedicated to gay and lesbian issues. Therapists are trained at the center to provide clinical support during the coming out process. The Evelyn Hooker Center provides therapy and runs a variety of coming out groups. The center can be contacted for more information.

Gay and Lesbian Alliance Against Defamation (GLAAD)
Telephone: (800) GAY-MEDIA
http://www.glaad.org/org/index.html

GLAAD informs and educates the media to change the way gay, lesbian, bisexual, and transgender (GLBT) persons are depicted in the entertainment and news industry. It is "dedicated to promoting and ensuring fair, accurate, and inclusive representation of individuals and events in all media as a means of eliminating homophobia and discrimination based on gender identity and sexual orientation." GLAAD has primary locations in Los Angeles and New York City, and some chapters have combined their talents to create media resource centers throughout the nation. The website is complete with current news about GLBT persons, and a search button link will retrieve information on this population of youth.

The Gay, Lesbian, and Straight Education Network (GLSEN)
121 West 27th Street, Suite 804
New York, NY 10001
Telephone: (212) 727-0135
http://www.glsen.org/templates/index.html

GLSEN is a national organization whose mission is to create safe schools for gay, lesbian, bisexual, and transgender youth. Members want all youth, regardless of their sexual orientation, to be respected and valued for who they are. The network's home page has many articles and current news related to GLBT and button links to a resource center, an action center, a bookstore, and gay-straight associations. A button link is available to search their website.

Hetrick-Martin Institute
2 Astor Place
New York, NY 10003
Telephone: (212) 674-2400
http://www.hmi.org/main.html

The HMI is devoted to gay, lesbian, bisexual, questioning, and transgender youth. They offer a wide range of services for this population of youth (age twelve to twenty-one) and their families, including housing and a counseling center. HMI created the first school for GLBQT, the Harvey Milk School. The website is extensive, with resources, FYI fact sheets, publications, and a button link to search databases.

LAMBDA GBLT Community Services
P.O. Box 31321
El Paso, TX 79931-0321
Telephone: (915) 562-GAYS
http://www.lambda.org/

LAMBDA's main goal is to reduce "homophobia, inequality, hate crimes, and discrimination by encouraging self-acceptance, cooperation, and nonviolence." Its website features current news items related to being gay, lesbian, bisexual, and transgender. Various links are available to other gay support networks, and additional information is available through the *Youth OUTreach* button link.

Massachusetts Governor's Commission on Gay and Lesbian Youth
State House, Room 111
Boston, MA 02133
Telephone: (617) 828-3039
http://www.state.ma.us/gcgly/

The commission was created in 1992 in response to a growing number of suicidal deaths among gay and lesbian youth. Now in its ninth year, the commission works to curtail the suicide rate and the violence some of these youth encounter. Its website offers access to publications, *The Gay and Lesbian Student Rights Law, The Safe Schools for G/L Students,* Gay Youth Pride posters, and the 1999 *Massachusetts Youth Risk Behavior Survey.*

National Coalition for Gay, Lesbian, Bisexual, and Transgendered Youth
OutProud
369 Third Street, Suite B-362
San Rafael, CA 94901-3581
http://www.outproud.org

The coalition serves as a resource center for youth and educators. Its home page posts the latest news related to gay, lesbian, bisexual, and transgender issues. Button links can locate coming out stories shared by other youth, community role models, a library, online brochures related to sexual orientation, community sources of support, and other educational links.

National Institute for Gay, Lesbian, Bisexual, and Transgender Education
3932 Broadway, Box 45600
Kansas City, MO 64171
Telephone: (816) 960-7200
http://www.thenationalinstitute.org/

The institute is committed to individuals, families, religious communities, corporations, and professionals that contend with gay, lesbian, bisexual, and transgender issues. The institute works toward abolishing any form of oppression, inequity, and discrimination these individuals face. Its online magazine, *Authenticity,* is available on its website, as well as a resource center, a speakers and trainers bureau, and a bookstore. More information on the institute's *Endangered Youth Project* and *Youth Recognition Project* can be accessed on its home page.

Office for Civil Rights
Customer Service Team
Mary E. Switzer Building
330 C Street, SW
Washington, DC 20202
Telephone: (800) 421-3481
http://ed.gov/offices/OCR

The OCR functions out of the U.S. Department of Education and ensures that all youth have an equal opportunity to succeed in school. Its website offers a button link to a full spectrum of educational projects and products. A search button link will retrieve information on gay, lesbian, bisexual, and transgender youth.

Project 10
7850 Melrose Avenue
Los Angeles, CA 9004
Telephone: (213) 651-5200 extension 244
http://www.lausd.k12.ca.us/lausd/offices/glec/p10_flyer.html

Project 10 is foremost a dropout prevention program that serves youth in the Los Angeles Unified School District. The project was started in 1984 in response to concerns for gay, lesbian, bisexual, and transgender youth who were considered at risk for suicide, alcohol/substance abuse, and HIV/AIDS. As a support program for youth who need emotional support or information and resources on others like themselves, the project also offers workshops and school site counseling.

Project 10 East, Inc.
P.O. Box 382401
Cambridge, MA 02238
Telephone: (617) 864-GLBT
http://www.project10east.org/

Project 10 East is committed to helping schools and communities create and sustain safe spaces in schools for all youth regardless of their sexual orientation. To this end, the project offers weekly meetings for youth at local high schools, training to schools about sexual GLBT issues, and a curriculum for teachers to implement in their classrooms. The project's home page has two button links to additional GLBT resources.

Safe and Drug Free Schools Program
Office of Elementary and Secondary Education
400 Maryland Avenue, SW
Washington, DC 20202
Telephone: (202) 401-0113
http://www.ed.gov/offices/OESE/SDFS/

This federal project's primary goal is to reduce drug use and violence in schools. Its website has access to current news related to drug abuse and violence, and a button link will retrieve the publication, *Preventing Youth Hate Crimes*.

Youth Project
National Center for Lesbian Rights
870 Market Street, Suite 570
San Francisco, CA 94102
Telephone: (800) 528-6257
http://www.nclrights.org/index.html

The National Center for Lesbian Rights works "through direct litigation and advocacy . . . to change discriminatory laws and to create new laws and policies benefiting lesbians and other oppressed members of the queer community." The center also sponsors a toll-free hot line for youth who are experiencing abuse and harassment. Its publication button link will locate a sample of a school board antiharassment policy, legal perspectives on sexual harassment in schools, and guidance to develop effective state laws.

Advocacy

American Civil Liberties Union (ACLU)
Lesbian and Gay Rights Project
125 Broad Street, 18th Floor
New York, NY 10004
Telephone: (212) 549-2627
http://www.aclu.org/
http://www.aclu.org/issues/gay/safe_schools.html

The ACLU has been advocating on behalf of the liberties of the American people since 1920. No matter a person's color, creed, religious background, age, gender, or sexual orientation, the ACLU will do what it takes to ensure his/her civil rights. One of the ACLU projects works specifically with gay, lesbian, bisexual, and transgender persons. Its publication *Making School Safe for LGBT Youth* is accessible through their *Lesbian and Gay Rights* button link.

The Human Rights Campaign
919 18th St., NW, Suite 800
Washington, DC 20006
Telephone: (202) 628-4160
http://www.hrc.org/

The HRC advocates for the equal rights of gay, lesbian, bisexual, and transgender persons. Its home page offers current news related to its fight for equal rights and various button links to its outreach efforts. A button link is available to search the site for issues related to GLBT youth. The HRC sponsors the *National Coming Out Project.*

National Gay and Lesbian Task Force
1700 Kalorama Road, NW
Washington, DC 20009-2624
Telephone: (202) 332-6483
http://www.ngltf.org/

The task force is a network of people committed to social justice for gay, lesbian, bisexual, and transgender persons. The members are actively engaged in research and public policy. Its website has a link to its library and publications.

National Youth Advocacy Coalition (NYAC)
1638 R Street NW, Suite 300
Washington, DC 20009
Telephone: (202) 319-7596
http://www.nyacyouth.org

The NYAC advocates for youth who are gay, lesbian, bisexual, or transgender, and it seeks to end homophobia, discrimination, and any inequities these youth encounter. It has a full spectrum of projects that work toward a youth's empowerment and healthy development: Development of National Infrastructure; Bridges Projects; HIV/SDT Prevention Project; Values, Youth Leadership, and Involvement; National Advocacy; and the Annual National Summit. The coalition's home page has a resource and database button link.

Parents, Families and Friends of Lesbians and Gays (PFLAG)
1726 M Street, NW
Suite 400
Washington, DC 20003
Telephone: (202) 461-8180
http://www.pflag.org.

PFLAG is a national network of members committed to supporting persons who are gay, lesbian, bisexual, or transgender. The members firmly believe that such persons are normal, healthy U.S. citizens and their sexual orientation is a characteristic of the whole. They acknowledge that such persons have a unique set of needs that can be met through unconditional love and support. The organization offers a wide range of services to keep these persons safe and their families united. With over 460 chapters, PFLAG also educates society about the inherent dangers of homophobia. Its website has links to resources for schools and youth and a button to search its database.

P.E.R.S.O.N. Project
http://www.youth.org/PERSONproject/

P.E.R.S.O.N. stands for *Public Education Regarding Sexual Orientation Nationally* and serves to provide public school youth "fair, accurate, and unbiased" information about gay, lesbian, bisexual, and transgender persons. Members advocate for the transformation of public school curricula and textbook adoption policies to include relevant and accurate descriptions of GLBT persons and sexual orientation. The website contains current news related to the GLBT issues and a resource button link.

Safe Schools Coalition of Washington
Telephone: (800) 307-9275
http://www.safeschools-wa.org/

Members of this coalition collaborate to make Washington schools safe places where youth, teachers, and families feel they belong. Their website has many resources on issues related to gay, lesbian, bisexual, and transgender youth. Current news, a resource guide, reports and publications, legislative updates, and direct help for youth are a few of the links found on their website.

Support Services

Cool Page for Queer Teens
http://www.bidstrup.com/cool.htm

Youth will find that this website has a series of rubrics that deal with some aspect of being queer. Each rubric has a set of questions about the topic and links to their answers.

Elight Gay Youth 'Zine
Youth Guardian Services Inc.

Attention: Elight!
8665 Sudley Road #304
Manassas, VA 20110-4588
Telephone: (877) 270-5152
http://www.youth.org/elight

This website is featured as an online community for gay, lesbian, bisexual, and transgender youth. Through various button links, youth can read others' coming out stories, create cyber friendships, and share their experiences with other GLBT youth.

Gay and Lesbian National Hotline
PMB #296
2261 Market Street
San Francisco, CA 94114
Telephone: (888) THE-GLNH
http://www.glnh.org/

The toll-free, confidential hot line answers callers' most basic questions and counsels those who are experiencing a stressful or anxious event in their life. The hot line serves as referral center and provides callers information on HIV/AIDS.

Horizons Community Services
961 West Montana Street
Chicago, IL 60614-2408
Telephone: (773) 684-5329
Lesbian and Gay Helpline: (773) 929-HELP
Anti-Violence Hotline: (773) 871-CARE
Crises Line: (800) AID-AIDS
http://www.horizonsonline.org/main.html

Horizons is a social service agency for the Midwest community of gay, lesbian, bisexual, and transgender persons. With its mission "to support healthy and integrated lives within the lesbian and gay community," its services include: the Anti-Violence Project; Education and Support; Lesbian and Gay Helpline; Illinois State Hot Line; Legal Services; Mature Adult Program; Psychotherapy Services; Speaker Services; and Youth Services. Its youth program provides youth (fourteen to twenty-three years old) a social outlet and offers them counseling services, health education, disease prevention training, and leadership skills development.

Oasis
http://www.oasismag.com/

Oasis in an online magazine for gay youth made up of feature columns, profiles in courage, news and events, and arts and entertainment.

Queer America
http://www.queeramerica.com/

Queer America is a database of resources for gay, lesbian, bisexual, and transgender youth. Visitors to the website can enter information into three fields, and a customized list of organizations will be generated. Queer America is sponsored by OutProud, The National Coalition for Gay, Lesbian, Bisexual and Transgender Youth.

The Trevor Project
The Trevor Helpline
Telephone: (800) 850-8078
http://www.trevorproject.com/

The helpline is a twenty-four-hour, seven-days-a-week operation available for gay youth considering suicide. The project is based largely on an Academy Award–winning short film about a gay youth who survives a suicide attempt. Gay and questioning youth can call the hot line to receive assistance, support, and referrals from trained counselors.

Youth Resource
http://www.youthresource.com/

The website, dedicated to gay, lesbian, bisexual, and transgender youth, is sponsored by Advocates for Youth. Visitors to this website can enter a cyber chat room and connect with others and read an advice column.

SEX EDUCATION AND YOUTH WITH DISABILITIES

Professional Associations

Many organizations are devoted to youth with disabilities, and many must address sex education in their national and local meetings. However, after an extensive search, the following organizations were the only ones that intentionally discussed sex education on their website.

ARC of the United States
1010 Wayne Avenue, Suite 650
Silver Spring, MD 20910

Telephone: (301) 565-3842
http://thearc.org/

ARC is a national organization for and of persons with mental retardation and related developmental disabilities and their families. ARC seeks to enhance the quality of life for these persons and their families, as well as conduct research in the prevention of mental retardation. Their position statement on sexuality education can be located via the button link "About the ARC."

Association for Persons with Severe Handicaps
29 West Susquehanna Avenue, Suite 210
Baltimore, MD 21204
Telephone: (410) 828-8274
http://www.tash.org/

As its name implies, this association is devoted to persons who live with severe disabilities. A search button will retrieve the organization's resolution on sexuality for persons with severe disabilities.

Council for Exceptional Children
1110 North Glebe Road, Suite 300
Arlington, VA 22201-5704
Telephone: (800) 328-0272
http://www.cec.sped.org/

The Council for Exceptional Children (CEC) is devoted to improving the education and lives of persons and youth with exceptionalities and those considered gifted. CEC is an advocate for the advancement and empowerment of these persons and is actively involved in developing federal policies, professional standards, and professional development for those who serve these people. The council's website offers various button links that include access to its publications and products. A search button will retrieve a bibliography on sex education and youth with mental retardation.

Chapter Eight

●❖ Resources and Selected Publications

An overwhelming amount of material is available on sexuality and sex education through books, journal articles, and reports. This chapter presents some of the sources that are a vital medium of information. Following the list of professional journals, significant collections of printed and on-line resources are found in the following areas: general resources on sex education; sexual abuse and harassment; sexual orientation; and youth with disabilities. Each of these categories is divided into books, journal articles, and reports and studies available on-line.

PROFESSIONAL JOURNALS

Learned societies are dedicated to their disciplines and equally committed to developing and advancing their professional fields through active research. This research and scholarly discourse is disseminated through professional journals. The following journals represent professional fields that discourse issues related to sex education. For the most part, the journal title is indicative of the research focus. These journals regularly publish articles that examine some aspect of sexuality or sex education with regard to the myriad social, physical, and emotional phenomena that youth encounter.

Adolescence
Libra Publishers, Inc.
3089C Clairemont Dr., Suite 383
San Diego, CA 92117
Telephone: (619) 571-1414

AIDS Education and Prevention
International Society for AIDS Education
c/o Guilford Publications, Inc.

72 Spring St., 4th Fl.
New York, NY 10012
Telephone: (212) 365-7006

American Journal of Health Behavior
American Academy of Health Behavior
c/o PNG Publications
PO Box 4593
Star City, WV 26504-4593
Telephone: (304) 293-4699

American Journal of Health Promotion
American Public Health Association
c/o Valerie James, Publisher
1660 Cass Lake Road
Keego Harbor, MI 48320
Telephone: (800) 783-9913

American Psychologist
American Psychological Association
750 First Street, NE
Washington, DC 20000-4242
Telephone: (202) 336-5568

The American School Board Journal
National School Boards Association
1680 Duke Street
Alexandria, VA 22314
Telephone: (703) 838-6722

Child and Adolescent Psychiatric Clinics
W. B. Saunders
Harcourt Health Services
11830 Westline Industrial Drive
St. Louis, MO 63146
Telephone: (800) 325-4177

Child Welfare
Child Welfare League of America, Inc.
440 First St., NW, 3rd Fl.
Washington, DC 20001-2085
Telephone: (202) 638-2952

Clinical Psychology Review
Pergamon Press
Elsevier Science Publishing Company
PO Box 945
New York, NY 10010
Telephone: (888) 437-4636

Family Planning Perspective
The Alan Guttmacher Institute
120 Wall Street, 21st Floor
New York, NY 10005
Telephone: (212) 248-1111

Health and Sexuality
Association for Reproduction Health Professionals
2401 Pennsylvania Avenue, NW, Suite 350
Washington, DC 20037-1718
Telephone: (202) 466-3825

Health Education & Behavior (formerly Heath Education Quarterly)
Society for Public Health Education
c/o Sage Publications, Inc.
2455 Teller Rd.
Thousand Oaks, CA 91320
Telephone: (805) 499-0721

Health Promotion Practice
Society for Public Health Education
750 First Street, NE, Suite 910
Washington, DC 20002-4242
Telephone: (202) 408-9804

Journal of Adolescent Health
Society for Adolescent Medicine
1916 N.W. Copper Oaks Circle
Blue Springs, MO 64015
Telephone: (816) 224-8010

Journal of Adolescent Research
Sage Publications, Inc.
2455 Teller Rd.
Thousand Oaks, CA 91320
Telephone: (805) 499-0721

Journal of School Health
American School Health Association
7263 State Route 43
P.O. Box 708
Kent, OH 44240
Telephone: (330) 678-1601

Journal of the American Academy of Child and Adolescent Psychiatry
American Academy of Child and Adolescent Psychiatry
3615 Wisconsin Avenue, NW
Washington, DC 20016-3007
Telephone: (202) 966-7300

The Nation's Health
American Public Health Association
800 I Street, NW
Washington, DC 20001
Telephone: (202) 777-2742

Pediatrics
The American Academy of Pediatrics
141 Northwest Point Boulevard
Elk Grove Village, IL 60007-1098
Telephone: (847) 434-4000

GENERAL SEX EDUCATION

Books

American Academy of Child and Adolescent Psychiatry. 2000. *Your Adolescent: Emotional, Behavioral, and Cognitive Development from Early Childhood through the Teen Years.* New York: HarperCollins Publishers.

This comprehensive, encyclopedia-like text addresses issues related specifically to the adolescent. The content is divided into four parts: the life of an adolescent; day-to-day problem behaviors; serious problems and abnormalities; and seeking help. Various aspects of sexuality are addressed throughout the book with recommendations for parents.

Castro, Wendy. 1998. *Welfare Reform and Abstinence Education.* Washington, DC: Child Welfare League of America.

The text discusses the Personal Responsibility and Work Reconciliation

Act of 1996 that mandated that the federal government allot $50 million per year for abstinence-only education programs. The text is designed for policy makers, service providers, and those with a keen interest in abstinence education programs. The author addresses abstinence-education, the controversy over the abstinence versus comprehensive education debate, and recent findings in program implementation.

Columbia University's Health Education Program. 1998. *The "Go Ask Alice" Book of Answers: A Guide to Good Physical, Sexual, and Emotional Health.* New York: Henry Holt and Company.

This book is intended for adolescents and young adults with the entire content presented in a question and answer format. The questions are divided into sections devoted to: Relationships; Sexuality; Sexual Health; Emotional Health; Fitness and Nutrition; Alcohol, Nicotine, and Other Drugs; and General Health Questions. The questions range from waiting for the first kiss to specifics about penile penetration. The answers are direct, nonjudgmental, open-minded, and fact based.

D'Emilio, John, and Estelle B. Freedman. 1997. *Intimate Matters: A History of Sexuality in America.* Chicago: University of Chicago Press.

The book traces sexuality in the United States from 1600 to the present day. The content addresses the historical roots of sexuality and discusses the impact that sexual crusades and revolutions have had on societal standards of sex today.

Eberwein, Robert. 1999. *Sex Ed: Film, Video, and Framework for Desire.* New Brunswick, NY: Rutgers University Press.

This comprehensive text provides an in-depth discussion of sex education films by historical genres. The films are divided into categories: the initial phase, 1914–1939; World War II and the attack on venereal disease; youth and their bodies; films and videos for adults, 1946–present; and learning about pleasure. The films are described in detail as the author explains the purposes the films served and their impact on the audiences. A series of original photographs and film stills enhance the discussions.

Feldman, S. S., and G. R. Elliott. 1990. *At the Threshold: The Developing Adolescent.* Cambridge, MA: Harvard University Press.

The book provides an overview of research on issues that revolve around adolescent development. Chapters are written by field experts from education and the social sciences. Sexuality issues are addressed throughout the text.

Hedgepeth, Evonne, and Joan Helmich. 1996. *Teaching about Sexuality and HIV: Principles and Methods for Effective Education*. New York: New York University Press.

The text was designed for the sex education professional. The thirteen chapters cover effective sexuality and HIV education; creating a productive learning environment; theory and research for teaching about sexuality and HIV; meeting special challenges; planning and facilitating sexuality education sessions; introspective methods: helping learners see relevance; giving and gathering information and examining concepts, facts, and ideas; and methods for helping learners develop skills and reflect on attitudes.

Klein, Susan S. 1992. *Sex Equity and Sexuality in Education*. New York: State University of New York Press.

Much of this seventeen-chapter text explores gender equity issues in education. Authors from various fields cover sexuality issues such as homosexuality, puberty, harassment, etc. and the impact these have on sex education and opportunities in general education.

Laumann, Edward O., John H. Gagnon, Robert T. Michael, and Stuart Michaels. 1994. *The Social Organization of Sexuality: Sexual Practices in the United States*. Chicago: University of Chicago Press.

The text is a compilation of numerous studies on sexual behavior in the United States. The studies range from sexual practices (e.g., number of partners over time) to sexual health and happiness (e.g., sexual satisfaction and dysfunction). Empirical data on sex practices can be found in the text.

Mackay, Judith. 2000. *The Penguin Atlas of Human Sexual Behavior: Sexuality and Sexual Practices around the World*. New York: Penguin Putnam, Inc.

This atlas is composed of statistics of sex practices throughout the world. The statistics are divided into nine areas: sexuality; mating; reproduction; sexual health; the business of sex; sexual rites; sex crimes; evolutions; and tables. A world map is provided for each of the statistics with graphics placed accordingly. Although very little text accompanies the statistics, the visual elements are easy to interpret.

McKay, Alexander. 1999. *Sexual Ideology and Schooling: Towards Democratic Sexuality Education*. New York: State University of New York Press.

The author explores sexuality and sexuality education from restrictive and permissive ideologies and the impact these have on sex education. Democracy in sex education is explained in depth with discussions on how to maintain a democratic approach to sexual orientation, gender equality, and unwanted pregnancies.

Melody, M. E., and Linda Peterson. 1999. *Teaching America about Sex: Marriage Guides and Sex Manuals from the Late Victorians to Dr. Ruth.* New York: New York University Press.

The text provides an overview of sexuality in the United States from the late nineteenth century to 1995. The authors explore influential sex and marriage manuals of this genre and discuss the impact these and sex crusaders have had on society.

Millstein, Susan G., Anne C. Petersen, and Elena O. Nightingale. 2001. *Promoting the Health of Adolescents: New Directions for the Twenty-first Century.* New York: Oxford University Press.

This text provides a comprehensive overview of factors that contribute to good health-related behaviors. In this vein, readers can learn practical strategies that promote healthy behaviors among adolescents. Adolescent sexuality issues are discussed in-depth.

Pipher, Mary. 1994. *Reviving Ophelia: Saving the Selves of Adolescent Girls.* New York: Ballatine Books.

This *New York Times* best-seller describes life circumstances and events that some girls experience and struggle with in our culture today. Divorces, drugs and alcohol, and sexual violence are a few of the topics addressed in this text that potentially alter girls' images, self-esteem, and confidence. The author provides real-life accounts and advice for other girls who may find themselves in similar challenging situations.

Pollack, William S. 2000. *Real Boys' Voices: Boys Speak Out about Drugs, Sex, Violence, Bullying, Sports, School, Parents, and So Much More.* New York: Random House.

The author of this *New York Times* best-seller explores the perceptions of boys in the United States today. Boys' thoughts and feelings about their emotional lives, rage and suicide, reaching out to one another, dealing with loneliness and shame, and their venture into the real world are compiled into this twenty-four-chapter book. Boys speak about sex throughout the chapters.

Ridini, Steven P. 1998. *Health and Sexuality Education in Schools.* Westport, CN: Bergin and Garvey.

The text covers sex education programs by comparing how two communities educate youth about sex. Subsequent chapters provide suggestions for how to best implement a sex education program.

Roles, Patricia. 1990. *Facing Teenage Pregnancy: A Handbook for the Pregnant Teen.* Washington DC: Child Welfare League of America.

This book is designed for the pregnant adolescent in search of a solution. The content addresses the options available to pregnant adolescents, yet does not suggest a particular solution. The author uses a supportive, nonjudgmental approach to guide the youth in a critical time of decision making.

Rosemond, John. 2000. *Teen Proofing: Fostering Responsible Decision Making in Your Teenager.* Kansas City, MO: Andrew McNeel Publishing.

The text is written in an advice-style format whereby parents can learn how to best interact with and meet the needs of their adolescent. A chapter on sexuality explores the sex education debate and how parents can structure discussions about sex.

Tannahill, Reay. 1992. *Sex in History.* New York: Scarborough House.

This book investigates how various cultures throughout history have perceived sex. The author traces the sexual behavior and attitudes from ancient civilizations (3000 BC) to society in 1980.

Westheimer, Ruth K. 2000. *Encyclopedia of Sex.* New York: Continuum.

Aspects of sex are addressed in dictionary style. The first entry in the text, for instance, is abortion; the last entry is zoophilia (sex with animals). A glossary of terms and sexual slang accompanies the text.

Journal Articles

Blake, Susan M., Linda Simkin, Rebecca Ledsky, Cheryl Perkins, and Joseph M. Calabrese. 2001. **"Effects of a Parent-Child Communications Intervention on Young Adolescents' Risk for Early Onset of Sexual Intercourse."** *Family Planning Perspective* 33(2): 52–61.

Braverman, Paula K. 2000. **"Sexually Transmitted Diseases in Adolescents."** *Adolescent Medicine* 84(4): 869–889.

The author provides an overview of 25 sexually transmitted diseases (STD), and specifically examines the eight most common STDs among youth. Psychosocial issues, health care access, and ethnic and racial differences are among the topics addressed with regard to infection rates. The article concludes by underscoring the importance of providing youth with the information to protect themselves from acquiring an STD.

Centers for Disease Control and Prevention. 1999. **"Trends in HIV-related Sexual Risk Behaviors among High School Students—Selected U.S. Cities, 1991–1997."** *Journal of School Health* 69(7): 255–257.

The CDC summarizes the HIV infection data among high school youth from the Youth Risk Behavior Surveys of 1991, 1993, 1995, and 1997. The sexual behavior and the demographic characteristics of the samples are analyzed and discussed.

Donovan, Patricia. 1998. **"School-based Sexuality Education: The Issues and Challenges."** *Family Planning Perspectives* 30(4): 188–193.

The sex education state of affairs is addressed in the article with a complete discussion on the abstinence-only versus comprehensive sex education debate. The author writes that teachers are not prepared to teach sex education, and that because of the controversy surrounding sex education, many teachers are fearful of teaching about sexuality. A discussion ensues about the impact this has in the classroom. Recommendations for the provision of sex education conclude the article.

Elia, John D. 2000. **"The Necessity of Comprehensive Sexuality Education in the Schools."** *The Educational Forum* 64: 340–347.

A historical perspective begins the article and leads to current practices in sex education. The author emphasizes the need to teach youth about sexuality through a comprehensive approach. The crux of the article is a critical discussion on the need to teach youth about all aspects of sexuality.

Eyre, Stephen L., Nancy W. Read, and Susan Millstein. 1997. **"Adolescent Sexual Strategies."** *Journal of Adolescent Health* 20(4): 286–293.

The aim of the study was to investigate the strategies youth used to promote sexual encounters. The findings indicate that boys and girls differ in their strategies. Boys use coercion tactics (i.e., pressuring, raping), lying, and getting girls drunk, while girls tend to signal sexual availability. Both genders indicate they communicate commitment. The authors conclude the article with recommendations on intervention strategies.

Forsyth, Brian W.C. 2000. **"The AIDS Epidemic."** *Child and Adolescent Psychiatric Clinics of North America* 9(2): 267–277.

The author presents an overview on AIDS with a discussion of the epidemic's past, present, and future. International and national demographics are presented in terms of the epidemic's impact on women, adolescents, and children. A discussion of the prevention efforts concludes the article.

Hacker, Karen A., Yared Amera, Nancy Strunk, and Leslie Horst. 2000. **"Listening to Youth: Teen Perspectives on Pregnancy Prevention."** *Journal of Adolescent Health* 26(4): 279–288.

The authors' purpose in conducting this study was to determine the viewpoint of high school youth regarding teen pregnancy. The study found that 63 percent of the sample had had sex and only 35 percent of these youth used a condom consistently. The youth mentioned that having more information on pregnancies and birth control would prevent them from becoming pregnant.

Haffner, Debra W. 1997. **"Sexual Health for American Adolescents."** *Journal of Adolescent Health* 22(6): 453–459.

This article is a reprint of a Haffner lecture. The author provides statistics on the sexual behavior of youth and underscores the need for youth to receive a comprehensive sex education.

Kirby, D. 1999. **"What Does the Research Say about Sexuality Education?"** *Education Leadership* 58(2): 72–76.

Kirby discusses research on the effects of abstinence-only and abstinence-plus sex education programs. The purpose of the article is to answer whether abstinence-only programs delay the onset of sexual intercourse and decrease the sexual behavior of youth. A section of the article outlines common characteristics of effective curricula, and concluding remarks indicate a support for abstinence-plus programs.

Koch, Kathy. 1998. **"Encouraging Teen Abstinence."** *CQ Researcher* 8(25): 577–599.

This article is a comprehensive discussion on the sexual behavior of youth and the arguments surrounding the sex education debate. Tables and graphs illustrate demographic trends among youth, and a series of informational inserts (i.e., chronology section and "For More Information") complement the issue at hand.

Strasburger, V. C. 2000. **"Getting Teenagers to Say No to Sex, Drugs, and Violence in the New Millennium."** *Adolescent Medicine* 84(4): 787–810.

The author explores the lives of adolescents today as compared to prior generations. Some critical issues surrounding adolescence—primarily violence, sex, and drug use—are discussed with some views about the role media has in influencing adolescents. Solutions to these issues conclude the article.

Whitehead, Barbara D. 1994. **"The Failure of Sex Education."** *The Atlantic Monthly:* 55–80.

As the title indicates, much of Whitehead's discussion centers on the failure of the then current sex education model. The author uses statistics and research to support that sex education in the eighties and early nineties was disastrous.

Wilson, Susan N. 2000. **"Sexuality Education: Our Current Status, and an Agenda for 2010."** *Family Planning Perspectives* 32(5): 252–254.

In this viewpoint piece from *Family Planning Perspectives,* the author discusses sex education in 1999. At the time, 14 percent of public school districts had a comprehensive sex education policy, 51 percent had an abstinence-plus policy, and 35 percent instituted an abstinence-only policy. Additional statistics are provided on the sexual behavior of youth, in addition to a series of research questions that need to be addressed in the future. The author concludes with an agenda for advocacy.

Reports and Studies Available On-Line

These publications provide an overview of sex education today. The reports discuss the sex education debate, general statistics on sex education provisions, and guidelines and recommendations for sound sex education programs.

Abstinence vs. "Safer Sex" Sexuality Education: A Comparison
The Medical Institute for Sexual Health
http://www.medinstitute.org/products/index.htm

But Does It Work? Improving Evaluations of Sexuality Education, 2001
Sexuality Information and Education Council of the United States
http://www.siecus.org/pubs/evals/eval0000.html

Changing Emphasis in Sexuality Education in U.S. Public Secondary Schools, 1988–1999, 2000
The Alan Guttmacher Institute
http://www.agi-usa.org/pubs/journals/3220400.html

Guidelines for Comprehensive Sexuality Education, 1996
SIECUS
http://www.siecus.org/pubs/guidelines/guidelines.pdf

Hungry Hearts: Evaluating the New Curricula for Teens on Marriage and Relationships, 2000
American Values 2001
http://www.americanvalues.org/html/r_hungry_hearts.shtml

Marriage in America: A Report to the Nation, 1995
American Values 2001
http://americanvalues.org/html/r_marriage_in_America.shtml

National Guidelines for Sexuality and Character Education
The Medical Institute for Sexual Health
http://www.medinstitute.org/products/index.htm

National School Health Strategies, 2001
Centers for Disease Control and Prevention
http://www.cdc.gov/nccdphp/dash/coordinated.htm

National Survey of Public Secondary School Principals: The Politics of Sex Education, 1999
Kaiser Family Foundation
http://www.kff.org/content/1999/1560/Toplines.pdf

Prevention and Abstinence Education Efforts: Survey Results on the Use of TANF and Title V Funds, 1999
American Public Human Services Association
http://www.aphsa.org/publicat/teenpreg.pdf

Report Says Sex Ed Can Reduce Teen Pregnancy, Jury Out on AB Only, 2001
The Alan Guttmacher Institute
http://www.agi-usa.org/pubs/journals/gr010203.html

Science or Politics? George W. Bush and the Future of Sexuality Education in the United States, 2001
Advocates for Youth
http://www.advocatesforyouth.org/publications/factsheet/fsbush.pdf

Sex Education in America: A View from Inside the Nation's Classrooms, 2000
Kaiser Family Foundation
http://www.kff.org/content/2000/3048/SexED.pdf

Sex Education: Politicians, Parents, Teachers and Teens, 2001
The Alan Guttmacher Institute
http://www.agi-usa.org/pubs/ib_2–01.html

Sex in the 90s: Kaiser Family Foundation/ABC Television 1998 National Survey of Americans on Sex and Sexual Health, 1998
Kaiser Family Foundation
http://www.kff.org/content/archive/1430/abc.pdf

Sexuality, Contraception, and the Media (RE 0038), 2001
American Academy of Pediatrics
http://aap.org/policy/re0038.html

Sexuality Education for Children and Adolescents, 2001
American Academy of Pediatrics
http://www.aap.org/policy/008.html

Should We Teach Only Abstinence in Sexuality Education, 1997
Center for AIDS Prevention Studies
http://www.caps.ucsf.edu/abstinence.html

Teaching Our Teachers to Teach: A SIECUS Study on Training and Preparation for HIV/AIDS Prevention and Sexuality Education, 2001
SIECUS
http://www.siecus.org/pubs/teach/teac0000.html

Teaching Your Children about Sexuality, 2000
American College of Obstetricians and Gynecologists
http://medem.com.

Toward a Sexually Healthy America: Roadblocks Imposed
by the Federal Government's Abstinence-Only-Until-Marriage
Education Program, 2001
Organizations: Advocates for Youth, SIECUS
http://www.advocatesforyouth.org/publications/abstinenceonly.pdf

What Statistics Don't Tell about Sexuality Education, 1999
SIECUS
http://www.siecus.org/pubs/srpt/srpt0022.html

Whatever Happened to the Adolescent Family Life Act? 1998
The Alan Guttmacher Institute
http://www.agi-usa.org/pubs/journals/gr010203.html

Who Are We? 2001
American Values 2001
http://americanvalues.org/html/jean_s_talk.shtml

What's Wrong With Abstinence-Only Sexuality Education
Programs? 2001
SIECUS
http://www.siecus.org/policy/SReport/srep0003.html

The following reports provide an in-depth investigation of the sexual behavior among youth. Statistical findings are generally available on these reports as well as discussions on the profiles of youth at risk for pregnancy, sexually transmitted diseases, and HIV/AIDS.

Adolescent Health: State of the Nation—Mortality Trends, Causes of
Death, and Related Risk Behaviors among U.S. Adolescents, 1993
Centers for Disease Control and Prevention
http://www.cdc.gov/nccdphp/dash/ahson/foreword.htm

Children on the Brink, 2000
USAID
http://www.usaid.gov/pubs/hiv_aids/childrenreport.pdf

Kinsey and Children, 1998
Kinsey Institute
http://www.indiana.edu/~kinsey/controv-akchild.html

Recent Findings from the 'Add Health' Survey: Teens and Sexual Activity, 2001
The Alan Guttmacher Institute
http://www.agi-usa.org/pubs/journals/gr040401.html

Sexual Activity and Contraceptive Practices among Teenagers in the United States, 1988 and 1995, 2001
Centers for Disease Control and Prevention
http://www.cdc.gov/nchs/data/series/sr_23/sr23_21.pdf

Sexual Health Care and Counsel Survey, 2001
Kaiser Family Foundation
http://www.kff.org/content/2001/3113/Final%20Summary.pdf

Trends in Sexual Risk Behaviors among High School Students—United States, 1991–1997
Centers for Disease Control and Prevention
http://www.cdc.gov/nccdphp/dash/4736mmwrfile/mmhtm

These five publications investigate factors that influence the sexual behavior of youth. In each of these, youth articulated their perceptions of intimacy, sex, and parent and familial communication and support.

The Cautious Generation: Teens Tell Us About Sex, Virginity, and "The Talk," 2000
National Campaign to Prevent Teen Pregnancy
http://www.teenpregnancy.org/cautious.pdf

Family Communication About Sex: What Are Parents Saying and Are Their Adolescents Listening? 1998
Centers for Disease Control
http://www.cdc.gov/hiv/wad/miller.pdf

Family Matters: A Research Synthesis of Family Influences on Adolescent Pregnancy, 1998
National Campaign to Prevent Teen Pregnancy
http://www.teenpregnancy.org/iresearc.htm

Kaiser Family Foundation Survey on Teens and Sex: What They Say Teens Need to Know, and Who They Listen To, 1996
Kaiser Family Foundation
http://www.kff.org/content/archive/1159/teentop.pdf

National Survey of Teens: Teens Talk About Dating, Intimacy, and Their Sexual Relationships, 1998
Kaiser Family Foundation
http://www.kff.org/content/archive/1373/datingrep.pdf

The following publications address youth pregnancy in terms of pregnancy demographics and trends, factors that contribute to pregnancy, and the effectiveness of pregnancy prevention programs.

Communities Responding to the Challenges of Adolescent Pregnancy Prevention, 1998
Advocates for Youth
http://www.advocatesforyouth.org/publications/catalog.htm

Condom Availability and Responsible Sexuality Education, 2000
Planned Parenthood Inc.
http://www.plannedparenthood.org/articles/sexed.html

Do Condoms Work? 1995
Center for AIDS Prevention Studies
http://www.ama-assn.org/spcial/hiv/preventn/prevent2.htm.

Emerging Answers: Research Findings on Programs to Reduce Teen Pregnancy, 2001
National Campaign to Prevent Teen Pregnancy
http://www.teenpregnancy.org/053001/emeranswsum.pdf

Explaining Demographic Trends in Teenage Fertility, 1980–1995, 2000
The Alan Guttmacher Institute
http://www.agi-usa.org/pubs/journals/3216600.html

Meeting the Needs of Young Clients: A Guide to Providing Reproductive Health Services to Adolescents, 2000
Family Health International
http://www.fhi.org/en/fp/fpother/adolhand/adolchap1.html#anchor383693

The National Evaluation of the Children's Aid Society Carrera-Model Program to Prevent Teen Pregnancy, 2001
The Children's Aid Society
http://www.childrensaidsociety.org/cas/teen_preg/program_report.html

No Easy Answers: Research Findings on Programs to Reduce Teen Pregnancy, 1997
National Campaign to Reduce Teen Pregnancy
http://www.teenpregnancy.org/fmnoeasy.htm

Peer Education: Promoting Health Behaviors, 1997
Advocates for Youth
http://www.advocatesforyouth.org/publications/factsheet/fspeered.htm

SafeSmarts: Safer Sex, Condoms and "the Pill" Survey, 2000
Kaiser Family Foundation
http://www.kff.org/content/2000/3081/SafeSexToplines.pdf

Teenage Pregnancy: Overall Trends and State-by-State Information, 1999
The Alan Guttmacher Institute
http://www.agi-usa.org/pubs/teen_pre_stats.html

Teenager's Pregnancy Intentions and Decisions, 1999
The Alan Guttmacher Institute
http://www.agi-usa.org/pubs/or_teen_pre_survey.html

Trends in Pregnancies and Pregnancy Rates by Outcome: Estimates for the United States, 1976–1996
Centers for Disease Control and Prevention
http://www.cdc.gov/nchs/releases/00facts/trends.htm

U.S. Teenage Pregnancy Statistics: With Comparative Statistics for Women Aged 20–24, 2001
The Alan Guttmacher Institute
http://www.agi-usa.org/pubs/teen_preg_sr_0699.html

Why is Teenage Pregnancy Declining? The Roles of Abstinence, Sexual Activity and Contraceptive Use, 1999
The Alan Guttmacher Institute
http://www.agi-usa.org/pubs/or_teen_pre_decline.html

These eight reports and studies provide additional insight into HIV/AIDS among youth and among the general population. Some of the reports are qualitative in nature and others are empirically data driven.

Hearing Their Voices: A Qualitative Research Study on HIV Testing and Higher-Risk Teens, 1999
Kaiser Family Foundation
http://www.kff.org/content/1999/1492/HearingVoices2.PDF

HIV/AIDS and HRC
Human Rights Campaign
http://www.hrc.org/issues/hiv_aids/background/aidstimeline.pdf

HIV Infection and AIDS in Adolescents, 2000
Society for Adolescent Medicine
http://www.adolescenthealth.org/html/hiv_infection_and_aids.html

Meeting the Needs of Children, Youth, Women, and Families Affected by HIV and AIDS through Medicaid Managed Care
AIDS Policy Center for Children, Youth, and Families
http://www.aidspolicycenter.org/library/PDFs/meetingtheneeds.pdf

National Survey of Teens on HIV/AIDS, 2000
Kaiser Family Foundation
http://www.kff.org/content/2000/3092/Teensurveyonhiv.pdf

Peer Education and HIV/AIDS: Past Experiences,
Future Directions, 2000
Population Council
http://www.popcouncil.org/pdfs/peer_ed.pdf

USAID Efforts to Address the Needs of Children Affected
by HIV/AIDS, 2001
USAID
http://www.usaid.gov/pubs/hiv_aids/2166_ovchild10.pdf

Youth and HIV/AIDS 2000: A New American Agenda
Office of National AIDS Policy, The White House
http://www.aidspolicycenter.org/library/PDFs/youth_report1.pdf

These reports emphasize the pervasiveness of sexually transmitted diseases today. Some of these reports provide general statistics, prevention efforts, and awareness-building activities.

An Introduction to Sexually Transmitted Diseases, 1999
National Institutes of Health
http://www.niaid.nih.gov/factsheets/stdinfo.htm

National STD Action Plan, 2001
American Social Health Association
http://ashastd.org/stdaction/index.html

New SexSmarts Study on Teens and Sexually Transmitted Diseases, 2001
Kaiser Family Foundation
http://www.kff.org/content/2001/3148/SummaryofFindings.pdf

What Teens Know and Don't (But Should) about Sexually Transmitted Diseases, 1999
Kaiser Family Foundation
http://www.kff.org/content/archive/1465/stds_t.pdf

SEXUAL ABUSE AND SEXUAL HARASSMENT

Books

Allen, Craig. 1991. *Women and Men Who Sexually Abuse Children: A Comparative Analysis.* Brandon, VT: Safer Press.

Araji, Sharon K. 1997. *Sexually Aggressive Children: Coming to Understand Them.* Thousand Oaks, CA: Sage Publications.

Besharov, Douglas J. 1990. *Recognizing Child Abuse: A Guide for the Concerned.* New York: Free Press.

Brandenburg, Judith B. 1997. *Confronting Sexual Harassment: What Schools and Colleges Can Do.* New York: Teachers College Press.

Carich, Mark, and Steven E. Mussack. 2001. *The Handbook of Sexual Abuser Assessment and Treatment.* Brandon, VT: Safer Press.

Colton, Matthew, and Maurice Vanstone. 1996. *Betrayal of Trust: Sexual Abuse by Men Who Work with Children—In Their Own Words.* New York: Free Association Books.

Costin, Lela B., Howard J. Kareger, and David Stoesz. 1995. *The Politics of Child Abuse in America.* New York: Oxford University Press.

Cunningham, Carolyn, and Kee MacFarlane. 1996. *When Children Abuse: Group Treatment Strategies for Children with Impulse Control Problems*. Brandon, VT: Safer Press.

Durham, Duane, John Keating, Andrew Leggett, and Margaret Osmond. 1998. *Treating the Aftermath of Sexual Abuse: A Handbook for Working with Children in Care*. Washington, DC: Child Welfare League of America.

Freeman-Longo, Robert E., and Gerald T. Blanchard. 1998. *Sexual Abuse in America: Epidemic of the 21st Century*. Brandon, VT: The Safer Society Press.

Gilmartin, Pat. 1994. *Rape, Incest, and Child Sexual Abuse: Consequences and Recovery*. New York: Garland.

Havelin, Kate. 2000. *Sexual Harassment: "This Doesn't Feel Right!"* Mankato, MN: Capstone Press.

Herman, Judith L. 2000. *Father-Daughter Incest*. Cambridge, MA: Harvard University Press.

Hoghughi, Masud S., Surya R. Bhate, and Finlay Graham. 1997. *Working with Sexually Abusive Adolescents*. Thousand Oaks, CA: Sage Publications.

Hunter, Mic. 1990. *Abused Boys: The Neglected Victims of Sexual Abuse*. New York: Fawcett Columbine.

Kaminker, Laura. 1999. *Everything You Need to Know about Dealing with Sexual Assault*. New York: The Rosen Publishing Group.

Kinnear, Karen. 1995. *Childhood Sexual Abuse: A Reference Handbook*. Santa Barbara, CA: ABC-CLIO.

Knopp, Fay Honey. 1991. *The Youthful Sex Offender*. Brandon, VT: Safer Press.

Levesque, Roger J.R. 1999. *Sexual Abuse of Children: A Human Rights Perspective*. Bloomington, IN: Indiana University Press.

Levy, Barrie. 1997. *In Love and In Danger: A Teen's Guide to Breaking Free of Abusive Relationships*. Berkeley, CA: Publishers Group West.

Levy, Barrie. 1998. *Dating Violence: Young Women in Danger.* Berkeley, CA: Publishers Group West.

Levy, Barrie, and Patricia Occhiuzzo Giggans. 1995. *What Parents Need to Know about Dating Violence.* Seattle, WA: Seal Press.

Lowenthal, Barbara. 2001. *Abuse and Neglect: The Educator's Guide to the Identification and Prevention of Child Maltreatment.* Baltimore: Paul H. Brookes Publishing Company.

Mach, Kathleen F. 1994. *The Sexually Abused Child: A Parents Guide to Coping and Understanding.* Williamsburg, MI: Family Insights Books.

Mendel, Matthew Parynik. 1995. *The Male Survivor: The Impact of Sexual Abuse.* Thousand Oaks, CA: Sage Publications.

Parrot, Andrea. 1999. *Coping with Date Rape and Acquaintance Rape.* New York: The Rosen Publishing Group.

Prendergast, William E. 1996. *Sexual Abuse of Children and Adolescents: A Preventive Guide for Parents, Teachers and Counselors.* New York: Continuum.

Prendergast, William E. 1996. *Sexual Abuse of Children and Adults.* New York: Continuum Publishing Company.

Prentky, Robert, and Stacey Bird Edmunds. 1997. *Assessing Sexual Abuse: A Resource Guide for Practitioners.* Brandon, VT: The Safer Society Press.

Pryor, Douglas, W. 1996. *Unspeakable Acts: Why Men Sexually Abuse Children.* New York: New York University Press.

Ryan, Gail, and Sandy Lane. 1997. *Juvenile Sex Offending: Causes, Consequences, and Correction.* San Francisco: Jossey-Bass Publisher, Inc.

Sabella, R. A., and R. D. Myrick. 1995. *Confronting Sexual Harassment: Learning Activities for Teens.* New York: Education Media Corporations.

Schaefer, Karen. 1993. *What Only a Mother Can Tell You about Child Sexual Abuse.* Washington, DC: Child Welfare League of America.

Shoop, R. J., and D. L. Edwards. 1994. *How to Stop Sexual Harassment in Our Schools: A Handbook and Curriculum Guide for Administrators and Teachers*. New York: Paramount Publishing.

Sperekas, Nicole B. 2001. *But He Says He Loves Me*. Brandon, VT: Safer Press.

Stein, Nan. 1999. *Classrooms and Courtrooms: Facing Sexual Harassment in K–12 Schools*. New York: Teachers College Press.

Stein, Nan, and Lisa Sjostrom. 1994. *Flirting or Hurting? A Teacher's Guide on Student-to-Student Sexual Harassment in Schools*. West Haven, CT: NEA Professional Library.

Strauss, Susan, and Pamela Espeland. 1992. *Sexual Harassment and Teens: A Program for Positive Change*. Minneapolis: Free Spirit Publishing, Inc.

Wetzel, Roberta, and Nina W. Brown. 2000. *Student-Generated Sexual Harassment in Secondary Schools*. Westport, CN: Bergin and Garvey.

Whetsell-Mitchell, Juliann. 1995. *Rape of the Innocent: Understanding and Preventing Child Sexual Abuse*. Washington, DC: Accelerated Development.

Wright, Lesley Bailey, and Mindy Loiselle. 1997. *Boys on Track: Boys Dealing with Sexual Abuse*. Brandon, VT: The Safer Press.

Journal Articles

Crisci, George S. 1999. **"When No Means No: Recognizing and Preventing Sexual Harassment in Your Schools."** *American School Board Journal* 186(6): 25–29.

Finkelhor, D., and Jennifer Dziuba-Leatherman. 1994. **"Victimization of Children."** *American Psychologist* 49 (3): 173–183.

Jones, Rebecca. 1999. **"'I Don't Feel Safe Here Anymore': Your Legal Duty to Protect Gay Kids from Harassment."** *American School Board Journal* 186: 26–31.

Rickert, V. J., and C. M. Weimann. 1998. **"Date Rape among Adolescents**

and Young Adults." *Journal of Pediatric Adolescent Gynecology* 11: 167–175.

Saywitz, Karen J., Anthony P. Mannarino, Lucy Berliner, and Judith A. Cohen. 2000. **"Treatment for Sexually Abused Children and Adolescents."** *American Psychologist* 55(9): 1040–1049.

Stein, Nan. 2001. **"Students Sexually Harassing Students."** *Choices in Preventing Youth Violence* 8: 9.

———. 2001. **"Students Sexually Harassing Students."** *Choices in Preventing Youth Violence* 8: 9.

2001. **Violence in Schools: Gender and Sexual Harassment: Schools as the Training Grounds for Domestic Violence.** Wellesley, MA: Wellesley College Center for Research on Women.

Stock, Jacqueline L., Michelle A. Bell, Debra K. Boyer, and Frederick A. Connell. 1997. **"Adolescent Pregnancy and Sexual Risk-Taking among Sexually Abused Girls."** *Family Planning Perspective* 29(4): 213–216.

Reports and Studies Available On-Line

An Annotated Summary of the Regulations for Title IX of the Education Amendments of 1972, 1997
NOW Legal Defense and Education Fund
http://www.nowldef.org/html/pub/pubdet.shtml#education

Bruised Inside: What Our Children Say about Youth Violence, What Causes It, and What We Need to Do about It, 2000
National Association of Attorneys General
http://www.keepschoolssafe.org/bruised.pdf

Case Law on Sexual Harassment in Schools
Equal Rights Advocates
http://www.equalrights.org/sexhar/school/caselaw.html

Characteristics of Crimes Against Juveniles, 2000
Office of Juvenile Justice and Delinquency Prevention
http://www.ncjrs.org/pdffiles1/ojjdp/179034.pdf

Child Abuse and Neglect: State Statutes Elements: Mandatory Reporters of Child Abuse and Neglect, 2000
National Clearinghouse on Child Abuse and Neglect Information
http://www.calib.com/nccanch/pubs/sag/mandarep.pdf

Child Abuse and Neglect: State Statutes Elements: Reporting Procedures, 1999
National Clearinghouse on Child Abuse and Neglect Information
http://www.calib.com/nccanch/pubs/stats01/report.pdf

Child Maltreatment 1999
U.S. Department of Health and Human Services
http://www.acf.dhhs.gov/programs/cb/publications/cm99/index.htm

Child Rape Victim 1992, 1994
Office of Justice Programs, U.S. Department of Justice
http://www.ojp.usdoj.gov/bjs/pub/pdf/crv92.pdf

Children as Victims, 1999 National Report Series
Office of Juvenile Justice and Delinquency Prevention,
U.S. Department of Justice
http://www.ncjrs.org/pdffiles1/ojjdp/180753.pdf

The Commonwealth Fund Survey of the Health of Adolescent Girls, 1997
The Commonwealth Fund
http://www.cmwf.org/programs/women/adoleshl.asp

Criminal Victimization 1999: Changes 1998–1999 with Trends 1993–1999, 2000
Office of Justice Programs, U.S. Department of Justice
http://www.rainn.org/test/ncvs99.pdf

Current Trends in Child Abuse Prevention, Reporting, and Fatalities: The 1999 Fifty State Survey
Prevent Child Abuse America
http://www.preventchildabuse.org/research_ctr/fact_sheets/1999_50_survey.PDF

Dating Violence, 2000
Centers for Disease Control
http://www.cdc.gov/ncipc/factsheets/datviol.htm

The Dimensions of an Adolescent Lesbian Sexual Identity: A Pilot Test of a Measure, 1998
Wellesley Centers for Women
http://www.wcwonline.org/title273.html

Do the Right Thing: Understanding, Addressing, and Preventing Sexual Harassment in Schools; A Practical Guide for Educators, Parents, and Students, 1998
Organization(s): National Women's Law Center, Council of Chief State Officers, National School Boards Association
http://www.nwlc.org

Domestic and Sexual Violence Data Collection: A Report to Congress under the Violence against Women Act, 1996
Organization(s): National Institute of Justice, Bureau of Justice Statistics
http://www.ncjrs.org/pdffiles/alldom.pdf

Federal Activities Addressing Violence in Schools, 2000
Centers for Disease Control
http://www.cdc.gov/nccdphp/dash/violence/violenceactivities.pdf

Full Report of the Prevalence, Incidence, and Consequences of Violence against Women: Finding from the National Violence against Women Survey, 2000
Office of Justice Programs, National Institute for Justice, U.S. Department of Justice
http://www.rainn.org/test/fullnvawsurvey.pdf

Guidelines for the Evaluation of Sexual Abuse of Children: Subject Review (RE 9819), 1999
American Academy of Pediatrics
http://www.aap.org/policy/re9819.html

Hate Crime: A Sourcebook for Schools Confronting Bigotry, Harassment, Vandalism and Violence, 1991
Southwest Center for Education Equity, Southwest Regional Laboratory
http://www.WestEd.org

The Health of Adolescent Boys: Commonwealth Fund Survey Findings
The Commonwealth Fund
http://www.cmwf.org/programs/women/boysv271.asp

Hostile Hallways: AAUW Survey on Sexual Harassment in America's Schools, 1993
American Association of University Women
http://www.aauw.org/2000/hh.html

Hostile Hallways: Bullying, Teasing, and Sexual Harassment in School, 2001
American Association of University Women
http://www.aauw.org/2000/hostile.html

Juvenile Offenders and Victims: 1999 National Report
U.S. Department of Justice
http://www.ncjrs.org/html/ojjdp/nationalreport99/toc.html

Juvenile Sex Offenders, Research Biography
National Youth Violence Prevention, U.S. Department of Justice
http://ojjdp.ncrs.org/juvsexoff/sexbibtopic.html

Juveniles Who Have Sexually Offended, 2001
National Center for Juvenile Justice
http://www.ncjrs.org/pdffiles1/ojjdp/184739.pdf

Key Facts on Youth, Crime, and Violence, 2000
Children's Defense Fund
http://www.childrensdefense.org/crime_keyfacts.htm

Know the Rules, Just in Case . . . , 1998
National Center for Missing and Exploited Children
http://www.missingkids.org/

Know the Rules: Public Awareness Campaign for Teen Girls, 1998
National Center for Missing and Exploited Children
http://www.missingkids.org/

Perspectives on Acquaintance Rape, 1997
American Academy of Experts in Traumatic Stress
http://www.aaets.org/arts/art13.htm

Preventing and Countering School-Based Harassment—A Resource Guide for K–12 Educators, 1997
Center for National Origin, Race and Sex Equity, Northwest Regional Education Laboratory
http://nwrel.org/cnorse

Preventing Youth Hate Crime—A Manual for Schools and Communities, 1998
Safe and Drug-Free Schools Program, U.S. Department of Education
http://www.ed.gov/offices/OESE/SDFS/news.html

Protecting Students from Harassment and Hate Crime: A Guide for Schools, 1999
Office of Civil Rights, U.S. Department of Education
http://www.ed.gov/pubs/Harassment/policy1.html

Protective Effects of Sports Participation on Girls' Sexual Behavior, 2000
Wellesley Centers for Women
http://www.wcwonline.org/title336.html

Reproductive Health in Teens: Data and Sources, 2001
Centers for Disease Control
http://www.cdc.gov/nccdphp/dash/ahson/datasour.htm

Revised Sexual Harassment Guidance: Harassment of Students by School Employees, Other Students, or Third Parties, 2001
Office of Civil Rights, U.S. Department of Education
http://www.ed.gov/offices/OCR/shguide/index/html

Righting the Wrongs: A Legal Guide to Understanding, Addressing, and Preventing Sexual Harassment in Schools, 1998
National Women's Law Center, Council of Chief State School Officers, National School Boards Association
http://www.nwlc.org; http://www.nsba.org/resources.htm

School Health Programs: An Investment in Our Nation's Future, 2001
Centers for Disease Control
http://www.cdc.gov/nccdphp/dash/ataglanc.htm

School Violence, 2001
National Youth Violence Prevention
http://www.safeyouth.org/topics/school.htm

Secrets in Public: Sexual Harassment in Our Schools, 1993
NOW Legal Defense and Education Fund, Wellesley College Center for Research on Women
http://www.wcwonline.org/title118.html

Sex Offenses and Offenders: An Analysis of Data on Date Rape and Sexual Assault, 1997
Office of Justice Programs, U.S. Department of Justice
http://www.ojp.usdoj.gov/bjs/pub/pdf/soo.pdf

Sexual Assault of Young Children as Reported to Law Enforcement: Victim, Incident, and Offender Characteristics (NCJ 182990), 2000
National Center for Juvenile Justice
http://www.ojp.usdoj.gov/bjs/pub/pdf/saycrle.pdf

Sexually Transmitted Diseases and Child Sexual Abuse: Portable Guides to Investigating Child Abuse, 1996
Office of Justice Programs, Office of Juvenile Justice and Delinquency Prevention
http://www.ncjrs.org/pdffiles/stdandab.pdf

Student to Student Sexual Harassment: A Legal Guide for Schools, 1998
National School Boards Association
http://www.nsba.org/resources.htm

Uniform Crime Reports, 1999
Federal Bureau of Investigation
http://www.fbi.gov/ucr/ucr0699.pdf

SEXUAL ORIENTATION

Books

Bass, Ellen, and Kate Kaufman. 1996. *Free Your Mind: The Book for Gay, Lesbian, and Bisexual Youth and Their Allies.* New York: HarperCollins Publishers.

Bernstein, Robert A. 1995. *Straight Parents, Gay Children: Inspiring Families to Live Honestly and with Greater Understanding.* New York: Thunder's Mouth Press.

Chandler, Kurt. 1995. *Passages of Pride: Lesbian and Gay Youth Come of Age.* New York: Times Books/Random House.

Clendinen, Dudley, and Adam Nagourney. 1999. *Out for Good: The Struggle to Build a Gay Rights Movement in America.* New York: Simon and Schuster.

D'Augelli, Anthony R., and Charlotte J. Patterson. 2001. *Lesbian, Gay, and Bisexual Identities and Youth: Psychological Perspectives.* New York: Oxford University Press.

Fone, Byrne. 2000. *Homophobia: A History.* New York: Henry Holt and Company.

Gay and Lesbian Educators of British Columbia. 2000. *Challenging Homophobia in Schools: A K–12 Resource.* New York: GLSEN.

GLSEN. 2000. *Ending Anti-gay Bias in Schools: A Training of Trainers Manual.* New York: GLSEN.

GLSEN. 2001. *The GLSEN Workbook: A Developmental Model for Assessing, Describing and Improving Schools for Lesbian, Gay, Bisexual and Transgender (LGBT) People.* New York: GLSEN.

Gray, Mary L. 1999. *In Your Face: Stories from the Lives of Queer Youth.* Binghamton, NY: The Hawthorne Press, Inc.

Harbeck, Karen M. 1992. *Coming Out of the Classroom Closet: Gay and Lesbian Students, Teachers, and Curricula.* New York: Harrington Park Press.

Harris, Mary B. 1997. *School Experiences of Gay and Lesbian Youth: The Invisible Minority.* Binghamton, NY: The Hawthorne Press.

Hogan, Steve, and Lee Hudson. 1998. *Completely Queer: The Gay and Lesbian Encyclopedia.* New York: Henry Holt and Company.

Hunter, Ski, Coleen Shannon, Jo Knox, and James L. Martin. 1998. *Lesbian, Gay, and Bisexual Youth and Adults: Knowledge for Human Services Practice.* Thousand Oak, CA: Sage Publications.

Latham, Bob. 2000. *The Invisible Minority: GLBTQ.* New York: GLSEN.

Lipkin, Arthur. 1999. *Understanding Homosexuality: Changing Schools.* Boulder, CO: Westview Press.

Mallon, Gerald P. 1999. *Social Services with Transgendered Youth.* New York: The Hawthorne Press, Inc.

Mastoon, Adam. 1997. *The Shared Heart: Portraits and Stories Celebrating Lesbian, Gay, and Bisexual Young People.* New York: William Marrow: Lothrop, Lee, and Shepard Books.

Owens, Robert E. 1998. *Queer Kids: The Challenges and Promise for Lesbian, Gay, and Bisexual Youth.* New York: Harrington Park Press.

Remafedi, Gary (ed). 1994. *Death by Denial: Studies of Suicide in Gay and Lesbian Teenagers.* Boston, MA: Alyson Publications.

Ryan, Caitlin, and Donna Futterman. 1998. *Lesbian and Gay Youth: Care and Counseling.* New York: Columbia University Press.

Savin-William, Ritch C. 1990. *Gay and Lesbian Youth: Expressions of Identity.* New York: Hemisphere Publishing Corporation.

Stewart, Gail. 1997. *Gay and Lesbian Youth.* San Diego, CA: Lucent Books.

Unks, Gerald. 1995. *The Gay Teen: Education Practice and Theory for Lesbian, Gay, and Bisexual Adolescents.* New York: Routledge.

Woog, Dan. 1995. *School's Out: The Impact of Gay and Lesbian Issues on America's Schools.* Los Angeles: Alyson Books.

Journal Articles

Buckel, David S. 2000. **"Legal Perspectives on Ensuring a Safe and Nondiscriminatory School Environment for Lesbian, Gay, Bisexual, and Transgendered Students."** *Education and Urban Society* 32: 390–398.

Fontaine, J. H. 1998. **"Evidencing a Need: School Counselors' Experiences with Gay and Lesbian Students."** *Professional School Counseling* 1: 8–14.

Giorgis, C., K. Higgins, W. McNab. 2000. **"Health Issues of Gay and Lesbian Youth: Implications for Schools."** *Journal of Health Education* 31: 28–36.

Grossman, A. K., and M. S. Kerner. 1998. **"Support Networks of Gay Male and Lesbian Youth."** *Journal of Gay, Lesbian, and Bisexual Identity* 3: 27–46.

Remafedi, Gary, James A. Farrow, and Robert W. Deisher. 1991. **"Risk Factors for Attempted Suicide in Gay and Bisexual Youth."** *Pediatrics* 87(6): 869–875.

Remafedi, Gary, S. French, M. Story, M. D. Resnick, and R. Blum. 1998. **"The Relationship between Suicide Risk and Sexual Orientation: Results of a Population-Based Study."** *American Journal of Public Health* 88(1): 57–60.

Robinson, K. E. 1994. **"Addressing the Needs of Gay and Lesbian Students: The School Counselor's Role."** *School Counselor* 41: 326–332.

Saewyce, Elizabeth, Linda H. Bearinger, Rover William Blum, and Michael D. Resnick. 1999. **"Sexual Intercourse, Abuse and Pregnancy among Adolescent Women: Does Sexual Orientation Make a Difference?"** *Family Planning Perspective* 31(3): 127–131.

Sanders, G. L., and I. T. Kroll. 2000. **"Generating Stories of Resilience; Helping Gay and Lesbian Youth and Their Families."** *Journal of Marital and Family Therapy* 26: 433–442.

Reports and Studies Available On-Line

Adding Sexual Orientation and Gender Identity to Discrimination and Harassment Policies in School, 2000
GLSEN and ACLU
http://www.glsen.org/binary-data/GLSEN_ARTICLES/pdf_file/37.pdf

Adolescence, Sexual Orientation and Identity: An Overview
OutProud, Inc, reprinted with permission from Warren J. Blumenfeld
http://www.outproud.org/article_sexual_identity.html

Creating Safe Schools for Lesbian and Gay Students: A Resource Guide for School Staff, 1997
Youth Pride, Inc
http://members.tripod.com/~twood/guide.html

Defending Gay/Straight Alliances and Other Gay-Related Groups in Public Schools Under the Equal Access Act: Questions and Answers, 1998
Lambda Legal Defense and Education Fund
http://www.lambdalegal.org/cgi-bin/pages/documents/record?record=251

Each Child That Dies: Gay and Lesbians in Your Schools, 1995
OutProud, Inc., reprinted from *Multicultures, Unity Through Diversity—*

Focus on Gays, Lesbians, and Bisexuals, 2000
National Education Association
http://www.nea.org/bt/1-students/gays.pdf

Gay/Straight Clubs Formed by Public School Students: Why School Officials Need to Treat Them Equally, 1996
American Civil Liberties Union
http://www.aclu.org/issues/gay/equalacc.html

Gay/Straight Student Alliances and Other Gay-Related Student Groups: What Did Congress Have to Say in Passing the Equal Access Act? 1996
Lambda Legal Defense and Education Fund
http://www.lambdalegal.org/cgi-bin/pages/documents/record?record=147

HIV/STD Prevention and Young Men Who Have Sex with Men, 1999
Advocates for Youth
http://www.youthhiv.org/l_ymsm2.htm

Homosexuality and Adolescence, 1993
American Academy of Pediatrics
http://www.medem.com

Just the Facts about Sexual Orientation and Youth: A Primer for Principals, Educators, and School Personnel, 1999
American Council Association
http://www.apa.org/pi/lgbc/publications/justthefacts.html

Making Schools Safe for Gay and Lesbian Youth: Breaking the Silence in Schools and in Families: Education Report, 1993
Massachusetts Governor's Commission on Gay and Lesbian Youth
http://www.state.ma.us/gcgly/publicationsofthecommission.html

A Monograph of Diversity in the Field of Education, edited by Jean M. Novak and Louis G. Denti, Volume 1, 1995.
http://www.outproud.org/article_each_child.html

PFLAG's From Our House to the School House: A Recipe for Safe Schools
PFLAG
http://pflag.org/schools/ourhouse.htm

Preventing Youth Hate Crimes: A Manual for Schools and Communities
Safe and Drug Free Schools
http://www.ed.gov/pubs/HateCrime/start.html

Prevention of Health Problems among Gay and Lesbian Youth: Making Health and Human Services Available and Effective for Gay and Lesbian Youth, 1994
Massachusetts Governor's Commission on Gay and Lesbian Youth
http://www.state.ma.us/gcgly/publicationsofthecommission.html

Schools Shouldn't Hurt: Lifting the Burden from Gay, Lesbian, Bisexual and Transgendered Youth, 1996
Rhode Island Task Force on Gay, Lesbian, Bisexual and Transgendered Youth
http://members.tripod.com/~twood/safeschools.html

Stopping Anti-Gay Abuse of Students in Public Schools: A Legal Perspective, 1998
Lambda Legal Defense and Education Fund
http://www.lambdalegal.org/sections/library/stopping.pdf

Strengthening the Learning Environment: A School Employees' Guide to Gay and Lesbian Issues, 1999
National Education Association
http://home.nea.org/books/showitem.cfm?pubid=258

Tackling Gay Issues in School: A Resource Module, 1998
Gay, Lesbian and Straight Education Network of Connecticut and Planned Parenthood of Connecticut, Inc.
http://www.outinct.com/glsen

Taking the Lead: How School Administrators Can Provide the Leadership Necessary to Creating Schools Where All People are Valued, Regardless of Sexual Orientation, 1999
GLSEN
http://www.glsen.org/templates/resources/record.html?section=14&record=384

They Don't Even Know Me: Understanding Anti-Gay Violence and Harassment in Schools, 1999
Safe Schools Coalition of Washington State
http://www.safeschools-wa.org/theydontevenknowme.pdf

Understanding Gay and Lesbian Students Through Diversity, 2000
National Education Association
http://www.nea.org/bt/1-students/gayles.pdf

Violence Against Gay, Lesbian, and Bisexual Youth
Organizations: National Youth Violence Prevention, Center for Mental Health Services, Substance Abuse and Mental Health Services Administration
http://www.cdc.gov/nccdphp/dash/violence/synthesisandapplication.htm

Youth Speak: GLSEN's School Climate Survey, 1999
GLSEN
http://208.178.40.179/binary-data/GLSEN_ARTICLES/pdf_file/24.pdf

Youth Violence, 2000
Centers for Disease Control
http://www.cdc.gov/ncipc/factsheets/yvfacts.htm

YOUTH WITH DISABILITIES

Books

Ducharm, Stanley H., and Kathleen M. Gill. 1997. *Sexuality after Spinal Cord Injury: Answers to Your Questions.* Baltimore: Paul H. Brookes Publishing Company.

Eisenberg, Myron G., and Robert L. Gluekauf. 1999. *Medical Aspects of Disability: A Handbook for the Rehabilitation Professional.* New York: Springer Publishing Company.

Fegan, Lydia, Anne Rauch, and Wendy McCarthy. 1995. *Sexuality and People with Intellectual Disability.* Baltimore: Paul H. Brookes Publishing Company.

Garell, Dale C. 1994. *The Encyclopedia of Health: Medical Disorders and Their Treatment.* New York: Chelsea House Publishers.

Karp, Gary. 1999. *Life on Wheels: For the Active Wheelchair User.* Sebastopol, CA: O'Reilly and Associates, Inc.

Kriegsman, Kay, H., Elinor L. Zaslow, Jennifer D'Zmura-Rechsteiner. 1992. *Taking Charge: Teenagers Talk about Life and Physical Disabilities.* Bethesda, MD: Woodbine House, Inc.

Marinelli, Robert P., and Arthur E. Dell Orto. 1999. *The Psychological and Social Impact of Disability.* New York: Springer Publishing Company.

Osman, Betty B. 1982. *No One to Play With: The Social Side of Learning Disabilities.* New York: Random House.

Pueschel, Siegfried M., and Maria Sustrova. 1997. *Adolescents with Down Syndrome: Toward a More Fulfilling Life.* Baltimore: Paul H. Brookes Publishing Company.

Schmerzler, Audrey, and Jane Walsh. 1998. *Disability Fact Finder: Nursing Management of Individuals with Disabilities.* Philadelphia: Lippincott Williams & Williams.

Schwier, Karin Melberg, and Dave Hingsburger. 2000. *Sexuality: Your Sons and Daughters with Intellectual Disabilities.* Baltimore: Paul H. Brookes Publishing Company.

Smith, Corrine, and Lisa Strick. 1997. *Learning Disabilities: A to Z: A Parent's Complete Guide to Learning Disabilities from Pre-School to Adulthood.* New York: The Free Press.

Journal Articles

Berman, Helene, Dorothy Harris, Rick Enright, Michelle Gilpin, Tamzin Cathers, and Gloria Bukovy. **"Sexuality and the Adolescent with a Physical Disability: Understandings and Misunderstandings."** *Issues in Comprehensive Pediatric Nursing* 22: 183–196.

Blum, R. W., M. D. Resnick, R. Nelson, and A. St. Germaine. 1991. "Family and Peer Issues among Adolescents with Spina Bifida and Cerebral Palsy." *Pediatrics* 88: 280–285.

Brantlinger, E. 1992. **"Sexuality Education in the Secondary Special Ed-**

ucation Curriculum: Teachers' Perceptions and Concerns." *Teacher Education and Special Education* 15: 32–40.

Brookes, Jane P. 1992. **"Sex Education for Students with Moderate Mental Retardation."** *Teaching Exceptional Children* 24(4): 56–57.

Carter, Jade K. 1999. **"Sexuality Education for Students with Specific Learning Disabilities."** *Intervention in School and Clinic* 34(4): 220–223.

Clark, Edith Marie, and Jack W. Farley. 1990. **"Sex Education for Young Children with Special Needs."** *Preventing School Failure* 34(2): 222.

Colson, Steven E., and Judith K. Carlson. 1993. **"HIV/AIDS Education for Students with Special Needs."** *Intervention in School and Clinic:* 262–274.

Cromer, B. A., B. Enrile, K. McKoy, M. Gerhardstein, M. Fitzpatrick, and J. Judis. 1990. **"Knowledge, Attitudes, and Behavior Related to Sexuality in Adolescents with Chronic Disability."** *Developmental Medicine and Child Neurology* 32: 602–609.

Garwood, Monique, and Marita P. McCabe. 2000. **"Impact of Sex Education Programs on Sexual Knowledge and Feelings of Men with a Mild Intellectual Disability."** *Education and Training in Mental Retardation and Developmental Disabilities* 35(3): 269–283.

Huntley, Cristy F., and Susan M. Benner. 1993. **"Reducing Barriers to Sex Education for Adults with Mental Retardation."** *Mental Retardation* 31(4): 215–220.

Ingraham, Cynthia L., McCay Vernon, Brenda Clemente, and Linda Olney. **"Sex Education for Deaf-Blind Youths and Adults."** *Journal of Visual Impairment and Blindness* 94(12): 756–761.

Kinross, Louise. 2001. **"Trying Their Wings."** *Exceptional Parent* 31(7): 46–50.

Lero, Marc. 1994. **"Teaching Adolescents about AIDS."** *Teaching Exceptional Children* 26(4): 49–51.

Mansell, Sheila, Dick Sobsey, and Rosemary Moskal. 1998. **"Clinical**

Findings among Sexually Abused Children with and without Developmental Disabilities." *Mental Retardation* 36(1): 12–22.

May, Deborah C., and D. K. Kundert. 1996. **"Are Special Educators Prepared to Meet the Sex Education Needs of Their Students? A Progress Report."** *The Journal of Special Education* 29(4): 433–441.

McCabe, Marita P. 1993. **"Sex Education Programs for People with Mental Retardation."** *Mental Retardation* 31(6): 377–387.

Nelson, Robert M. 1999. **"Sterilization of Minors with Developmental Disabilities."** *Pediatrics* 104(2): 337–401.

Romaneck, Greg M., and Robert Kuehl. 1992. **"Sex Education for Students with High-Incidence Special Needs."** *Teaching Exceptional Children* 25(1): 22–24.

Sundram, Clarence J., and Paul F. Stavis. 1994. **"Sexuality and Mental Retardation: Unmet Challenges."** *Mental Retardation* 32(4): 255–264.

Ward, K. M. 2001. **"Community Services, Issues, and Service Gaps for Individuals with Developmental Disabilities Who Exhibit Inappropriate Sexual Behaviors."** *Mental Retardation* 39(1): 119.

Whitehouse, Michele A., and Marita P. McCabe. 1997. **"Sex Education Programs for People with Intellectual Disability: How Effective Are They?"** *Education and Training in Mental Retardation and Developmental Disabilities* 31: 229–240.

Reports and Studies Available On-Line

Sexuality: Position Statement #9, 1996
ARC
http://thearc.org/posits/sex.html

Sexuality Education of Children and Adolescents with Developmental Disabilities, 1996
American Academy of Pediatrics
http://www.aap.org/policy/01225.html

Chapter Nine

⚫⟶ **A Different World**

The idea for this book first came to me during the advent of the Christmas 2000 commercials. I was watching a prime time sitcom when a commercial appeared for the popular, convenient, "point and click" disposable cameras. The commercial depicted a small group of adolescent girls, perhaps thirteen or fourteen years old, sporting the cameras, walking up to a home. The girls ring the doorbell, and a younger boy, perhaps seven or so, answers the door with a frustrated face. The girls ask to see the boy's brother, apparently smitten by him, and the youngster, disgusted with the girls, sighs something to the effect of "he's upstairs." The girls sneak upstairs to a bedroom and begin taking pictures of a handsome, adolescent boy who is only wearing his underwear. The girls then walk out of the home giggling.

I have never studied marketing and may be incorrect about the camera maker's intent, but it seems that the purpose of the commercial was to show the adolescent market that the cameras can be fun and that this one instance is just one of many ways the cameras can be used. This was a very imaginative commercial no doubt, but I was taken aback at what I saw. It has been twelve years since I was in high school, and I never imagined that I would see a commercial of young girls pursuing a boy in his underwear. I may have read more into this commercial than most, but this commercial solidified for me that youth aren't as innocent about sex as many believe. I did some preliminary, superficial research of sex in our culture to see what youth are exposed to and found that images of sex are pervasive, especially on premium cable channels, the Internet, and magazines in the grocery store aisles. The extent of their influence is widely debated and nearly impossible to quantify, but the fact remains that youth can learn about sex by simple exposure to the media. Just take former President Bill Clinton's prevarication about his relationship with Monica Lewinsky. Many youth for the first time learned about the parameters of sex and oral sex just by watching the news coverage.

We live in such a different world than just a decade ago. I realize that every generation seems to find that the current generation of youth has unprecedented liberties, but this is evident when I see commercials such as this one or I watch prime time sitcoms. If today's youth watched the *Friends* 2000–2001 season, they learned that Monica and Chandler were living together, having sex, despite the fact that they were unmarried. The 2001–2002 season found Rachel pregnant after a one-night stand with Ross. If they caught an episode of *Will and Grace*, they learned that Grace contemplated a ménage à trois, and her peers Will, Jack, and Karen had experienced one in the past. If they caught an episode of MTV's *Real World*, they watched real, attractive young adults (perhaps role models for younger generations) talk about their sexual relationships or attractions. One episode dealt with girls that boys consider "panty droppers." If youth managed to catch HBO's *Sex and The City* or Showtime's *Queer as Folk*, they learned some graphic details about how some people choose to live their sex lives. These are popular shows that have received accolades for their entertainment value, and some of the actors and scriptwriters have received awards, but the sexual content in these (and other shows for that matter) is for mature audiences. How appropriate can these be for the youth who watch these shows? In addition, what impact does watching them have on their sexual behavior? Alternatively, do these shows simply reflect what youth already know? This is where sex education plays a critical role. This chapter discusses some final thoughts regarding sex education and are presented in the following sections: Recommendations; Chronology of Sex Education; Sex Education and Sexual Violence; Gay, Lesbian, Bisexual, and Transgender Youth; Youth with Special Needs; and Summary.

RECOMMENDATIONS

Youth need sex education. Most people agree with this statement—conservative and liberal factions alike. In addition, large-scale polls seem to suggest that people across the nation believe that youth need certain skills that can be learned in sex education. Exactly when youth should begin to study sex education and what they should study remains in contention. I believe that sex education should start as early as kindergarten, with youth exposed to sex education throughout their education, and young adults should be required to take a human sexuality course as an undergraduate requirement. This does not mean that kindergartners should study the male and female anatomy or the human reproductive system, and first graders should learn about condoms and contraceptives; sex education should be age- and developmentally appropriate. Kindergartners can learn about families, the responsibilities of mothers and fathers, and so forth. First graders can learn about the birth of household pets, how to protect themselves from strangers, how to respect personal boundaries.

There are some inherent challenges that come with implementing sex education early on. As a former second grade teacher, I can attest to the fact that teachers are inundated with curricular material they must implement in addition to teaching the essentials. Adding another critical subject to teachers' workload may not be feasible. Moreover, teachers may not feel comfortable enough to teach sex education or know enough about sexuality to impart the information to their students. However, schools need to make a concerted effort to teach sex education because youth will learn about sex one way or another. Professionals in the field of sex education hope that the youth learn from parents, teachers, church, or community programs, but chances are that the youth will learn from friends and the media. It makes better sense for youth to learn about sex from reliable sources in comfortable, supportive learning environments.

However, what should they learn—abstinence-only, abstinence-plus, or the works? No doubt about it, youth should abstain from sex. Abstinence is the only effective contraception and the only method of keeping safe from sexually transmitted diseases and the virus that causes AIDS. Concerned adults should do everything in their power to instill this in youth. All sex education programs should preach abstinence. Despite my stance, I remain unconvinced that all youth will abstain from sex simply because concerned adults and statisticians tell them to. This fact is evident in studies that have found that 39 percent of ninth grade youth have had sex, 65 percent of twelfth graders have had sex, 40 percent of girls become pregnant before the age of 20, and 60 percent of HIV positive adults became infected when they were in their teens (cited in Association of Reproductive Health Professionals 2001). For this reason alone, youth should also learn about safe sex practices. A conservative faction is diametrically opposed to this, but no abstinence message or "no, not for me" role-playing is going to stop all youth from having sex. Period. However, learning to use contraceptives might help some avoid becoming pregnant or acquiring an STD.

Every school and community should investigate its needs and determine the type of program that best meets those needs. One sex education program does not fit and cure all. If an abstinence-only program works for a district in Austin, Texas, and an abstinence-plus program works for Chicago, Illinois, so be it. I know first hand that some youth would balk at discussions of abstinence, and other youth would not even consider sex before marriage and take to heart those catchy abstinence mantras. Professionals should look at the continuum found in figure 1.1, determine the knowledge, values, and skills they want their youth to have and the type of program that would work best for them, and implement away. Sex is a wonderful, essential part of life, and youth engage in sex because it feels good. This cannot be ignored. However, youth need to understand that sex should be reserved for when they are emotionally and mentally mature and able to contend with the consequences that come with a sexual relationship.

The statistics about youth found in chapter 1 seem to suggest that youth are dating at younger ages, having sex at younger ages, and although the pregnancy and birth rates are currently in decline, the rates are still high. Moreover, the STD rate of infection for youth is staggering—over three million cases a year. Sex education could alleviate many of the untoward consequences of sex, and parents should be expected to play a part in the sex education process. Research seems to support the idea that parents that communicate their disapproval of sex outside of a committed, sound relationship are likely to have children that will postpone sex. Many parents may feel awkward and uncomfortable when it comes to the sex talk, but they need to realize that talking about sex is beyond talking about the penis, sperm, and vagina. Sex education is the sharing of values and instilling in youth respect for one another, how to protect themselves and their future, and teaching them to exercise responsibility. Parents need to know this. They should therefore have some form of sex education themselves that could be provided through training sponsored by local PTAs, churches, or community organizations.

Chronology of Sex Education

In the early twentieth century, sex education was the instruction of heterosexual copulation, reproduction, and, because of the outbreak of venereal diseases among soldiers of the great wars, sex education could be found in the army barracks. Society was very conservative during this period of our history. With the Comstock Laws in effect, anyone caught with so-called obscene sexual material—information on contraceptives, abortions, prostitution, or the open display of nudity—or distributing it was arrested and fined. Any form of public display of sexuality other than reproduction was considered reprehensible, offensive, obscene, and grounds for open social censure. One author, for instance, was arrested for his work on marsupials. Imagine the shock Comstock would feel about the sexual behavior of society today.

The idea of an organization monitoring sex in society is not necessarily a horrific idea, and some of these watchdog organizations do exist. However, these organizations should study sex among youth and, based on their studies, provide communities and schools with recommendations. People should not be judged for the way they conduct their sex lives and they certainly should not be forced to conform to the standards of yesteryear. So when schools report that gay youth are having a difficult time being accepted by their peers, for instance, adults shouldn't shirk their responsibility to teach a student body to respect all people regardless of sexual orientation.

Sexual hygiene renegades such as Prince Morrow, Maurice Bigelow, and Margaret Sanger made it possible for sex education to progress as it did. Morrow and Bigelow were concerned and alarmed with the social diseases of their time and, through the Society of Sanitary and Moral Prophylaxis, strove "to promote the appreciation of the sacredness of human sexual relations, and thereby to minimize the moral and physical evils resulting from ignorance and vice" (cited in Kirkendall 1981, 3). These individuals firmly believed in sex as it relates to love, marriage, and families and were nonetheless conservative. (Much of the historical literature on sex and sex education rarely talked about the act of copulation.) Most of the early literature (for instance, Gaffney 1914) stressed the importance of teaching about nature—the significance of seeds, animals, eggs, a nurturing mother—and youth were expected to make the connection to human sexuality. Some authors reported advice for parents—be direct, unashamed, and do not "pretend that men and women are angels" (Geddes and Thomson 1915)—and others shared values that hold true today, for example, boys respecting women (Ellis 1914). As the decades passed, most experts in sex education remained conservative and the message was generally the same:

- Youth do not get enough information at home.
- Youth should learn about sex in school.
- Youth will learn about sex from questionable sources if they do not get the information from concerned adults.
- Sex education should be integrated in the subjects with teachers elaborating on sex when opportunities present themselves.
- Schools, parents, and churches should collaborate to impart sexual knowledge.
- Parents and teachers need sex education themselves.
- Sensitive topics such as masturbation, homosexuality, sex before marriage, and so on were not tolerated and were discussed in the pejorative.

➡ In addition to learning about reproduction and family, youth should also learn about such "social evils" as prostitution, sexually transmitted diseases, and abortion.

Perhaps the most interesting aspect of the historical literature was an insert in a 1945 issue of the *Journal of Social Hygiene* that provided girls with some dating advice (see figure 9.1). Amazingly, girls were believed (at least by the organization responsible for the pamphlet) to be so immature they needed advice to gather their "scatter brains" and bear some of the dating responsibility. How times have changed, from dating advice that included going out in public after a movie, to today with girls taking a picture of a boy in his underwear.

So many events have unfolded in our history that affect the way we perceive sex, but three significant events occurred since the 1960s that changed society forever: the pill and the women's rights movement; the gay rights movement spurred by New York City's Stonewall Revolution; and AIDS. The sexual revolution began with the pill, as it afforded people the freedom to have sex without fear of pregnancy. Before that time, women were urged to exercise sexual restraint (Melody and Peterson 1999), but thereafter women could make choices about sex that best fitted their needs. Historically, it was axiomatic that gay, lesbian, bisexual, and transgender persons led double lives. Those who did not were severely persecuted. Things have changed for these people, and some communities accept them when they choose to live openly. Others still risk physical danger in their communities. These three events have empowered people, and a whole new generation of youth recognizes that diverse voices in their communities are insightful and not a cause for alienation. We need to continue to teach youth to invite and respect diversity.

No one can debate the fact that AIDS is a tragedy. So many lives have been lost to AIDS, and fear of death (or at least a lifetime of medications and consistent doctor visits) has definitely ended or curbed the sexual revolution. Youth understand AIDS to some degree, but we fail them when we do not teach them abstinence or how to practice safe sex. One recent study by the Alan Guttmacher Institute found that youth often equate sex with intercourse alone, and youth further believe that oral sex is a form of abstinence and a way to avoid pregnancies and sexually transmitted diseases. Needless to say, youth still risk acquiring the virus that causes AIDS when they engage in oral sex, and schools are evidently doing a poor job of teaching them this fact.

Figure 9.1. Dating Advice for Girls: Circa 1945

Do's and Don'ts for Girls

Discussing dates with her girls, Dr. Stephens finds that they like the half dozen suggested below to help them maintain their emotional balance:

1. Know your date if at all possible. If you are going on a blind date, be sure it's a double date and that the other girl is in sympathy with your point of view. Two girls can get their way, where it may be hard for one to do so.
2. Think of something interesting to do. You can't just talk all evening, especially if you hardly know the boy. You can't expect him to have all the ideas. Collect your "scatter brains" and put them to some useful purpose.
3. Be quick to see the possibilities in your situation and prevent it before it occurs. For example, after seeing a sexy movie, you'd better eat with a crowd than go for a ride by yourselves.
4. Remember, any girl with her wits about her has the upper hand in the situation. Don't lead your date on and then wonder what's the matter with him.
5. If you must "put him in his place" do it kindly. Take the blame yourself; maybe you are more devastating than you think, and if you have that much glamour you can afford to be gracious. Then don't forget to give the guy a second chance if you like him. Maybe you could even invite him to something you've planned, just to show that you don't hold a grudge. Of course, if it happens the second time then you have to decide whether he's worth your trouble.
6. Don't drink alcoholic beverages—not even a little—when on a date.

Source: From "Do's and Don'ts for Girls," by District of Columbia Social Hygiene Society. In *Journal of Social Hygiene*, Volume 31 (4), insert.

Sexual Violence among Youth

The prevalence of child sexual abuse is disturbing, and far more distressing is the fact that schools are not mandated to implement sexual abuse curricula. Sexual abuse seems to occur in all cultures regardless of family constellation, socioeconomic status, ethnicity, or gender. Sometimes the perpetrators are adults, and sometimes they are youth, and they are as heterogeneous as their victims are. There is no question that youth need to learn to protect themselves and to respect the boundaries of others. Incidents such as the one that follows should not be occurring. On October 18, 2000, the *Chicago Sun-Times* reported that an eleven-year-old boy allegedly sexually assaulted a twelve-year-old girl in the closet of a special education classroom. A teacher and thirteen students were in the classroom when the assault occurred. What is more troubling about the story is that school administrators allegedly ignored teachers' and parents' complaints of other sexual abuse among the students. One teacher reported that a girl had previously been assaulted on the school playground, and a group of boys had forced another boy to perform oral sex. The emotional repercussions of these attacks are devastating and will last a lifetime. This incident managed to catch the media's attention, but imagine all the other cases of sexual abuse that go unreported or are ignored. Schools need to take proactive measures and implement sexual abuse prevention programs. Schools can accomplish this in three ways, according to the Colorado Coalition Against Sexual Assault (1999):

1. Implement programs that stress positive life skills that build youth's self-esteem, teach conflict resolution skills, and train them in assertiveness. These types of programs rarely address sexual assault and abuse explicitly.
2. Implement risk reduction programs that increase youth's sexual abuse awareness through discussions of incidence, prevalence, and circumstances. Youth learn to identify potential abusers and how to prevent an abuse from happening.
3. Implement social change programs that teach youth about the issue and abuse of power. Youth learn about victimization (bullying, sexual abuse, sexual harassment); some facts about sexual abuse; developing empathy and respect for one another; and assertiveness skills.

The Colorado Coalition Against Sexual Assault has a comprehensive website (http://ccasa.org/compend.htm) complete with curricular resources on each of these types of programs. Concerned parents, teachers, school officials, and child caregivers should review the site and bibliography.

As far as sexual harassment is concerned, the American Association of University Women revealed in 1993 and again in 2001 that a relatively large number of youth know what sexual harassment is and have experienced sexual harassment at school (83 percent for girls, 79 percent for boys). Despite the fact that the 2001 study found that more schools have implemented a sexual harassment policy (70 percent of schools have a policy compared to 26 percent in 1993), sexual harassment is still pervasive. Some school officials dismiss sexual harassment among youth as naïve banter or innocent flirting, but there is nothing naïve or innocent about the humiliation of youth by youth (having their clothes pulled off, being groped, being forced to do something sexual, or being the targets of sexual rumors). The emotional pain that these youth will endure is a deep one. The U.S. Department of Education (1999) has an excellent resource that school officials should become familiar with, *Protecting Students from Harassment and Hate Crime: A Guide for Schools.* The document outlines strategies for developing a schoolwide sexual harassment policy and methods for creating a safe school climate that supports diversity.

Youth also have to be taught about the possible dangers of online interaction. Mitchell et al. (2001) found that among 1,501 youth (ten to seventeen years of age) who use the Internet, one in five were targets of unwanted sexual solicitations (engage in sex, sex talk, or request for personal sexual information), some of which were requested by adults. Although 25 percent of the sample mentioned they were distressed by the solicitation, 3 percent indicated that someone tried to contact them offline and none suffered any form of physical abuse. Figure 9.2 illustrates how quickly sex becomes an item in the chat rooms popular among youth. Exactly which of the online identities is an adult is nearly impossible to tell, but youth need to learn to safeguard themselves from the dangers that lurk in cyberspace.

Gay, Lesbian, Bisexual, and Transgender Youth

There is no doubt that gay, lesbian, bisexual, and transgender youth have many barriers to overcome. Not only do these youth struggle with the emotional and physical milestones that all youth contend with, these youth have to contend with: (a) their sexual orientation; (b) the stigma that is associated with being gay; (c) their peers' attitude and behavior toward their sexuality; and (d) their family's attitude and behavior toward their sexuality. All the while, many of these youth feel isolated, with little or no support system and no role models in proximity. One gay youth described his situation to an agency committed to gay youth:

> I don't know what to do anymore. I'm 14. I'm gay. I'm still in the closet. Nothing seems to be getting better with my life. I am doing home studies because I just couldn't handle being picked on at school anymore, even by people I didn't know. I hate being in the closet because I feel like I'm living a lie. My life is sh*t. I've lost almost all hope. I am almost at the point that I just don't care anymore. I am writing to you in hopes that you can somehow help me find someone, a guy around my age who can hug me when I really need one. I am only asking you this as a last resort. But I have no other choice. Please help if you can. Thank you sooooo much.—Dave. (Glatze and Nycum 2001, 54)

Figure 9.2. Sex in a Chat Room

Web Talks Often Cross the Line

As afternoon boredom sets in, activity picks up in Internet chat rooms targeted at teens and preteens. We sampled the most popular rooms of America Online Tuesday afternoon and didn't have to look hard to find examples of sexually charged content. A sampling:

Britney Spears Chat Room, 3:10 p.m.
animalboy7654: any girls have a nude pic
ballr4ly0921: a/s/l [age/sex/location] check
Novembertopez: n e [any] guys wanna chat im [instant message] me
   (i got pic)

'N Snyc Chat Room, 3:15 p.m.
Code PhreeZe: any girls want to play truth or dare?
RchhpS: any hott girl wanna chat press 128 (14/m/nh) [14-year-old
   boy in New Hamshire]

Dawson's Creek Chat Room, 3:20 p.m.
LilSeetty 79110: Any cute guys wanna chat? Check out a couple
   revealing pics my x-boyfriend took! Click the link

Bridget Jones Chat Room, 3:40 p.m.
SweetChic748: hey whats shakin?
BadGir62626: my hips
BadGir62626: lol [laughing out loud]
SweetChic748: haha
punkrawk458: any girls 13+wanna cyber? [have cyber sex, an intimate
   online conversation]
BadGir62626: ewww
BadGir62626: loser
FLgirl0622: ew 13??
Flgirl0622: i know
SweetChic 748: I am 13
BadGir62626:somepeoples need a life
BadGir62626: I'm 13 and I don't cyber

Source: From "Web Talks Often Cross the Line" by Debra Pickett. In *Chicago Sun-Times,* June 20, 2001, (p. 6). Reprinted by permission.

The October 2001 issue of *Out* magazine ran a very interesting article that captures the state of gay, lesbian, bisexual, and transgender (GLBT) youth in America today. Glatze and Nycum (2001), two journalists determined to increase the awareness of GLBT youth, documented their travel and exchanges with GLBT youth throughout the country. (For access to interviews, stories, and photographs visit their website at www.younggayamerica.com). The journalists ultimately knew that being gay is a struggle in and of itself and set out "to give (gay youth) a better way to express themselves, feel less isolated, learn from each other's experiences, and come to understand their importance in the world" (56).

Their trek of forty-five cities (rural and urban communities) produced a plethora of stories—one youth reported that the school intentionally omitted his picture from the school's senior yearbook, another youth described how other youth terrorized him at his place of employment, and another discussed how he was spit on daily. The fact that these youth are taunted goes without saying. However, what became evident to the journalists was that gay youth can be found in all types of communities, and some type of support group can be found within 100 miles of where some gay youth live. Some youth manage to find one another traveling great distances (two mothers drive their fifteen-year-old sons three hours just to see each other), and others connect with one another on the Internet. Some youth are shocked to discover that there are other gay youth living in similar situations. The journalists also discovered that youth are coming out at earlier ages than previous generations, and this generation of youth seems to be more comfortable with being gay. In fact, these youth are not discouraged by their circumstances, they recognize that their desires are part of who they are, and they are determined to do something about the way society treats them.

Some people may not see a connection between sexual orientation and sex education, but the fact remains that sexual orientation is an aspect of sexuality and youth should know that there are diverse sexual orientations in this world. I don't necessarily agree that everyone has to celebrate that this diversity exists (I respect those who are uncomfortable with gay, lesbian, bisexual, and transgender issues), but people should certainly tolerate diversity and accept the fact that some people are different. Moreover, schools should teach youth to respect one another, and discussions of homosexuality should not be conducted in the pejorative. A sex education curriculum alone cannot teach youth about factors associated with sexual orientation; instead, schools should implement policies that create safe school learning environments. Schools can have policies that do not tolerate harassment of any kind; sponsor support groups for gay, lesbian, bisexual, and transgender youth; train teachers in ways to teach about social justice in the content areas; and have resources and materials available for these youth. Schools that foster a positive regard for these youth will ultimately transform the way society treats gay, lesbian, bisexual, and transgender persons.

Youth with Special Needs

Throughout history, a person with a disability was considered an asexual being with no physical or mental capacity for love and sex. They were rarely taught about sex, and those who exhibited any signs of sexual activity were sedated or sterilized. This is a different world, and for youth with disabilities, this is a golden age of opportunity (Smith 2001). This generation of American youth with disabilities has rights that previous generations of youth with disabilities could not have imagined. Significant strides have been made since the 1970s, and federal laws now ensure their civil rights. Persons with disabilities can and are expected to live normal, productive lives in communities far from the institutions of yesteryear. In fact, persons who are blind can now use slot machines that are Brailled and/or audio assisted. Persons in wheelchairs participate in marathons, and others are mountain climbers. Moreover, wheelchairs that walk and climb rough terrain are now available for those who enjoy outdoor activities.

Persons and youth with disabilities in mainstream society and general education environments need sex education because they now have greater opportunities for personal interaction. In order for them to have successful friendships and relationships, they need the same sexual knowledge and cognitive skills as youth without disabilities. Moreover, because some of these youth cannot fully process social cues, they are often vulnerable to victimization. For these reasons alone, they must be allowed to learn the mechanics and consequences of dating and sex and how to protect themselves from abuse and harassment.

The literature on sex education and youth with special needs is sparse. Most authors offer recommendations for a sound sex education program for youth with special needs, and others attest that sex education works for these youth. However, very little data can empirically conclude that any sex education programs for these youth are effective. More research is needed in this area. In particular, studies should address the following:

- What types of sex education programs are available for youth with mild disabilities? How often are they implemented? How many of these youth actually receive sex education?
- How often is sex education addressed in the IEP as a short- or long-term goal? Is there a difference between the goals stated for students with mild disabilities and those with more severe disabilities?
- Is sex education effective for these youth? Why or why not?

How do the sexual knowledge and skills of youth with disabilities compare to those of youth without disabilities?

•• Who is teaching these youth sex education? What are their qualifications? How are the instruction and materials adapted? In what settings should youth with disabilities receive sex education, segregated or integrated settings? One author suggested that youth with learning disabilities need concrete and graphic sex education examples to better understand the content. However, the very examples they need may not be tolerated in local communities (Osman 1982).

•• How well can all students with disabilities identify and prevent sexual abuse? How aware are they of intervention strategies?

•• How well do students with physical disabilities understand the sexual implications of their disability?

If questions such as these remain unanswered (empirically speaking), we may never know the full extent of sexual health and knowledge of youth with disabilities.

SUMMARY

Times have changed, and sex is pervasive in society. Youth will learn about sex one way or another; it just makes better sense that they learn factual, accurate, unbiased information through sex education. An ancient Persian proverb captures the sentiment of this chapter, "A foolish man waters an elephant with a spoon" (Scheffler 1997, 32). Providing youth with bits and pieces of sex education on an as-needed basis is foolish. Youth need to know about all aspects of sexuality if society expects them to have healthy, fulfilled lives in these times.

REFERENCES

American Association of University Women. 1993. *Hostile Hallways: The AAUW Survey on Sexual Harassment in America's Schools. Bullying, Teasing, and Sexual Harassment in School.* Washington, DC: AAUW.

American Association of University Women. 2001. *Hostile Hallways: Bullying, Teasing, and Sexual Harassment in School.* Washington, DC: AAUW.

Association of Reproductive Health Professionals, "Surgeon General's Report on Sexual Health Encourages Comprehensive Sex Education," http://www.arhp.org/pr/99–54.html (cited September 17, 2001).

Colorado Coalition Against Sexual Assault, "Compendium of Sexual Violence and Harassment Educational Prevention Resources for Youth," http://www.ccasa.org/compen.htm (cited October 11, 1999).

Ellis, Grace F. 1914. "Sex Instruction in a High School." *Journal of Social Hygiene* 1: 271–272.

Gaffney, Charles E. 1914. "A Father's Plan for Sex Instruction: Instruction within the Home." *Journal of Social Hygiene* 1: 270–271.

Geddes, Patrick, and J. Arthur Thomson. 1915. "Sex Education." *Journal of Social Hygiene* 2: 330.

Glatze, Mike, and Benjie Nycum. 2001. "Youthquake: San Francisco-Based Journalist Mike Glatze and Benjie Nycum Hit the Road to Document the State of Young Gay America—a Joyful, Heartbreaking, and Sometimes Harrowing Adventure. *Out*, October, 54–62.

Kirkendall, Lester. 1981. "Sex Education in the United States." In *Sex Education in the Eighties: The Challenge of Healthy Sexual Evolution*, ed. by Lorna Brown. New York: Plenum Press.

Main, Frank, and Carlos Sadovi. 2000. "Alleged Attacks Stun Parents: Ex-teacher Claims Sexual Assaults at Howe School." *Chicago Sun Times:* 18 October 2000.

Melody, M. E., and Linda M. Peterson. 1999. *Teaching America about Sex: Marriage Guides and Sex Manuals from the Late Victorians to Dr. Ruth.* New York: New York University Press.

Mitchell, Kimberly J., David Finkelhor, and Janis Wolak. 2001. "Risk Factors for and Impact of Online Sexual Solicitation of Youth." *Journal of the American Medical Association* 285(3): 3011–3014.

Osman, Betty B. 1982. *No One to Play With: The Social Side of Learning Disabilities.* New York: Random House.

Scheffler, Alex. 1997. *Let Sleeping Dogs Lie and Other Proverbs from Around the World.* Hauppauge, New York: Barron's Educational Series, Inc.

Smith, Deborah Deutsch. 2001. *Introduction to Special Education: Teaching in an Age of Opportunity.* Boston: Allyn and Bacon.

U.S. Department of Education. 1999. *Protecting Students from Harassment and Hate Crimes: A Guide for Schools.* Washington, DC: U.S. Department of Education.

⚭ U.S. Federal Codes Protecting Youth from Sexual Abuse

SEC. 2241. AGGRAVATED SEXUAL ABUSE

(a) By Force or Threat.—Whoever, in the special maritime and territorial jurisdiction of the United States or in a Federal prison, knowingly causes another person to engage in a sexual act

(1) by using force against that other person; or

(2) by threatening or placing that other person in fear that any person will be subjected to death, serious bodily injury, or kidnapping; or attempts to do so, shall be fined under this title, imprisoned for any term of years or life, or both.

(b) By Other Means.—Whoever, in the special maritime and territorial jurisdiction of the United States or in a Federal prison, knowingly—

(1) renders another person unconscious and thereby engages in a sexual act with that other person; or

(2) administers to another person by force or threat of force, or without the knowledge or permission of that person, a drug, intoxicant, or other similar substance and thereby -

(A) substantially impairs the ability of that other person to appraise or control conduct; and (B) engages in a sexual act with that other person; or attempts to do so, shall be fined under this title, imprisoned for any term of years or life, or both.

(c) With Children.—Whoever crosses a State line with intent to engage in a sexual act with a person who has not attained the age of 12 years, or in the special maritime and territorial jurisdiction of the United States or in a Federal prison, knowingly engages in a sexual act with another person who has not attained the age of 12 years, or knowingly engages in a sexual act under the circumstances described in subsections (a) and (b) with another person who has attained the age of 12 years but has not attained the age of 16 years (and is at least 4 years younger than the person so engaging), or attempts to do so, shall be fined under this title, imprisoned for any term of years or life, or both. If the defendant has previously been convicted of another Federal offense under this subsection, or of a State offense that would have been an offense under either such provision had the offense occurred in a Federal prison, unless the death penalty is imposed, the defendant shall be sentenced to life in prison.

(d) State of Mind Proof Requirement.—In a prosecution under subsection (c) of this section, the Government need not prove that the defendant knew that the other person engaging in the sexual act had not attained the age of 12 years.

SEC. 2243. SEXUAL ABUSE OF A MINOR OR WARD

(a) Of a Minor.—Whoever, in the special maritime and territorial jurisdiction of the United States or in a Federal prison, knowingly engages in a sexual act with another person who—

(1) has attained the age of 12 years but has not attained the age of 16 years; and (2) is at least four years younger than the person so engaging; or attempts to do so, shall be fined under this title, imprisoned not more than 15 years, or both.

(b) Of a Ward.—Whoever, in the special maritime and territorial jurisdiction of the United States or in a Federal prison, knowingly engages in a sexual act with another person who is -

(1) in official detention; and (2) under the custodial, supervisory, or disciplinary authority of the person so engaging; or attempts to do so, shall be fined under this title, imprisoned not more than one year, or both.

(c) Defenses.—(1) In a prosecution under subsection (a) of this section, it is a defense, which the defendant must establish by a preponderance of the evidence, that the defendant reasonably believed that the other person had attained the age of 16 years.

(2) In a prosecution under this section, it is a defense, which the defendant must establish by a preponderance of the evidence, that the persons engaging in the sexual act were at that time married to each other.

(d) State of Mind Proof Requirement.—In a prosecution under subsection (a) of this section, the Government need not prove that the defendant knew -

(1) the age of the other person engaging in the sexual act; or

(2) that the requisite age difference existed between the persons so engaging.

Source: Legal Institute Information. 2000. *Chapter 109A – Sexual Abuse.* Ithaca, NY: Cornell Law School.

Appendix B

⚓ The Walt Whitman Community School Philosophy

We believe that all young people, regardless of their sexual orientation, deserve a school situation which guarantees, as much as possible, personal security and physical safety. We believe that adolescence is a time in which people are searching for an identity, including sexual orientation.

We believe that many adolescents, in the process of establishing a genuine sexual orientation, experience extreme intolerance and punishment from most of their peers as well as from the adult society. Approximately one in three teen-age suicides results from the negative attitudes of society toward GLBTQ young people.

We believe that heterosexual adolescents whose parents are GLBT will benefit from a school situation which is free of intolerance and which encourages those young people to gain a realization of sexual orientation issues in order to allow a better understanding of and appreciation for their parents' lifestyles.

We believe that in order for young people to realize a healthy self-concept and esteem, a school situation in which positive reinforcement, access to positive adult role models of various sexual orientations, and an atmosphere of acceptance by their peers is necessary not only for academic success but also for personal growth.

We believe that our society can no longer afford to disenfranchise persons based on sexual orientation, because those individuals are often as not among the most creative, innovative, and intelligent members of the population. These young people may be those individuals who will eventually find the solutions to the problems our world is experiencing.

We believe that a sound education foundation is necessary so that these young people will be able to move successfully into the world of work or pursue further education without the hindrance of poor academic skills.

We believe that because this population of adolescents is at particular risk of contracting HIV/AIDS, a school situation should emphasize realistic and extensive health education.

We believe that GLBTQ young people require a specialized education which will prepare them for membership in a largely heterosexual society. Members of the GLBT community will be able to provide valuable assistance in representing and educating about those unique life issues which these young people will encounter.

We believe that all young people deserve to belong to a community which fosters and reinforces their lifestyles and the development of a sense of self-worth.

We believe that parental involvement in the education process and emotional support of their children is integral to the development of a healthy individual. A school designed to provide services for GLBTQ young people is in a position to provide services to parents as well as to their children. Many parents can benefit from communication-building opportunities and from participating in community activities with other parents struggling with the same issues.

We believe that all young people, including those belonging to minority groups, should receive civics education which emphasizes both community responsibility as well as constitutional rights. Young people who will live in a largely intolerant society will benefit from an educational process which also prepares them to deal with possible conflicts and harassment.

We believe that adolescents should be provided opportunities to donate time and energy to community service activities in order to foster an appreciation of the responsibility that all members of a community owe to the whole.

Source: From "The Walt Whitman Community School Philosophy," by Walt Whitman Community School, 2001. Reprinted with permission.

●◆ Index

●❖ About the Author

David Campos is assistant professor of elementary education in the College of Education at Roosevelt University. His experiences include teaching second grade and conducting corporate training and development for Advanced Micro Devices and Guiltless Gourmet, Inc. He has supervised student teachers and taught undergraduate and graduate courses in special education, multicultural education, and curriculum methods. In addition to his duties as an assistant professor, he has served as an assistant dean of academic affairs and as a project coordinator for a Title II Teacher Quality Enhancement Grant.